Dvořák's
Prophecy

BY THE SAME AUTHOR

Conversations with Arrau (1982)

Understanding Toscanini: How He Became an American Culture-God and Helped Create a New Audience for Old Music (1987)

The Ivory Trade (1990)

Wagner Nights: An American History (1994)

The Post-Classical Predicament: Essays on Music and Society (1995)

Dvořák and America (2003; for young readers)

Classical Music in America: A History of Its Rise and Fall (2005)

Artists in Exile: How Refugees from Twentieth-Century War and Revolution Transformed the American Performing Arts (2008)

Moral Fire: Musical Portraits from America's Fin-de-Siècle (2012)

"On My Way": The Untold Story of Rouben Mamoulian, George Gershwin, and "Porgy and Bess" (2013)

Dvořák's Prophecy

and the Vexed Fate of Black Classical Music

JOSEPH HOROWITZ

W. W. NORTON & COMPANY
Independent Publishers Since 1923

Copyright © 2022 by Joseph Horowitz
Foreword copyright © 2022 by George Shirley

For information about permission to reproduce selections from this book, write to
Permissions, W. W. Norton & Company, Inc., 500 Fifth Avenue, New York, NY 10110

For information about special discounts for bulk purchases, please contact
W. W. Norton Special Sales at specialsales@wwnorton.com or 800-233-4830

Manufacturing by Lake Book Manufacturing
Book design by Chris Welch
Production manager: Lauren Abbate

Library of Congress Cataloging-in-Publication Data

Names: Horowitz, Joseph, 1948– author. | Shirley, George, other.
Title: Dvořák's prophecy : and the vexed fate of black classical music / Joseph Horowitz ;
foreword by George Shirley.
Description: First edition. | New York : W. W. Norton & Company, 2022. |
Includes bibliographical references and index.
Identifiers: LCCN 2021025183 | ISBN 9780393881240 (hardcover) | ISBN 9780393881257 (epub)
Subjects: LCSH: Music—United States—History and criticism. | African Americans—Music—
History and criticism. | Music—United States—African American influences. | Music and race—
United States. | Dvořák, Antonín, 1841–1904.
Classification: LCC ML200 .H798 2022 | DDC 780.973—dc23
LC record available at https://lccn.loc.gov/2021025183

W. W. Norton & Company, Inc., 500 Fifth Avenue, New York, N.Y. 10110
www.wwnorton.com

W. W. Norton & Company Ltd., 15 Carlisle Street, London W1D 3BS

1 2 3 4 5 6 7 8 9 0

The American mind does not oppose tradition, it forgets it.

—GEORGE SANTAYANA

Contents

Foreword

George Shirley

When I began my career in 1959, there existed only a handful of notable African-American operatic artists, mainly abroad in Europe. Traditionally, American opera companies had been segregated. A rare early instance of acclaimed Black artists performing alongside white singers was Verdi's *Aida* at the Cleveland Stadium Opera in 1932, in which Caterina Jarboro and Jules Bledsoe sang Aida and Amonasro. Sometime later, the New York City Opera began engaging Black singers with regularity. The turning point was Marian Anderson's belated Metropolitan Opera debut—she was already fifty-eight years old and past her vocal prime—in 1955. I joined the Met in 1961 as a result of winning the national auditions, and made my debut there as Ferrando in Mozart's *Così fan tutte* in October 1961—as it happened, some ten months after Leontyne Price's Met debut in *Il trovatore*. That same first season, I sang Pinkerton in *Madama Butterfly* and Alfredo in *La traviata*—and so became the first African-American tenor to sing lead roles at the leading American opera house.

Not long after, I was asked by Nathaniel Merrill if I would consider singing Sporting Life in a production of *Porgy and Bess* that he was planning to stage during the summer. Merrill was the Met's resident stage director, someone I had worked with. But I refused because I knew the history of Black male operatic singers who after achieving success singing the leading roles in *Porgy* then found themselves unable to secure contracts for roles in the standard repertoire. I wanted to be recognized as a tenor who could sing Verdi, Puccini, and Strauss, and also Schubert and Schumann. I am reminded of a wonderful cartoon by the Black cartoonist Ollie Harrington. It's set in a meeting room at a university—you can see the clock tower through a window—with a long table at which a number of white gentlemen are seated. At the head of the table a Black gentleman is standing with a sheaf of papers in his hand. The chairman of the committee says, "Mr. Brown, before you deliver your paper on the effects of gamma rays, how about a good old spiritual?" I wanted to disarm that knee-jerk expectation if I could, as I was determined to establish my career as both an interpreter of European classical music and the music of my native heritage.

And so I didn't sing Sporting Life until I was in my late sixties—in Bregenz, Austria. This was a rather famous Götz Friedrich production. It turned out to be one of the most thrilling and spiritually satisfying experiences of my career. I've sung in a lot of opera houses, but I've never elsewhere had such a feeling of family. It is a memory I will always treasure.

Gershwin's masterpiece surpasses all other operas based on American life. It speaks profoundly to the human condition. It explores the same human aspects that define white, brown, "red," or "yellow" life, aspects peculiar to the human animal, ethnic origins notwithstanding. (I prefer the word "ethnicity" to "race" because there is only one race and that is the human race.) *Porgy and Bess* is typically criticized for "negative" human portraits created by a white composer. But consider Mascagni's *Cavalleria rusticana* and Leoncavallo's *I pagliacci*—two of the most beloved *verismo* operas in the international repertoire. They focus on the dark side of life, as do Verdi's *Tosca* and Puccini's *Il tabarro*. Berg's *Lulu* and *Wozzeck*, William Bolcom's *A View from the Bridge* and *McTeague*, and Carlisle Floyd's *Susannah* each reveal blemishes in white life. The images of Blacks in *Porgy and Bess* bother me much less than many representations of Black life that we see and hear in entertainment media today.

One has to ask: What is the value of theater if it is devoid of meaningful reflection of reality? I grew up in Detroit surrounded by characters like Sporting Life, Crown, Bess, and Porgy. They were real and lived their lives as best they knew how. What is more: as Joe Horowitz writes in *Dvořák's Prophecy*, Gershwin's characters are not "stereotypes," as countless Gershwin critics have maintained. Rather, they are archetypes, defined by the dictionary as "original models from which all things of the same type are representations." They do not, as stereotypes do, embody "a standardized mental picture," "over-simplified" and "uncritical." In a sense, you can take Gershwin's characters and make them whomever you want. You will have the person who is addicted and lacks the strength to resist. You will have the person who is crippled and yet possesses dignity enough to keep going.

The "new paradigm" for American classical music proposed in *Dvořák's Prophecy* rightfully situates *Porgy and Bess* at the very center of things, as the highest creative achievement in American classical music. What Joe calls the "standard narrative," so influentially propagated by Aaron Copland and others, treated George Gershwin as a marginal figure. But that is no longer viable. Joe begins his story very differently: with Antonin Dvořák's prophecy that "negro melodies" would foster a "great and noble school" of American classical music. In other words, he starts with Black musical roots: the sorrow songs Dvořák embraced, songs equally esteemed (as Joe chronicles) by Mark Twain, and also by Frederick Douglass and W. E. B. Du Bois. Dvořák was an honest man who spoke and lived the truth. That truth was later "pushed under the rug." Joe shines a light on all of that.

As Joe puts it, classical music in America "stayed white." His new paradigm explores how and why that happened—and also proposes remedies. The resulting version of classical music in America is broader and deeper than before. It connects to *The Souls of Black Folk* and *Adventures of Huckleberry Finn,* to Walt Whitman, Herman Melville, and Ralph Ellison. It also yields many important musical benefits, not the least of which is bringing necessary context to the interwar "Black classical music" now being appreciatively unearthed. I myself have come late to the music of Nathaniel Dett, William Levi Dawson, and Florence Price. In the case of Dett's important oratorio *The Ordering of Moses*, many decades ago I was invited to take part in a performance in Denver, sponsored by the National Association of Negro Musicians. I was grateful for that invitation. But it wasn't possible to move on and perform it elsewhere, as I might with *Messiah*. In fact, I have yet to hear a live performance of Dawson's *Negro Folk Symphony*, or of any of the symphonies of Florence Price.

The "new paradigm" will fascinate and instruct not only music lovers, but lovers of American culture generally. And I must add something about its pertinence to the academy. It is unsurprising that few Black scholars have undertaken a study of classical music in the United States. That will now begin to change. In fact, the topic will change for everyone. Mark Clague, my colleague at the University of Michigan and a distinguished historian of American music, has called the American music story he himself was taught "malnourished." The disconnection between the rich history of Black American music and the classical music we typically hear has proved impoverishing. Because of our current conversation about race, we now observe a seemingly desperate effort to make up for lost time, to present Black faces in the concert hall. I think that's only fair. But if it's going to become a permanent new way of thinking, there has to be new understanding. *Dvořák's Prophecy* is on time, it's a bull's-eye. We have been left unprepared for the current cultural moment. *Dvořák's Prophecy* explains how we got there.

We worry today about "appropriation"—another theme that *Dvořák's Prophecy* importantly tackles. But it is impossible to prevent human beings from emulating what appeals to them. Blacks did not invent football, basketball, or baseball. And indeed Blacks were prevented from playing these sports professionally for decades because they were seen as white sports reserved for white players. Today, Blacks have appropriated these games to everyone's delight, except possibly those who still feel we have no right to play them because they did not spring from Black initiative.

Jazz was partly born of the experience of Black musicians working in brothels—the seamy side of American society. We "appropriated" Western musical instruments and imposed our own rhythmic and harmonic rules on Western musical forms—and created music that is purely American. White musicians emulated the improvised sounds and rhythms that poured from the bells of cornets, the bowels of pianos, the reeds of clarinets and saxophones. And they capitalized on it, oftentimes earning more than the musicians that gave it birth. Not because they were better performers, necessarily, but because they held the unfair advantage of being white.

Those of us who as Black singers and instrumentalists have appropriated the music of European composers, and have performed successfully in concert halls and opera houses worldwide, have pursued the path that human beings naturally follow. I have no right to tell anyone they cannot perform the music of Black folk if they have the desire and ability to do so with proper respect for its content and distinctiveness. And no one has the right to tell me that I cannot perform the music of Europe, or the Middle East, or Asia or Africa, so long as I possess the ability to do so with respect for diverse musical languages.

If I am going to sing the Duke in *Rigoletto* with respect for the language and the style, then I can sing the Duke in *Rigoletto*. You don't have to be Ethiopian to sing Aida, or Japanese to sing Madama Butterfly. We see or hear something for which we have an affinity and we are drawn to it, no matter its origin. If it speaks to us as a way of life, we have no reason not to pursue it. Music is like that; it belongs to no one person or ethnic entity.

Dvořák's Prophecy proposes a bigger world of American classical music than what we have known before. It is more diverse and more equitable. And it is more truthful.

Preamble

Using the Past

In 1893 the Bohemian composer Antonín Dvořák, residing in New York City, predicted that a "great and noble school" of American classical music would be founded upon America's "negro melodies." This prophecy was famous, influential, and controversial. In retrospect, it was shrewd, compassionate—and naïve. The Black musical motherlode migrated into popular realms: the music that defines America to this day. But classical music in America stayed white. How and why that happened is a central thread of this book. The barriers to integration were both institutional and aesthetic.

My larger theme is a failure of historical memory. Classical music in the United States, I argue, is crippled by a condition of "pastlessness." A misleading narrative, popularized by Aaron Copland, Virgil Thomson, and Leonard Bernstein, maintained that there was no American music of consequence before 1910. During interwar decades when literary historians and writers identified a "usable past" that included Ralph Waldo Emerson and Henry David Thoreau, Walt Whitman and Herman Melville, American composers decided they had none. This act of amnesia was supported by a clean modernist aesthetic that devalued Emersonian "mud and scum." It mistrusted the vernacular. It distanced American composers and institutions of performance from Dvořák's prophecy and from the astonishing sorrow songs that Dvořák esteemed a folk music protean with melody, rhythm, and sentiment. The same amnesia overlooked the music of Black concert composers in Dvořák's wake. And it diminished the reputation and influence of two great creative talents—Charles Ives and George Gershwin—whose music found deep roots in vernacular song and dance. To this day, classical music in America remains Eurocentric. American orchestras and opera companies mainly perform foreign repertoire. The anchoring American canon Dvořák anticipated never materialized.

Additionally, there exist new impediments to recovering our musical past. These include misplaced accusations of "cultural appropriation." With the passage of time, appreciating Dvořák's prophecy, and the era in which it occurred, seemingly becomes harder, not easier.

As a cultural historian specializing in the history of classical music in the United States, I have spent three decades immersed in the Gilded Age and *fin-de-siècle*, 1865 to World War I. For American classical music, this was a period of brisk ascent and peak achievement. What came after was an equally swift downward slope forecast by wartime Germanophobia and sealed by the failure to secure a native canon. (This two-part trajectory is the central premise of my *Classical Music in America: A History of Its Rise and Fall* [2005].) In American historiography generally, my fifty-year swath is oddly volatile, subject to radically different interpretations. A melee of historical actors, trends, and events—political, social, cultural—has been variously explored or neglected, used or abused.

This book argues for a new understanding of the history of classical music in America—one that strives to "use the past" with open ears. I begin by focusing on a pair of seminal pre–World War I achievements by Mark Twain and Charles Ives. *Adventures of Huckleberry Finn* and Ives's Symphony No. 2 are twin landmarks in defining a distinctively American style in fiction and concert music via vernacular speech and song.

I next consider subsequent readings of the same prewar period, beginning with the search for a usable past influentially undertaken by Van Wyck Brooks and Lewis Mumford beginning around 1915, and subsequently by Copland, Thomson, and Bernstein (acting as music historians). I observe that the quest for literary forebears, revisiting 1865–1915, led somewhere, and that the musical quest did not. Pastlessness does not notably afflict American literature or visual art; there exists a viable canon of American novels and poems, and also of American art and architecture. Mark Twain's achievement led to Hemingway and Faulkner. Ives's, however, was not "used" by Copland and his contemporaries: modernists attuned to the future. Their mistrust of all possible forebears discouraged honest retrospection.

This Oedipal predilection equally overlooked the sorrow songs in which Dvořák discerned "music that suits itself to any mood or purpose." Dvořák's perspective—"there is nothing in the whole range of composition that cannot be supplied with themes from this source"—was shared by important American musicians and musical thinkers around the turn of the century. And yet the post–World War I bifurcation of American music—"popular" versus "classical"—was an unhappy bifurcation of Black versus white. Indeed, an aversion to jazz, less virulent abroad, became a defining feature of the interwar musical high culture of the United States. An aversion to Gershwin among American-born classical musicians was part of the same skewed picture. So was the unjust obscurity cloaking William Dawson's *Negro Folk Symphony*, Nathaniel Dett's *The Ordering of Moses*, and Florence Price's Symphony No. 3—formidable creative achievements whose lineage is indeed traceable to Dvořák and his milieu.

My excavation of a past denied and forgotten ultimately yields a new paradigmatic narrative for American classical music, starting with the sorrow songs and privileging Ives, Gershwin, and other Americans for whom vernacular resources seemed vitally proximate, and whose democratic largesse resonated with a capacious cultural saga that includes Twain, Whitman, and Melville. Stressing nineteenth-century beginnings, I discover an unexpected convergence of musical and literary pasts. In effect, the vexed fate of classical music in the United States generally, and of "Black classical music" specifically, furnishes a case study of how generations of chroniclers, cumulatively burdened with inherited assumptions, can fail to use the past profitably. Freshly revisiting Dvořák's prophecy of 1893—a prediction that was also a diagnosis— yields opportunities to reexamine how the New World went about importing Old World musical traditions that Americans have fitfully attempted to make their own.

In fact, I believe that Americans in general are losing touch with the past, with our history and cultural inheritance. We live in an age of instant gratification. We no longer know our forebears. This is one reason we feel so fractured today. Dvořák was bent on excavating roots. This exercise has never seemed more timely.

Ultimately, *Dvořák's Prophecy* is a call for action—for better understanding the American past, and hence better appreciating the challenges and opportunities of our fraught contemporary moment.

THE STORY OF American music imposes a dense nexus of culture and race, of historical, political, and moral reckonings. We are a nation stained with twin original sins. What was done to the indigenous Americans who came first, and to the enslaved Africans who came after, can neither be undone nor—it increasingly seems—wholly overcome. How should such bitter knowledge inflect historical understanding and interpretation?

After three decades of experience producing concerts, I find that I am more than ever disposed to use music to poke at the fissures of the American experience. This exercise can be cathartic; it also invites opposition and frustration. Above all, it reveals how little we know our musical past and the uses, constructive or otherwise, to which it may be put.

However much I have marveled at this discovery, I had never thought to write a book based on it until 2016. A book review assignment from the *Wall Street Journal* became a last straw. The book was the Library of

America's 1,600-page Virgil Thomson compendium *The State of Music & Other Writings*. Its predominant subject matter was the history of American music.

I had long known the caustic prose of Virgil Thomson. He enjoys a heroic cameo in my *Understanding Toscanini: How He Became an American Culture-God and Helped Create a New Audience for Old Music* (1987). Thomson's guerilla reviews for the *New York Herald Tribune* (1940–1954) bore lonely witness to the excesses of a cult venerating the Italian conductor Arturo Toscanini—a form of worship that penalized American and contemporary music, and privileged celebrity performers over mere composers. These corrosive hit-and-run jobs were widely inflammatory and influential. Thomson was also a minor composer of consequence. In post-Toscanini decades he became an *éminence grise*, sermonizing from a high pulpit at the *New York Review of Books*.

I felt the need to revisit Thomson's use of history. Like Van Wyck Brooks and Lewis Mumford, he rode an interwar revisionist wave that condemned the American past as unusable. For Brooks and Mumford, previous generations of American writers produced nothing to build upon. For Thomson, no previous generation of American composers— no previous American composer, period—offered a springboard toward the American school that Antonín Dvořák, visiting from Bohemia, had once famously and influentially espoused in predicting that the music of African Americans would become the fundament of an American classical music of world importance.

Brooks and Mumford were propelled by an Oedipal revolt that harkened far back to Ralph Waldo Emerson and Henry David Thoreau for inspiration. Once the catalytic thrust of their rebellion took effect, they softened and made room for Herman Melville and Walt Whitman. Thomson never softened—he ever after condemned pre–World War I Americans as superfluous European clones.

Rereading Thomson for the *Wall Street Journal,* I was stunned by his insouciance. He made things up. He pursued the chimera of a useless past. Are George Chadwick's symphonic compositions merely "a pale copy of . . . continental models"? Did Thomson even know Chadwick's music? It is more than doubtful. But his assumptions were echoed in the ubiquitous American music narratives popularized by Copland and Bernstein.

The very considerable music of Chadwick and others consigned by Thomson to "a sort of adolescence" remains insufficiently familiar. What should nevertheless have canceled conventional wisdom was the gradual disclosure of the genius of Charles Ives. Ives had written great American music by 1900. By 1920—around the time Thomson, Copland, and Bernstein believed American concert music to have begun its ascent toward world importance—Ives had amassed a body of work surpassing any oeuvre Thomson, Copland, or Bernstein would bequeath. How they dealt with "the Ives case" is a topic for my Chapter 4.

None of this was wholly new to me. And yet writing my review, I stumbled into an epiphany of sorts. The modernists of the interwar decades applied a criterion of newness; important creators exerted some notable degree of originality. They looked forward. Concomitantly, they disparaged any sustained, appreciative backward gaze as "nostalgic" and "sentimental." Previous generations of American artists and thinkers had more cherished the past. They treated history as a cradle or bedrock. This seemed a consequential realization.

MANY OF US today are understandably discomfited by the naked interplay of culture and race during Dvořák's vibrant American decade. The murder of George Floyd symbolizes a fresh awakening to our abysmal history of racial injustice. We are newly sensitized. In our eagerness to fix the present, however, we become prone to distort the past in ways that may diminish understanding of our common national experience.

Virgil Thomson rigged the past: he used it as a whipping boy. A broad panoply of usage—honoring or ignoring the past, abusing it, censoring it, discovering in it an inspiration or goad or consolation—

is documented in this book. My own recourse to the past here includes the personal pasts of Mark Twain and Charles Ives, the pre–World War I literary past surveyed by Van Wyck Brooks and other interwar writers, and the pre–World War I musical past that Virgil Thomson, Aaron Copland, and Leonard Bernstein claimed to have surveyed but did not.

In effect, I have treated classical music in America as a case study of how the past has been remembered, distorted, or denied. My governing conviction is that the past greatly matters.

Additional resources of interest to readers of *Dvořák's Prophecy*—including links to six documentary films and playlists exploring the author's "new paradigm"—can be found at www.josephhorowitz.com.

Dvořák's
Prophecy

Chapter One

Dvořák, American Music, and Race

Dvořák's Prophecy—Dvořák's Progeny: Burleigh and
Coleridge-Taylor—The Black Symphonists—Porgy and Bess—
The Appropriation Debate

Dvořák's Prophecy

Indelible accounts of plantation song were set down by Frederick Douglass and W. E. B. Du Bois—the one born into slavery (and so with no birth date), the other born in 1868 and hence a witness to former slaves and their songs. In his 1845 "narrative" of an "American slave," Douglass remembers the "wild songs" slaves would sing tramping through the woods to the Great House Farm, "revealing at once the highest joy and the deepest sadness."

They would sometimes sing the most pathetic sentiment in the most rapturous tone, and the most rapturous sentiment in the most pathetic tone. . . . They told a tale of woe which was then altogether beyond my feeble comprehension; they were tones loud, long, and deep; they breathed the prayer and complaint of souls boiling over with the bitterest anguish. Every one was a testimony against slavery, and a prayer to God for deliverance from chains. The hearing of those wild notes always depressed my spirit and filled me with ineffable sadness. I have frequently found myself in tears while hearing them. The mere recurrence of those songs, even now, afflicts me; and while I am writing these lines, an expression of feeling has already found its way down my cheek.

Du Bois wrote in the *The Souls of Black Folk* (1903):

Little of beauty has America given the world save the rude grandeur God himself stamped on her bosom; the human spirit in this new world has expressed itself in vigor and ingenuity rather than in beauty. And so by fateful chance the Negro folk-song—the rhythmic cry of the slave—stands to-day not simply as the sole American music, but as the most beautiful expression of human experience born this side the seas. It has been neglected, it has been, and is, half despised, and above all it has been persistently mistaken and misunderstood; but notwithstanding, it still remains as the singular spiritual heritage of the nation and the greatest gift of the Negro people.

What are these songs, and what do they mean? I know little of music and can say nothing in technical phrase, but I know something of men, and knowing them, I know that these songs are the articulate message of the slave to the world. . . . They are the music of an unhappy people, of the children of disappointment; they tell of death and suffering and unvoiced longing toward a truer world, of misty wanderings and hidden ways.

Through all the sorrow of the Sorrow Songs there breathes a hope—a faith in the ultimate justice of things. The minor cadences of despair change often to triumph and calm confidence. Sometimes it is faith in life, sometimes a faith in death, sometimes assurance of boundless justice in some fair world beyond. But whichever it is, the meaning is always clear: that sometime, somewhere, men will judge men by their souls and not by their skins. Is such a hope justified? Do the Sorrow Songs sing true?

The origins of these singular songs were equally singular. West Africa is pertinent, but so are Anglo-American hymns. The ring shout—circling singers, quickening in pace and intensity—was an African import. The drums of Africa were prohibited by slaveholders; clapping, foot-stomps, and the beating of sticks took their place. Slaves who went to church sang Protestant hymns before creating hymns of their own. Revivalist camp meetings, with their feverish vocalizing, were often interracial. Over time, these varied strains coalesced as a body of songs known as spirituals. They were sung in the praise house, on the campgrounds, in the fields, and in crude cabins flanking columned mansions.

The Fisk Jubilee Singers of Nashville, Tennessee, were the first to popularly purvey African-American spirituals in concert, beginning in 1871. Their formal renditions replaced raw timbres and impetuous improvising with synchronized harmonies and precise intonation. The arrangements were diatonic—not fancy, but homespun and sincere. Their first national tour, in 1872, impacted greatly. Abroad, beginning in 1873, their impact was if anything even greater. They spawned rival Jubilee troupes. The singers were invariably Black, the arrangements always choral. In contradistinction to blackface minstrels singing Stephen Foster, the Fisk Singers mainly purveyed the slave songs of the South, whose spiritual properties they both celebrated and preserved. They sang their share of Foster, too.

Among the many vivid witnesses to the Fisk phenomenon was Mark Twain. A connoisseur of vernacular speech, he naturally cherished vernacular song. Of his many musical affinities, he held in highest esteem not the Schubert songs and Wagner operas he knew, or the minstrel tunes he adored, but the concerts of the Fisk Jubilee Singers. He testified: "Arduous and painstaking cultivation has not diminished or artificialized their music." He wrote a publicity blurb for the Singers' 1873 European tour:

> I think these gentlemen and ladies make eloquent music—and what is as much to the point, they reproduce the true melody of the plantations, and are the only persons I ever heard accomplish this on the public platform. The so-called "negro minstrels" simply

mis-represent the thing; I do not think they ever saw a plantation or heard a slave sing.

I was reared in the South, and my father owned slaves, and I do not know when anything has so moved me as did the plaintive melodies of the Jubilee Singers. It was the first time for twenty-five or thirty years that I had heard such songs, and heard them sung in the genuine old way—and it is a way, I think, that white people cannot imitate—and never can, for that matter, for one must have been a slave himself in order to feel what that life was and so convey the pathos of it in the music.

Twenty-four years later, Twain hosted a visit from the Jubilee Singers at his home in Lucerne, Switzerland. Six of the Singers were already known to him from an encounter in London in 1873. Of these, three were born in slavery and the others were children of slaves. He accompanied the group to a local beer hall crowded with Swiss and German imbibers—"self-contained and unimpressionable looking people, an indifferent and unposted and disheartened audience." The Jubilee Singers cast a spell. "No one was indifferent any more; . . . the camp was theirs. . . . Away back in the beginning—to my mind—their music made all other vocal music cheap; and that early notion is emphasized now. It is utterly beautiful, to me; and it moves me infinitely more than any other music can."

By the time Twain hosted the Fisk singers in Lucerne, the pathos and exaltation of the spirituals had spawned new African-American musical genres, remote from the cotton field. At every stage, their complex fate was pondered with amazement—not least by a famous European visitor whom they ambushed in Manhattan.

∽

ANTONÍN DVOŘÁK'S AMERICAN sojourn of 1892–95 is a protean topic that remains unknown to general practitioners of American cultural history.* The story begins with Jeannette Thurber, a visionary educator who sought to create an American music conservatory of international consequence. Her larger goal was to keep gifted young American musicians from studying abroad—and so further the creation of an "American school." America already had plenty of composers, even good ones. But they mainly evinced their German training. Thurber chose Antonín Dvořák to direct her National Conservatory of Music, on East 17th Street in Manhattan, knowing that he would instantly supply a pedigree.

Dvořák was one of two candidates for this 1892 appointment, the other being the Finn Jean Sibelius. Thurber chose Dvořák partly because she had heard that Sibelius was overly fond of drink. (She evidently was not apprised of Dvořák's own alcoholic propensities.) But her paramount criterion was musical: both Dvořák and Sibelius were cultural nationalists—believers that great art sprang from deep native soil. With Bedřich Smetana, Dvořák had created a Czech compositional style widely noticed and acclaimed. His *Slavonic Dances* of 1878 clinched his high European reputation, backed by Johannes Brahms, Joseph Joachim, and the German publisher Simrock. Dvořák proceeded to triumphantly apply his burgeoning style to the hallowed forms: symphony, opera, string quartet. These works pay knowing homage to Beethoven and Schubert, Brahms and Wagner. But their appeal equally derives from their rustic Bohemian stamp: a firm national bedrock. It was just what Jeannette Thurber wanted for America.

And Dvořák seized her mandate. He went looking for America's folk music. Naturally, he gravitated to Native Americans. And he discovered the sorrow songs: an epiphany. It struck with lightning speed.

Dvořák came to know Indian music from a variety of sources, including Buffalo Bill's Wild West in New York and the Kickapoo Medicine

---

* E.g., *Gotham: A History of New York City to 1898* by Edwin G. Burrows and Mike Wallace, while a tour de force (it deservedly won the 1999 Pulitzer Prize for History), did not find space in its 1,400 pages for Dvořák's New York sojourn. Wallace's prodigious volume two—*Greater Gotham* (2017)—is significantly richer in cultural history.

Show in Iowa (where he spent the summer of 1893). He also adored the most popular work of American literature: Henry Wadsworth Longfellow's *The Song of Hiawatha* (1855), a putative American *Beowolf.* Longfellow's vision of a noble savage, embodying a state of nature more benign than not, fired Dvořák's imagination.

Even more was Dvořák stirred by the sad fate of the Indian and the pathos of the slave. His empathy found expression in his Symphony *From the New World*—to this day, the most beloved orchestral work composed on American soil. It begins with a sorrow song and ends with an Indian dirge. Its most famous tune, later reconstituted as the synthetic spiritual "Goin' Home," memorializes the tragic servitude of Black Americans. The symphony's widely celebrated, widely debated premiere, on December 16, 1893, at Carnegie Hall, posed perennial questions: What is America? Who is an American? Very different answers materialized in New York and a few days later in Boston. Boston writers were incensed by Dvořák's assumption that "Black" and "red" Americans be considered representative or emblematic. Dvořák was denounced as a "negrophile." Invoking hierarchies of race, Boston critics scientifically categorized Dvořák's music as "savage" and "barbarian."

New York was another planet. Thurber was one of many convinced that African Americans owned America's musical seedbed—beginning in 1893, she would pack her conservatory with Black students on full scholarship. The "dean" of New York's music critics was Henry Edward Krehbiel of the *Tribune.* Krehbiel studied Black spirituals and Native American chant. At Chicago's World's Columbian Exposition in 1893, he assiduously reported the "ingenious use of contrasted rhythms" by the Kwakiutl Indians presented by Franz Boas. And he alone treated the war dances of the Dahomeyan village as other than animalistic; "the players showed the most remarkable rhythmical sense and skill that ever came under my notice," he wrote.

Any copious reception history of the *New World* Symphony and other Dvořák works in Boston and New York will discern that Boston defined "Americans" as descendants from the *Mayflower* and that New York more understood Americans as immigrants. The New York discourse on Dvořák is comparatively free of explicit racial bias; the ethnic ladder with Anglo-Saxons on top and "barbarian" Slavs down a rung—a fixture in turn-of-the-century American thought—is hardly applied. Leading New York critics did not write, as Boston's did, of "barbaric modulations" and "barbaric musical means" defacing Dvořák's *Requiem*, or complain of getting "heartily tired of the uncivilized in chamber and symphonic music."

Certainly Dvořák—a Bohemian outsider to Hapsburg Vienna—harbored no prejudice against the creative potential of Black Americans. His New World enthusiasms were many and varied. He absorbed the loneliness of the prairie. He studied the songs of the Kickapoo Medicine Show. He appreciated the novelty of New York's ethnic diversity and the range of musical inspiration it might afford. But his most audacious, most emphatic prophecy espoused the creative prowess of Black Americans.

I am now satisfied that the future music of this country must be founded upon what are called the negro melodies. This must be the real foundation of any serious and original school of composition to be developed in the United States. When I first came here last year I was impressed with this idea and it has developed into a settled conviction. These beautiful and varied themes are the product of the soil. They are American. . . .

These are the folk songs of America and your composers must turn to them. All of the real musicians have borrowed from the songs of the common people. I myself have gone to the simple, half-forgotten tunes of the Bohemian peasants for hints in my most serious work. Only in this way can a musician express the true sentiments of his people. He gets into touch with the common humanity of his country.

In the negro melodies of America I discover all that is needed for a great and noble school of music. They are pathetic, tender, passionate, melancholy, solemn, religious, bold, merry, gay or what you will. It is music that suits itself to any mood or any purpose. There is nothing in the whole range of composition that cannot be supplied with themes from this source.

What was Dvořák thinking? What did he know? In his lexicon, plantation song and Stephen Foster—"Swing Low" and "Camptown Races"— were all one thing: "negro melodies." Dvořák surely knew Foster to have been white—and his inspiration to have been partly Black. "Old Folks at Home"—for decades the most popular American song (better known to us as "Swanee River")—satisfied a criterion dear to Dvořák's heart: its authorship had already blurred into the anonymous realm of folk culture. Dvořák even transcribed it for soprano, baritone, chorus, and orchestra and—an event unthinkable in Boston—in 1894 conducted the premiere at the Madison Square Garden concert hall with a Black chorus and an interracial orchestra. The soloists were his African-American assistant Harry Burleigh (about whom more in a moment) and the most prominent Black concert artist of her day: Sissieretta Jones. Of "Old Folks at Home," with its repeated expostulations of "All the world is sad and dreary!", Jones said: "Is there a soul so insensible that it cannot be stirred to the very depths by the heartbroken cry of the poor old homesick darkey?"

As the most prominent composer for blackface minstrel entertainments, Foster of course today bears a taint. And yet, conditioned by his own marginality, he was an empathetic observer of the outcast. "Old Folks at Home" (1851) exhibits a developing political consciousness. Its slaves live happily enough, "way down on de Swanee Ribber." But its Black protagonist is adrift, longing for lost family and friends. Its mourning tone of existential loneliness was widely appreciated—not least by Dvořák, longing for verdant Bohemia in hectic Manhattan. With "My Old Kentucky Home" (1853), Foster dispensed with the dialect of de and dem. Its narrative of disruption and death depicts a family of slaves whose father figure has been sold downriver. No consoling vision of plantation cheer penetrates its imagery of backbreaking labor without surcease. Harriett Beecher Stowe's *Uncle Tom's Cabin* was published but one year earlier. Foster at first titled his song "Old Uncle Tom, Good Night." Its searing chorus stresses the verb "Weep!"

The music historian Dale Cockrell has portrayed Foster, in this final stage of his brief career, embracing a politics of radical change. Cockrell emphasizes the ambiguities of minstrelsy and the subversive power of music.

By the time of Dvořák's pronouncement, the blackface minstrel show had long been wildly popular. Its history had served to sharpen the lines in the ongoing public discourse on matters of race. Minstrelsy was, on the one hand, manifestly about degrading African-Americans in favor of white Americans. In these ways, and others less explicit, it was a powerful vehicle for affirming the values of the powerful. Yet it was not unambiguously that. In fact, entertainment has always served to some extent to disrupt the status quo; most fundamentally, people seek entertainment because their lives are colored by varying degrees of dullness, boredom, sadness, and insecurity. To be entertained by a surpassing national anxiety, such as race, paradoxically holds out the prospect of unmooring it.

This is something Dvořák might have sensed.

Dvořák's Progeny: Burleigh and Coleridge-Taylor

Dvořák's prophecy that "negro melodies" would found a great school of music, while essentially correct, did not and could not foresee that the great music school would turn popular: jazz and its offshoots. What he had in mind was a Black *classical*-music canon. And in fact, Dvořák bred such progeny—a lineage barely remembered today, but certain to surface in decades to come. It comprises interwar African-American symphonists, of whom the most remarkable was William Levi Dawson. And it also includes white composers, of whom the most remarkable was George Gershwin.

But the most immediate and tangible musical evidence of Dvořák's legacy was furnished by Dvořák's own assistant at the National Conservatory: Harry T. Burleigh, who survived both Dvořák and Gershwin, dying in New York in 1949 at the age of eighty-two. Though mainly forgotten, Burleigh was a major player in the history of American music. He also—as we will eventually discover—furnishes an example of the riskiness of generalizing about music and race.

That Dvořák chose as his assistant a twenty-six-year-old African American cannot be sufficiently pondered. Their mutual influence proved profound. Burleigh had arrived in New York from Erie, Pennsylvania, with a suitcase and a dream. The dream was to study composition with Antonín Dvořák. He failed the preliminary examination and wound up Dvořák's amanuensis instead. From Burleigh, Dvořák absorbed the songs Burleigh knew from his blind grandfather, a former slave. From Dvořák, Burleigh absorbed a fuller appreciation of his musical inheritance. After Dvořák died, it was Burleigh more than anyone else who transformed spirituals into concert songs. If you have heard Marian Anderson or Paul Robeson sing "Deep River," that is Burleigh's arrangement.

Burleigh's versions of the songs he sang for Dvořák are performed to this day. With their subtle trajectories and ambitious chromatic harmonies, they represent a high compositional achievement. It was Burleigh—as singer and transcriber—who made "Deep River" the iconic spiritual of the 1920s and '30s. To what degree Burleigh's "Deep River" is a Burleigh composition is an interesting question. As rendered by the Fisk Jubilee Singers in the 1870s, "Deep River" was a "Church Militant" spiritual. Burleigh slowed it down to achieve a hushed reverence reminiscent of Dvořák's *New World* Largo. In fact, one of Burleigh's "Deep River" variants—for male a cappella chorus—begins by citing the Largo's chordal introduction. It would not be presumptuous to infer that Dvořák was one source of inspiration for "Deep River" as we know it.

Blackface minstrelsy was a central impetus—Burleigh wanted to counteract its influence and to dignify his cultural legacy. For singers of his spiritual arrangements, Burleigh left a page of admonition, a fascinating document redolent of its time and place:

The plantation songs known as "spirituals" are the spontaneous outbursts of intense religious fervor, and had their origin chiefly in camp meetings, revivals and other religious exercises.

They were never "composed," but sprang into life, ready made, from the white heat of religious fervor during some protracted meeting in camp or church, as the simple, ecstatic utterance of wholly untutored minds, and are practically the only music in America which meets the scientific definition of Folk Song.

Success in singing these Folk Songs is primarily dependent upon deep spiritual feeling. The voice is not nearly so important as the spirit; and then rhythm, for the Negro's soul is linked with rhythm, and it is an essential characteristic of most all the Folk Songs.

It is a serious misconception of their meaning and value to treat them as "minstrel" songs, or to try to make them funny by a too literal attempt to imitate the manner of the Negro in singing them, by swaying the body, clapping the hands, or striving to make the peculiar inflections of voice that are natural with the colored people. Their worth is weakened unless they are done impressively, for through all these songs there breathes a hope, a faith in the ultimate justice and brotherhood of man. The cadences of sorrow invariably turn to joy, and the message is ever manifest that eventually deliverance from all that hinders and oppresses the soul will come, and man—every man—will be free.

This set of instructions, dated 1917, links to a body of writings espousing the preservation and propagation of plantation song. The pertinent authors include such white authorities as William Francis Allen, Thomas Wentworth Higginson, and Henry Krehbiel, and also Blacks such as W. E. B. Du Bois, whose essay "The Sorrow Songs" in *The Souls of Black Folk* contains hortatory sentences that Burleigh's admonition practically quotes at its close. But Burleigh's initiative was new: he placed his people's songs on the recital stage alongside Schubert and Brahms. And this was precisely his practice in concert. He was also an oratorio singer whose specialties included Mendelssohn's *Elijah*. We may intuit that for Burleigh this entire body of music, white and Black, was fundamentally united in its purpose and elevation.

Burleigh's achievement positioned him alongside those Harlem Renaissance artists and intellectuals who sought to refine the Black motherlode—and in opposition to ragtime, jazz, and other populist appropriations. And yet he was a good friend of Will Marion Cook, who belonged wholly in the second camp; in concert, he sang Cook's smash-hit show tune "Swing Along." Also, we know that in private Burleigh would "blacken up" with friends to have a good time. In fact, beginning in 1906 he served as music director of a series of blackface minstrel shows produced by the St. George's Men's Club. This was one of his responsibilities as baritone soloist at St. George's Episcopal Church—J. P. Morgan's congregation on East 16th Street. Burleigh obtained this position, which he prominently held for half a century, after auditioning behind a screen. Some on the audition committee rejected Burleigh's candidacy on grounds of race. Morgan himself cast the deciding vote. He and Burleigh became friends for life.

Among Dvořák's progeny, Burleigh did not, however, come first. Preceding him in this buried narrative is the once-famous Black British composer Samuel Coleridge-Taylor—who in the United States momentarily became a prized object of Dvořák's prophecy. The Coleridge-Taylor saga offers a snapshot of the density of compositional activity once engendered by the sorrow songs. Dvořák directly fostered a coterie of composers, of whom Burleigh proved the most important. The others, all composition students at the National Conservatory, produced now-forgotten concert works based upon "negro melodies." One was Black: Maurice Arnold, about whom Dvořák expressed high expectations. Another, William Arms Fisher, turned Dvořák's New World Symphony Largo into "Goin' Home." Rubin Goldmark, who later taught both Aaron Copland and George Gershwin, and whose Negro Rhapsody was once widely performed, was a former Dvořák student. So was Harvey Loomis, a leading figure in the Indianist movement in music alongside Arthur Farwell, who drew inspiration from Dvořák but did not study under him.*

But, remarkably, the two most established post-Dvořák, pre-Gershwin symphonic composers for whom "negro melodies" proved an indispensable inspiration were both European.† Frederick Delius, born in Yorkshire in 1862, was sitting on the porch of a Florida orange grove when he heard the songs of Black plantation workers from across the water. It was a revelation that turned him into a composer whose music—its frequent elegiac tone; its oscillations between sorrow and exaltation—was haunted by those Florida sounds ever after, not least in a series of works (1887–1903) explicitly evoking the American South. One of these, Appalachia: Variations on an Old Slave Song (1896–1903), is a veritable New World symphony. Decades later, in 1928, Delius predicted: "I believe that if America is one day to give the world a great composer, he will have colored blood in his veins."

Coleridge-Taylor, whose music Delius doubtless knew, did have colored blood. He was born in London in 1875. His father, Dr. Daniel Taylor,

---

* Will Marion Cook, whose In Dahomey (1903) was the first smash-hit all-Black Broadway musical, also briefly studied with Dvořák at the Conservatory, but there is no evidence that this relationship proved productive.

† A fascinating post-Gershwin instance is the Czech-born Bohuslav Martinů (1890–1959), whose style was highly inflected by American jazz even before he moved to the United States in 1941. Many pages of Martinu sound something like Dvořák intermingled with "negro melodies"—an inspired sequel to Dvořák's own American style.

was a Black physician from Sierra Leone. Dr. Taylor returned to Africa without knowing that Alice Martin, who was white, was pregnant with their child; she was the one who named and raised the prodigy composer. Coleridge-Taylor entered the Royal College of Music at fifteen. His 1898 cantata *Hiawatha's Wedding Feast*, composed when he was all of twenty-two, was a sensation on both sides of the Atlantic. Dvořák was an obvious influence on the young Coleridge-Taylor. But Black music was not. He began his creative life as a highly accomplished, highly acclaimed British composer who happened to be Black. Then, still in England, he met such African-American luminaries as Bob Cole, W. E. B. Du Bois, Paul Laurence Dunbar, James and J. Rosamond Johnson, and the leader of the Fisk Jubilee Singers: Frederick Loudin.

A landmark Coleridge-Taylor composition was his *Twenty-four Negro Melodies* for solo piano, composed in England but printed in Boston in 1905. Encouraged by Burleigh, by Dunbar and Booker T. Washington, Coleridge-Taylor had become part of the Dvořák legacy. Du Bois looked to Coleridge-Taylor as a beacon: the Black musical genius who would take the lead in adapting the sorrow songs of the South for symphony and opera. And it was Dvořák's former student William Arms Fisher, at Oliver Ditson & Company, who published the *Twenty-Four Negro Melodies*. Coleridge-Taylor's two visits to Washington, D.C., were peak moments in the early-twentieth-century history of African-American culture in that city. Nationally, the *Musical Courier*—a central repository of American musical opinion—reported of Coleridge-Taylor's 1904 D.C. sojourn: "The general impression in regard to the enterprise is of wonder and admiration, and an inspiring hope and ambition in many directions, the benefits of which cannot be sufficiently estimated."

Coleridge-Taylor died young: in 1912, of pneumonia. *Hiawatha's Wedding Feast* retained a sturdy place in the British choral repertoire for a time, then disappeared with the composer in tow. Today, Samuel Coleridge-Taylor is barely a name; he awaits rediscovery. Such works as *The Bamboula* (1910), adapting a Black Creole dance, and "Keep Me from Sinkin' Down" for violin and orchestra (1911), adapting a slave song, illustrate what Coleridge-Taylor's music eventually sounded like. Dvořák remains a strong influence on the second; the first, lavishly orchestrated, lacks the stomping physicality of Louis Moreau Gottschalk's 1845 setting of the same tune.

In *The Star of Ethiopia*, W. E. B. Du Bois's 1911 musical pageant about the African American experience, Coleridge-Taylor and *Hiawatha's Wedding Feast* occupy a privileged moment, cited as evidence of peak achievement by a Black artist in a white world. But this high station was never clinched, and whether Coleridge-Taylor ever surpassed his early triumph remains an open question. Certainly the Victorian musical culture in which he was raised was insular compared to that of France, Germany, or Russia. But he had time enough to escape it. Perhaps Coleridge-Taylor was constrained by a felt need to fit into the white mainstream. Perhaps the high example of Dvořák—his skill and success appropriating the American vernacular—was limiting as well as inspirational. Coleridge-Taylor's hostility to ragtime suits this picture. So does his decision, setting Paul Laurence Dunbar, to avoid Dunbar's dialect poems.* Comparably, Harry Burleigh—closely associated with Coleridge-Taylor in America—harbored a lifelong aversion to jazz.

It cannot be coincidental that Burleigh's first spiritual arrangement— "Deep River" (a choral version)—came in 1913: just after Coleridge-Taylor's death. He was picking up a thread. Burleigh's spirituals justifiably surpass Coleridge-Taylor's *Negro Melodies* in influence and resilience. At the same time, it remains undeniable that both Burleigh and Coleridge-Taylor are fundamentally decorous composers—more decorous than Gottschalk, than Dvořák, than Gershwin, than the sorrow songs as rendered by the Fisk Singers. They were explicitly intent upon dignifying their racial inheritance. Their aversion to "lower" styles of appropriation—to blackface minstrelsy, to coon songs—was visceral and defensive. Was their range of musical expression thereby narrowed?

---

* Coleridge-Taylor's seven *African Romances* for voice and piano (1897) set florid Dunbar poems. A seventh Dunbar setting by Coleridge-Taylor, "A Corn Song" (also 1897), uses a poem incorporating a short refrain in dialect.

The Black Symphonists

Samuel Coleridge-Taylor belongs in the history of American classical music—but there is no place to put him. He inhabits a post-Dvořák no-man's-land to the side of the standard narrative. The pertinent memory hole includes minstrelsy, its Black Broadway progeny, and its counterprogeny on the concert stage. Burleigh and Coleridge-Taylor, Will Marion Cook, James Reese Europe, and Clarence Cameron White are among the pertinent names. Another is Scott Joplin, the ragtime king, who considered himself a classical composer. By 1920, prejudice and habit had deflected most Black creative musical talent away from American classical music. But there remained a few survivors: highly trained Black musicians composing skillfully and ambitiously for orchestra. In this even deeper memory hole may be glimpsed the interwar orchestral output of Nathaniel Dett, William Dawson, William Grant Still, and Florence Price.

Here is an instance of cultural amnesia so extreme that a corrective effort is today inescapable, driven from without by social forces mandating a fuller understanding of American racial bias. A notable Dett event came first: his oratorio *The Ordering of Moses,* premiered by the Cincinnati Symphony in 1937, was in 2014 revived by the same orchestra, resulting in a Carnegie Hall performance and a much-noticed recording. While William Grant Still's Symphony No. 1 (the *Afro-American,* 1930) never wholly faded from view, the Los Angeles Philharmonic's 2019 minifestival "William Grant Still and the Harlem Renaissance," showcasing Still's First and Fourth Symphonies, was a notable initiative. Florence Price, previously unknown to the general musical public, leaped into view in 2018 when her two violin concertos, discovered in 2009, were released on CD. A full-page story in the Sunday *New York Times* ("Once Overlooked, Now Rediscovered") reported that Price's four symphonies would be recorded in fresh editions. The article queried: "The question is, who will perform [her music]. Even by late last year, when challenged by a group of local musicians to diversify their programming, the Boston Symphony replied that, while it was working on the problem, audiences still wanted to hear 'specifically the universal masterworks composed between 1600 [sic] and the mid-1900s.'" In fact, were the Boston Symphony to perform a Price symphony or concerto, a full house and national attention would follow. There is even a local connection: Price studied with George Chadwick at Boston's New England Conservatory. But the Boston Symphony abandoned Chadwick a century ago.

The discovery of a trove of Florence Price manuscripts in Chicago was happenstance. A considered inquiry into buried Black classical music would lead elsewhere. To begin with: the American Dvořák—denigrated or ignored by the standard narrators—becomes omnipresent.

When Samuel Coleridge-Taylor died, Du Bois eulogized:

> He came to America with strange enthusiasm. To his own people— to the sad sweetness of their voices, their inborn sense of music, their broken, half-articulate voices,—he leapt with new enthusiasm. From the fainter shadowings of his own life, he sensed instinctively the vaster tragedy of theirs. His soul yearned to give voice and being to this human thing. He turned to the sorrow songs.

Du Bois embraced Dvořák's prophecy, with Coleridge-Taylor as his agent. But Coleridge-Taylor failed to embed the sorrow songs in the concert hall with compelling originality. If William Dawson proved a likelier candidate, he utterly lacked the cachet in America that Coleridge-Taylor had enjoyed in Britain, where racial barriers were less harsh. In effect, Dawson's *Negro Folk Symphony* echoed in a void. He died an *éminence grise* in 1990 at the age of ninety-one, successful and admired within the sphere of spiritual arrangements—Burleigh's sphere. Though he had aspired to continue to compose for orchestra (he had first called his symphony "No. 1"), he never again did so. (I return to the interwar Black symphonists in Chapter 6.)

Any adequate attempt to understand Dawson's achievement—its

provenance and its fate—would necessarily compass whole chapters of the African-American experience in microcosm, an undertaking in which any degree of special pleading would be both superfluous and obtrusive. His fate—the fate of the gifted Black composer in American classical music—resembles Du Bois's own: surging promise; growing frustration and disappointment; escape to Ghana. Black American music escaped to jazz.

Porgy and Bess

But before jazz came ragtime and Scott Joplin, whose rags are composed pieces. In fact, Joplin's major undertaking was an opera, *Treemonisha* (1911). In effect, Joplin's gifted embodiment of Dvořák's prophecy—the smart syncopations of his rags, their physicality and steady energy—led in two directions: jazz and the concert hall. For Black musicians the first direction was by far the more productive. The result—much discussed in my pages to come—was a high/low schism more pronounced (and of course more racial) than any such musical schism abroad. Popular music was Black; classical music was white. In between—a brave opportunity to mediate—came George Gershwin's *Rhapsody in Blue* (1924). Another interloper was Duke Ellington, whom Alain Locke observed testing "his ability to carry jazz to the higher level." Beginning in 1935 with *Reminiscing in Tempo*, Ellington began experimenting with larger forms.

It bears stressing that the most notable fulfillment of Dvořák's prophecy—however much marginalized by the standard narrative—is the most notable creative achievement in American classical music, a work appreciated the world over, enthralling audiences in London, Paris, Berlin, Milan, and Leningrad, and exciting the approbation of such composers as Francis Poulenc and Dmitri Shostakovich and of such formidable critics as Max Graf and H. H. Stuckenschmidt. This of course is *Porgy and Bess*, which ingeniously mines the Black vernacular—and in so doing creates a New World variant of Old World grand opera.

When Gershwin's "folk opera" opened on Broadway in 1935, critics from both music and theater were confounded. "What is it?" they wanted to know—and could not tell. Their basic grievance was that Gershwin—famous as a songwriter and show composer—was an interloper. He did not belong to the world of Black ritual and music that *Porgy and Bess* appropriated. Nor was he a pedigreed classical musician entitled to compose for opera singers. Rather like Dvořák, he had no use for hierarchies of taste. And, like Dvořák, he trampled turf not his own.

Of many dozens of *Porgy* reviewers, one stood apart. He did not regard Gershwin as transgressive. He also happened to be the only writer old enough to remember Dvořák in New York. This was W. J. Henderson, born in 1855. No less than Henry Krehbiel, Henderson long espoused Black music as America's music. His 3,500-word review of the *New World* Symphony premiere, in the *Times*, had sounded this clarion call: "The American people—or the majority of them—learned to love the songs of the negro slave and to find in them something that belonged to America. If those songs are not national, then there is no such thing as national music." Assessing *Porgy* forty-two years later, Henderson wrote in the *New York Sun*:

> Art addresses itself to humanity; it cannot be monastic, nor can the artist live a hermit life. What he has to do is to study his own people and his own time and strive ever to bring his inner life into harmony with them. George Gershwin has done precisely that. He has not sought to align himself with Wagner or Mozart or Verdi. He has written a message to the people of Broadway and he has written it brilliantly. It is not grand opera; it is not folk opera; it is not pure Negro, but it is Gershwin talking to the crowd in his own way. And that is a very persuasive way.

The American musical landscape Gershwin straddled was fractured, crippled by a high/low schism pitting one man's music against another's. An outsider from an earlier century, Henderson singularly comprehended Gershwin as a remedial influence.

Gershwin himself was maddeningly comfortable in Harlem and Carnegie Hall both. His enthusiasms ranged from Stravinsky and Berg to Irving Berlin. His templates for *Porgy and Bess* included *Carmen* and *Die Meistersinger*. To study the speech and song of the Carolina Gullahs—the Black inhabitants of his opera's Catfish Row tenement—he went to a Folly Island church and "shouted" with the locals.

Gershwin held no degrees, not even from high school. He latterly taught himself how to orchestrate. He had never before attempted anything like a grand opera. And yet *Porgy and Bess* could not be ignored. No previous American opera had so held the stage. American composers asked themselves, "Why not one of us?" Virgil Thomson, in a much-cited *Modern Music* review, summarized *Porgy and Bess* as "an interesting example of what can be done by talent in spite of a bad set-up"—meaning a story and libretto laden with "fake folklore." Thomson recognized that by 1935 it was late for a white composer to craft a Black folk opera. In this regard (among others), he considered Gershwin a naïf. But for the most part, white reviews of *Porgy* were not concerned with issues of racial authenticity—the authenticity that mattered to them was purely artistic: Gershwin's opera was not really an opera; he was *aesthetically* naïve.

On the Black side of things, Gershwin's staunchest defenders were the members of the cast. Inhabiting Catfish Row, they found nothing "fake" about *Porgy and Bess*. They regarded Gershwin as an ally.* In

---

* Todd Duncan and Anne Brown, the original Porgy and Bess, loved their roles, loved the opera, and loved Gershwin as a man. In a 1990 interview, Duncan said, "It was a wonderful cast, highly educated, highly trained. We never had . . . moral troubles, morale troubles." Of Gershwin: "I fell in love with that man. . . . He was so honest and so true. . . . He was a genius, that man was. A real genius." Of "I Got Plenty o' Nuttin'": "When the song ends, . . . well then you have just told the audience what really is important to you, to the composer, to the lyricist and to Porgy. And also to me, Todd Duncan, as an artist and a Negro man. It became my credo: I got love, and I got God, and I got my song . . . the things that really matter in life under God are things that you can't buy." In a 1995 interview, Anne Brown said: "George Gershwin, to me, was a loveable big brother . . . he would come to my house, come to our parties. . . . My fondest memories of him were the times the two of us would have lunch alone in his apartment." From Robert Wyatt and John Andrew Johnson, eds., *The George Gershwin Reader* (2004), pp. 221–36.

the African-American press, Rob Roy of the *Chicago Defender* wished that J. Rosamond Johnson had been the composer (the "Negro National Anthem," "Lift Every Voice and Sing," was cocreated by Rosamond and his brother James). As Johnson in fact took the part of Lawyer Frazier, he knew both Gershwin and his opera at close quarters; at the Boston premiere, he grasped Gershwin's hand and whispered, "George, you've done it—you're the Abraham Lincoln of Negro music." Carl Diton, in the *Amsterdam News*, expressed "the sincerest hope" that *Porgy and Bess* would "never die." Ralph Matthews, in *Afro-American*, missed Hall Johnson's "sonorous incantations." Hall Johnson himself—whose choir famously purveyed his own spiritual arrangements—assessed *Porgy and Bess* at length for the distinguished "Journal of Negro Life" *Opportunity*. He attended four performances before deciding "that I do like it and that it is a good show." He cited "instances where Mr. Gershwin's music has missed a Negro feeling," and others that "succeeded in catching a real racial strain." *

In retrospect, none of these assessments fully apprehended Gershwin's indifference to issues of authenticity. He didn't care if he had composed an "opera." He made no claims to accurately represent African-American life. This confusion was compounded by the opera's source: DuBose Heyward's 1925 novella *Porgy*. A white Carolina writer fascinated by Gullah mores and physical types, Heyward perceived himself as a cultural anthropologist documenting a preindustrial subculture, a veritable state of nature. His novella is a regional cameo. His Porgy is an outcast goat-cart beggar who sinks into obscurity once Bess is gone. Gershwin's Porgy does not recede at the story's close; rather, he orders his neighbors to "Bring my goat!"—and sets off for New York

---

* The most publicized Black response to *Porgy and Bess* came from Duke Ellington, interviewed by Edward Morrow in *New Theatre*. Morrow's own sentiment that "the times are here to debunk such tripe as Gershwin's lamp-black Negroisms" was widely attributed to Ellington. Ellington subsequently disassociated himself from the Morrow article, but not without adding that Gershwin's music, though "grand," was "not distinctly or definitely Negroid." (See Howard Pollack, *George Gershwin* [2006], pp. 166–67.)

singing. This ceremonial ending is epic, metaphoric. No actual Catfish Row beggar would attempt to pilot a goat cart north to Manhattan.

The Appropriation Debate

If the Black press was conflicted by *Porgy and Bess* in the 1930s, something similar happened with Harry Burleigh and the concert spiritual. Not so very long after W. E. B. Du Bois and Antonín Dvořák extolled the sorrow songs as the fundament for a future American music, the artists and intellectuals of the Harlem Renaissance scoured the African-American musical past. One starting point was the cottonfield. And so it happened that Du Bois, his allies, and his adversaries pursued a now-legendary debate over the uses of a past known and acknowledged, wracked with pain and yet protean with possibility.

It is too little remembered that, like Dvořák, Du Bois was a Wagnerite. As a graduate student in Berlin, he came to know and embrace *The Ring of the Nibelung*. In the tradition of Wagner, Herder, and other German theorists of race, he linked collective purpose and moral instruction to "folk" wisdom: the soul of a people. That Wagner understands the pariah was doubtless also pertinent: Du Bois's favorite opera, *Lohengrin*, is (as ever with Wagner) about an outsider.* To Du Bois it was merely obvious that for Black Americans the sorrow songs comprised a usable past that, subjected to evolutionary development, would yield a desired native concert idiom—the same trajectory anticipated by Dvořák and Burleigh. Formal training and performance, for Du Bois, did not impugn the authenticity of folk sources; rather, a dialectical reconciliation of authority and cosmopolitan finesse would result. Concomitantly, ragtime, the blues, and jazz threatened Du Bois's cultural/political agenda. A child of the Gilded Age, born in tolerant Massachusetts in 1868, he endorsed uplift.

---

* A parallel case is Theodor Herzl in Vienna, for whom *Tannhäuser* excited visions of Jewish liberation.

Alain Locke, born in 1885, the sole offspring of a well-to-do Philadelphia couple, was like Du Bois a distinguished Black Harvard graduate.
His philosophy of the New Negro, a signature of the Harlem Renaissance, aligned with Du Bois's high-cultural predilections. "Negro spirituals," Locke wrote in 1925, could undergo "intimate and original
development in directions already the line of advance in modernistic
music. . . . Negro folk song is not midway in its artistic career yet, and
while the preservation of the original folk forms is for the moment the
most pressing necessity, an inevitable art development awaits them, as
in the past it has awaited all other great folk music." Like Du Bois, Locke
championed the tenor Roland Hayes, who succeeded Burleigh as the
preeminent exponent of the spiritual in concert. Like Du Bois, he mistrusted the popular musical marketplace in favor of elite realms of art.

The opposing camp included Harlem's loudest white cheerleader—
Carl Van Vechten—who deplored Hayes's refinements in favor of Paul
Robeson's "traditional, evangelical renderings" of the Burleigh arrangements.* This—and Van Vechten's celebration of the blues and jazz—
ignited a furious rebuttal from Du Bois, who discerned a decadent
voyeur in love with Black exoticism. But Van Vechten's revisionism was
supported by the Black writers Langston Hughes and Zora Neale Hurston. Many of Hughes's poems keyed on the dialect and structure of the
blues. He heard in jazz "the eternal tom-tom beating of the Negro soul."
He deplored the "urge toward whiteness" in the uses of Black music.

---

* Whatever one makes of Van Vechten's views of Black music and musical performance,
his writings as a classical-music critic—his initial calling—reveal a blowhard dilettante. A
specimen: "The program [was] made up entirely of Rachmaninoff's compositions, including a sonata in D minor, which is interesting, if very long. . . . Rachmaninoff plays with
much charm. . . . the composer's technique is quite sufficient for his needs, and if his tone
is not as beautiful as might be, it usually seemed to be adequate to the demands of the
piece in hand. In fact, he seemed to be always able to impart the spirit of his compositions
to the audience" (the New York Times, Nov. 21, 1909). Here, by way of comparison, is an
acute view, from W. J. Henderson: "The logic of the thing was impervious; the plan was
invulnerable; the proclamation was imperial. There was nothing left for us but to thank
our stars that we have lived when Rachmaninoff did and heard him" (The New York Sun,
Feb. 17, 1930).

Hurston deplored a "flight from Blackness." She heard concert spirituals "squeezing all of the rich Black juice out of the songs," a "sort of
musical octoroon." Du Bois's "idea that the whole body of spirituals are
sorrow songs" seemed to her "ridiculous." It left out the earthiness and
exuberance of the Black vernacular. To Hurston the sorrowful spirituals Du Bois espoused sounded submissive, to Locke the blues sounded
"dominated" by "self-pity." Pitting authenticity against assimilation, the
debate identified conflicting vernacular resources, old and new, rural
and urban.

If Harlem's internal debate over the legacy of plantation song anticipated today's preoccupation with issues of cultural appropriation, it was
Gershwin—or, more specifically, it was *Porgy and Bess*—that in the thirties ignited a nascent cultural-appropriation debate about interracial borrowings. Questions asked in 1935—could a white Brooklyn Jew catch a
"real racial strain"?—escalated during the following decades. With the
singular exception of a touring production that triumphed at home and
abroad, *Porgy and Bess* was little seen in the United States in the 1950s
and '60s. Both the National Association for the Advancement of Colored
People and the Council for the Improvement of Negro Theatre Arts urged
that Samuel Goldwyn's 1959 film version be boycotted by Black audiences
and performers. An advertisement placed by the latter organization in
the *Hollywood Reporter* read: "Dorothy and DuBose Heyward used the
race situation in the South to write a lot of allegories in which Negroes
were violent or gentle, humble or conniving, and given to erupting with
all sorts of going on after their day's work in the white folks' kitchen or
the white folks' yard was over, like sniffing happy dust, careless love,
crapshooting, drinking, topping it all off with knife play." Only beginning in the 1970s did *Porgy* enjoy wide and sustained American popularity as an opera of international stature—a pedigree coinciding with civil
rights legislation and the termination of Jim Crow laws. Today—times of
heightened racial sensitivity and fresh doubt—Gershwin's opera is again
questionable. Toni Morrison's reservations about Mark Twain's Jim, in
Adventures of Huckleberry Finn, are not irrelevant. Is Porgy's simplicity

overdrawn? Does it overecho minstrel-show caricatures? His moral stature notwithstanding, is Porgy in effect garbed in an "ill-made clown suit that cannot hide the man within"?

The most conspicuous recapitulation of the sixties view of *Porgy and Bess* as racially obtuse was a 2011 American Repertory Theater production directed by Diane Paulus, with the book and score adapted by Suzan-Lori Parks and Diedre L. Murray. With Audra McDonald as Bess, the ART *Porgy* became a hot Broadway ticket. The entire work was boldly reconceived: new speeches, new harmonies, new accompaniments, even virtually new numbers. Crucially, ostensible stereotypes were replaced with characters of ostensibly greater consequence. Bess was more robust, less pathetic. Porgy emerged wiser, more sophisticated, more specific. "When Gawd make cripple, He mean him to be lonely," sings Gershwin's Porgy. "He got to trabble dat lonesome road." The newly diminished Porgy sang, "When God made me, He made me to be lonely . . . I got to travel that lonesome road." McDonald's Bess was too savvy to credibly flee to New York with Sporting Life. Norm Lewis's Porgy was too sensible—too civilized—to plausibly attempt trekking one thousand miles in pursuit. What ART passed off as *Porgy and Bess*, widely seen and acclaimed, was a revisionist interpretation predicated on alleged offenses to fellow feeling. It shrank and recalibrated *Porgy and Bess* to fit the square world of identity politics.

In fairness, it must be conceded that the opera's tangled genesis ensures ambiguity. It even has two endings. The first—inherited from DuBose Heyward's dour novella—is tragic: "Oh Bess, oh where's my Bess?"; Porgy is bereft. The second is exalted: "I'm on my way to a heavenly land!"; it originates not with Heyward, not with Gershwin, but (as I had occasion to discover in the Library of Congress's Mamoulian Archive) with the immigrant director Rouben Mamoulian. Mamoulian directed both Gershwin's opera and, eight years previous, Heyward's play—the finale of which he reversed, having Porgy pick himself up and command: "Bring my goat!" Schooled in Russian experimental theater, Mamoulian detested realism. His governing template was the miracle play: allegoric, uplifting. When the Theatre Guild advertised *Porgy* as a true picture of Gullah life, Mamoulian was apoplectic. His reconceived *Porgy*—which made him a Broadway celebrity overnight—was no longer about discovering an exotic Carolina subculture. It was an epic communal rite, a universal saga of suffering and redemption.

So this was the *Porgy* that Gershwin saw at the Guild Theatre. And it was Gershwin who (over Heyward's objections) hired Mamoulian to direct *Porgy and Bess*. The final pages of the opera's libretto—previously attributed to Ira Gershwin and DuBose Heyward—were in fact written by Mamoulian in 1927.

This back story makes articulate the argument that Gershwin's characters are less Black stereotypes than they are universal archetypes. James Baldwin got Bess right when he likened her to Billie Holiday: she is a fallen woman—a victim who (unlike Heyward's Bess) fights her vulnerability strenuously, poignantly, but to no avail. As for Porgy, his debility sensitizes him; held in special regard by the community (as Heyward's Porgy is not), he in return becomes its moral beacon. His odyssey is twofold: he belatedly experiences love for the first time; summoning unsuspected strength, he rids the community of Crown. Gershwin's opera is in some part a fable, transcending race, about a cripple made whole, an agent of personal and communal redemption. One reason its characters are Black is that Gershwin adored Black music and needed Black people to sing it. If *Porgy and Bess* remains permanently controversial, so is the American experience of race it observes and haphazardly inhabits.

WHO BEST DECREED the destiny of American music? Of Black vernacular roots that equally aroused W. E. B. Du Bois and Mark Twain, Henry Krehbiel and Antonín Dvořák, Carl Van Vechten and Zora Neale Hurston, William Dawson and George Gershwin? The question remains unanswerable—not least because if certain Black Americans rejected American classical music, American classical music also rejected them.

Even though Roland Hayes and Paul Robeson enjoyed phenomenal success in recital, opera companies and orchestras resisted singers and instrumentalists of color. Notoriously, Marian Anderson had to wait until 1955 to sing at the Metropolitan Opera—an invitation engineered not by native-born Americans, but by four committed immigrants.

Anderson's account, in her 1956 autobiography, offers a chilling glimpse of her American-born manager Arthur Judson, who ruled America's preeminent classical-music business empire. Judson advised Anderson: "If you go to Europe it will only be to satisfy your vanity." She went anyway and was there discovered by Sol Hurok. It was Hurok (born in Russia) who propelled Anderson toward a major international career—and Verdi's *A Masked Ball* at the Met. The Met's Rudolf Bing (born in Vienna) was as eager to have her as his Canadian predecessor, Edward Johnson, had been resistant. Max Rudolf (born in Frankfurt) prepared her; Dimitri Mitropoulos (born in Athens) conducted her.

Such Black composers of symphonies, oratorios, and operas as Nathaniel Dett, William Grant Still, William Dawson, and Florence Price meanwhile comprised a shadowy half-presence within the precincts of American classical music. Duke Ellington's symphonic jazz at Carnegie Hall was a looming presence on the outskirts. George Gershwin, tainted by Harlem, was a presence less ignorable and yet unwanted.

The story I have just told begets another story: about the creation of a standard narrative for American classical music into which the sorrow songs and Dvořák's prophecy do not fit. Rather, it is a modernist narrative, a characteristic product of a time, empowered by newness, during which the present and future mattered more than any fond backward glance. This second story can best be observed from a height. I therefore commence in late-nineteenth-century New York City, and musical chroniclers who cherished retrospection over originality.

Chapter Two

In Defense of Nostalgia

*James Gibbons Huneker and the "Old Guard"—In Defense of
Nostalgia—Henry Edward Krehbiel and "Negro Melodies"—
The Fragmentation of Culture*

James Gibbons Huneker and the "Old Guard"

It is only natural when a man's hair begins to thin and he has
gout in the gums that he sadly turns to the "pleasures" of
memory, a bitter-sweet game . . . and one which always sets
the teeth on edge. . . .

I recall with intense amusement the New York restaurants and
cafes of a quarter of a century ago. Were they any better then than
now? is the inevitable question.

The answer is that we were younger then, our appetites and
teeth unafraid. . . . The young folk nowadays are not epicures.
Wine palates they have not; cocktails and the common consump-
tion of spirits have banished all sense of taste values. They are in
too much of a hurry to dance or to ride, to sit long at table and dine
with discrimination. . . .

The number of cheap, quick-fire food hells is appalling. . . .
Noisy bands of music-makers, ill-cooked food and hastily gobbled,
shrieking instead of conversation. . . . This is the order of the evening. . . . Eating and drinking are rapidly entering the category of

the lost fine arts. Bolting, guzzling, gum chewing, and film pic-
tures have driven them away.

   Some day, say hopeful prophets, they will return. I doubt it. Our
age is too materialistic.

The writer of this paean to the past was James Gibbons Huneker.
The year was 1915—when Huneker was fifty-eight years old. The most
flamboyant, most progressive American critic of his day, he was
a lonely herald of modernism. His enthusiasms, ranging across a
spectrum of music, literature, theater, and painting, included Ger-
hart Hauptmann, James Joyce, Stéphane Mallarmé, Edvard Munch,
August Strindberg, and Frank Wedekind, whose *Spring's Awakening*
he greeted as a landmark challenge to sexual taboos in the modern
theater. Huneker had his limits. But this did not preclude acute, open-
eared attention. Encountering Arnold Schoenberg's atonal *Pierrot
lunaire* in 1912, he registered

> the sound of delicate China shivering into a thousand luminous
> fragments. In the welter of tonalities that bruised each other as
> they passed and repassed, in the preliminary grip of enharmonies
> that almost made the ears bleed, the eyes water, the scalp to freeze,
> I could not keep a central grip on myself. It was new music, or new
> exquisitely horrible sounds, with a vengeance. The very ecstasy of
> the hideous! . . . If such music making is ever to become accepted,
> then I long for Death the Releaser.

   Huneker arrived in New York City in 1886 and found a tenth-floor
flat at Madison and 76th Street—from which elevation he could see
both the East and Hudson Rivers as well as the Statue of Liberty; the
looming "proximity of stone, steel, and brick," which he would in 1915
decry for robbing Manhattan of "earth, air, and moisture," had yet
to obscure the view. He was soon introduced to Moulds' on Univer-

sity Place, "a center for actors, writers, artists, musicians, as well as business and professional men. . . . There I ate . . . a bean soup without compare. And free!"*

But Huneker gravitated south to Union Square, then the city's hub for music, for German theater, and—Huneker's truest habitat—German beer saloons. This was the neighborhood of the Academy of Music and Steinway Hall, then the city's major opera house and concert venue; and of Jeannette Thurber's National Conservatory. The habitués of Maurer's and Brubacher's, of Lienau's, Fleischmann's, and Luchow's were artists already legendary—and yet not remote. Huneker observed the colossal Wagner tenor Albert Niemann—"a drinker that would have pleased Pantagruel"—downing cocktails from a beer glass till sunrise. Antonín Dvořák chased cocktails and beer with slivovitz. The resident composers also included Victor Herbert. The pianists were Rafael Joseffy, who had studied with Liszt, and with whom Huneker had studied; and Moriz Rosenthal, who had studied with Liszt and Joseffy both. The violinists included August Wilhelmj and Eugène Ysaÿe. These would remain great names for generations to come. Looking back in 1915, Huneker rhapsodized:

> There gathered . . . the very cream of the musical aristocracy. . . . a genuine atmosphere of Teutonic "Gemüthlichkeit" [sic] existed in those times that are no more. . . .
>
> Where Proctor's Theatre now stands . . . was a small brewery opened by Peter Buckel. Big trees pierced the floors of the piazza, and under them you could sit and enjoy yourself; opposite was Terrace Garden . . . The street then reminded me of a street in Vienna.
>
> The old Café Boulevard was worth while in the beginning, before it became a fashionable "slumming" attraction, and the old Fleischmann Vienna Café, next to Grace Church, was a cen-

---

* It was customary at such establishments to offer a free lunch to those who drank.

tre for conductor Anton Seidl, for Antonín Dvořák, the Bohemian
composer—I am forced to explain who these celebrated musicians
are, for the horde of philistines that invade our city know nothing
of art, little of manners, but much of money-getting. . . .

Down the street lay the Lower East Side, teeming with immigrants,
with bohemians and anarchists. Huneker there met Emma Goldman and
Ambrose Bierce. He was himself a great neighborhood celebrity, swill-
ing his libations, launching his orations, banging out "La Marsellaise"
and the "The Internationale" on smoke-stained pianos with rattling
keys. H. L. Mencken, a Huneker protégé, observed in 1909: "If a merci-
ful Providence had not sent James Gibbons Huneker into the world, we
Americans would still be shipping union suits to the heathen, reading
Emerson, sweating at Chautauquas and applauding the plays of Bronson
Howard." Mencken recorded in detail a five-hour Huneker monologue,
a "veritable geyser of unfamiliar names, shocking epigrams in strange
tongues, unearthly philosophies out of the backwaters of Scandinavia,
Transylvania, Bulgaria, the Basque country, the Ukraine." "I have never
encountered a man who was further removed from dullness; it seemed
a literal impossibility for him to open his mouth without discharging
some word or phrase that arrested the attention and stuck in the memory." The prodigious Huneker rant recorded by Mencken was thickly
layered with history and personal recollection: the topography of Liszt's
warts, Shaw's struggle to throw off Presbyterianism, what Cézanne
thought of his disciples, what George Moore said about German bath-
rooms, D'Annunzio's affair with Duse, the last words of Whitman.

In short: Huneker the prophet was equally a connoisseur of the past.
"As a nation," he grieved, "we are becoming as superficial in our reading as we are in our taste for the theatre. Our native theatre has nearly
touched low-water mark, and the film theatre . . . is only a degree lower;
stupidity and vulgarity in two instead of three dimensions." "Men [once]
seemed more vigorous to us . . . and seem more fidgety and nervous in
this year of grace . . . Really, personality counted then."

No reminiscence of James Gibbons Huneker known to me regards such mighty gusts of nostalgia as paradoxical or contradictory. They did not seem to signify a soft head or a lazy brain.

In Defense of Nostalgia

Jackson Lears is a cultural historian who has revisited the Gilded Age and discovered social and political ferment refuting stereotypes of hegemonic power linked to elitist institutions of high culture. Lears's influential *No Place of Grace: Antimodernism and the Transformation of American Culture, 1880–1920* (1981) explores a national craving for "intense experience" beginning around 1880. He surveys a variety of responses, including Wagnerism, spiritualism, and a vibrant arts and crafts revival. Vigorous alternatives to an impersonal industrial order are the core subject matter of his book.

A sequel 1998 essay is Lears's "Looking Backward: In Defense of Nostalgia." It begins with etymology. "Nostalgia" was first popularized by eighteenth-century European physicians. It designated a malady: homesickness, a failure to thrive in faraway lands. As recycled during World War II, it was a contagious disorder that could spread with epidemic speed through Army induction centers. Among provincial Americans, it could become pathological.

By 1950, "nostalgia" was widely understood as sentimental reverence for the past, freighted with political reaction. Prominent historians— Lears mentions Richard Hofstadter and Arthur Schlesinger, Jr.— invoked nostalgia to describe a failure of nerve, a refusal to grapple with modernity. The Populists of the 1890s—Dvořák's American decade— retreated toward an "agrarian myth." Later generations of nostalgists, Hofstadter wrote in 1948, displayed "a ravenous appetite for Americana" apprehended "in a spirit of sentimental appreciation rather than critical analysis." In 1965, Hofstadter discerned a "paranoid" strain of American politics; nostalgia was one of its symptoms.

The tide turned, Lears writes, in the sixties and seventies. Left-wing intellectuals acquired new appreciation for the preindustrial past. So did the emerging antiwar counterculture. Though "nostalgia" was "too tainted for scholars to reclaim [it] overtly," preindustrial custom and tradition in quest of "community" were rethought as "legitimate efforts to make sense of experience and not simply as symptoms of ignorance to be steamrolled by the forces of progress." A "respect for the pastness of the past" could "accompany a profound and nuanced sense of history." It could also inspire a humane and companionable lifestyle and progressive political thought. In the work of such historians as E. P. Thompson and Raymond Williams, "loving memories of the past" were shown to spark "rebellion against the present in the service of future generations." Thus were Britain's Luddites "heroic defenders of a humane way of life" rather than "quixotic fools."

In sum: "Isn't it time this much abused sentiment received its due? For centuries it has been the *bête noire* of every forward-looking intellectual, right, left, or center. Surely the longing for times lost deserves to be treated as more than a symptom of intellectual weakness. Surely the devotees of a past Golden Age deserve as much credibility as those whose Golden Age lies in the future. Why grant legitimacy to one form of sentimentality and not the other?"

∽

HUNEKER WAS PART of an Old Guard (so called by the critic Oscar Thompson in 1936) subsequently unequalled in prominence and influence in the annals of American musical journalism. His most remarkable compatriots were W. J. Henderson and Henry Krehbiel, music critics of the *Times* and the *Tribune,* respectively.

Though close friends, these writers diverged. Huneker was a virtuoso hyperstylist. Henderson practiced a plain English ahead of its time. Krehbiel was a practitioner of ponderous Germanic circumlocution, a pontificator whose tortuous sentences and vast paragraphs, leisurely yet intense, sag with luggage or acquire a cumulative locomotive velocity. Huneker taught piano at Jeannette Thurber's National Conservatory, where he also dispatched administrative responsibilities. Henderson's specialty was the human voice. Krehbiel, a prodigious autodidact, was not an instrumentalist. But he tackled every facet of music; he read six languages, translated opera librettos, composed exercises for the violin, and (among his dozen books) completed the first English edition of Alexander Wheelock Thayer's monumental *Life of Beethoven*.

Huneker, Henderson, and Krehbiel equally partook in the community of culture they observed, described, and assessed: later notions of "objectivity" did not register with them. After Word War I, Virgil Thomson was a lonely exception to a new etiquette prescribing arms-length distance from composers, performers, and managers. Before that, everyone dined at the same table. And New York was a musical feast. The Metropolitan Opera and Manhattan Opera, studded with international stars, fought for dominance. The depth of instrumental talent was unique. Anton Seidl, Artur Nikisch, Karl Muck, Gustav Mahler, Arturo Toscanini were the conductors. The critics took it all in—and from the inside. Krehbiel, accustomed to his eminence, dropped by when Seidl was teaching Albert Niemann the *Götterdämmerung* Siegfried in his East 62nd Street brownstone study. Henderson kept a salon. Huneker preferred his saloons. When Oscar Hammerstein, far the most colorful and accomplished of all American opera impresarios, locked himself in a room on a hundred-dollar bet that he could compose an opera in forty-eight hours, Huneker and other adversaries in the wager engaged organ grinders and a monkey to frustrate the great endeavor. But *The Kohinoor* was completed on time—and Hammerstein duly produced it. "The worst [opera] on record," Huneker called it. "The opening chorus consumed a third of the first act. . . . Two comic Jews, alternately, for half an hour sang 'Good morning, Mr. Morgenstern, Good morning, Mr. Isaacstein.'"

Of greater relevance to the present study: Huneker, Henderson, and Krehbiel were notable historians. Not only did these writers possess long memories; to a degree unknown among arts journalists a century later, they endeavored to study the pertinent past. Even Huneker, who lacked patience for scholastic exercise, authored an early history of the New York Philharmonic. Alongside a 1906 text of vocal instruction, Henderson's books include his *Early History of Singing* (1921); in tandem with the posthumous Henderson compendium *The Art of Singing*, it constitutes a narrative of "Golden Age" prowess and twentieth-century decline predicated on the author's favored criteria of vocal technique. It is Krehbiel, however, who indispensably documented musical history. His *The Philharmonic Society of New York* (1892) is a necessary but superseded early effort. But *Chapters of Opera* (1908) and *More Chapters of Opera* (1919), following "the Lyric Drama in New York from its earliest days down to the present time," have not been supplanted. If Virgil Thomson's *American Music Since 1910* is ephemeral synthetic history,* Krehbiel's twin volumes are a bedrock not merely for erudition; his charged verdicts are based on a long view. They both recount and use the past.

"Historical and Critical Observations and Records," reads Krehbiel's subtitle for *Chapters* and *More Chapters*. These 800 pages, partly derived from articles and reviews in the *New York Tribune*, assemble a copious data bank—a record of performances and venues. For most of the nineteenth century, opera in New York defied generalization. It was given in Italian, German, French, English. A typical American opera house might be the 4,000-seat Academy of Music, memorialized by Edith Wharton in *The Age of Innocence* as a playground for frivolous wealth. It might be the Bowery Theatre, where Walt Whitman observed audiences "packed from ceiling to pit with full-blooded young and middle-aged men, the best average of American-born mechanics . . . bursting forth in one of those long-kept-up tempests of hand-clapping . . . no dainty kid-glove business, but electric force and muscle from perhaps two thousand full-sinewed men." But by 1900 a single megavenue—the Metropolitan Opera House on 39th Street—ruled operatic taste and custom. One thread of Krehbiel's narrative, then, is an institutional history. Another follows the evolution of the art form via new repertoire as disclosed to

---

* See pages xx–xxii.

New York audiences: operas by Verdi and Wagner, operas by Debussy, Puccini, Strauss, plus countless others of lesser repute.

An anchoring factor—the ground bass of Krehbiel's tale—is a criterion of worth. At the turn of the twentieth century, Americans still widely cherished a belief that culture confers sweetness and light. Music, for Krehbiel, was a source of moral fortitude, an instrument for betterment. This may seem a Victorian myth. But before the Great War, before modernism, before the music lovers Hitler, Stalin, and Mussolini, it could be a living article of faith. Particular to Krehbiel's faith is his truculent insistence on a democratic ethos. The son of an immigrant German preacher, self-educated, self-made, he aspired to imbue Everyman with elite standards of humanizing art and learning. The result would be "American."

The Met began with no such aspirations. Its founders, in 1883, were newly wealthy boxholders-to-be, the boxes at the Academy of Music being full. To adorn the desired social cachet, they engaged Henry Abbey to give opera in Italian with celebrity singers. When that cost more than anticipated, they ditched Abbey and turned over the operatic part of their enterprise to Germans who could run it more cheaply. The result was seven seasons of German opera, mainly Wagner. One hundred twenty-two encircling boxes notwithstanding, glamour departed the vast tiered auditorium. A new audience, German and American, shushed those who paid the bills. The galvanizing figurehead of the new regime was not a star soprano or tenor, but a conductor: the raven-haired Wagner protégé and apostle Anton Seidl. The "intense excitation" Jackson Lears discovered in the late Gilded Age took a remarkable form. When the curtain fell on Isolde's "Liebestod," ladies in attendance—and the vast majority of American Wagnerites were female—would stand on their chairs and scream "for what seemed hours." The bill-payers—Morgans, Roosevelts, Vanderbilts, and others forging a new WASP elite—eventually had enough and expelled the Germans (including not a few German Jews). Opera in French and Italian resulted. But the Germans fought back until the Met virtually housed two companies, one

German and one not. A symbiotic status quo of opera in three tongues was subsequently established. But the idealism of the German experiment was not renewed.

Krehbiel never forgot the final performance of the German regime— *Die Meistersinger* on Saturday afternoon, March 21, 1891. The audience stayed put, standing, cheering, and applauding. The singers, bearing wreaths and bouquets, addressed the clamoring multitude. Some twenty minutes passed. At last Seidl, by Krehbiel's reckoning having already bowed some twenty times, stepped to the front of the stage to say: "Believe me, ladies and gentlemen, I understand the meaning of this great demonstration. For myself, the orchestra, and the other members of the company, I thank you." Only the appearance of workmen on the stage persuaded thousands to leave. Seventeen years later in *Chapters of Opera*, Krehbiel was still flaming with Olympian indignation. His analysis, a Jeremiad layered with historical understanding, must be quoted in full:

> To understand the story of the overthrow of German opera managed by the owners of the opera house, and the reversion to the system which had proved disastrous at the beginning and was fated to prove disastrous again, it is well to bear the fact in mind that instability was, is and always will be an element in the cultivation of opera so long as it remains an exotic; that is, until it becomes a national expression in art, using the vernacular and giving utterance to national ideals. The fickleness of the public taste, the popular craving for sensation, the egotism and rapacity of the artists, the lack of high purpose in the promoters, the domination of fashion instead of love for art, the lack of real artistic culture—all these things have stood from the beginning, as they still stand, in the way of a permanent foundation of opera in New York. The boxes of the Metropolitan Opera House have a high market value to-day, but they are a coveted asset only because they are visible symbols of social distinction. There were genuine notes of rejoicing in the stockholders' voices at the measure of financial success achieved in

the first three seasons of German opera, but the lesson had not yet been learned that an institution like the Metropolitan Opera house can only be maintained by a subvention in perpetuity; that in democratic America the persons who crave and create the luxury must contribute from their pockets the equivalent of the money which in Europe comes from national exchequers and the privy purses of monarchs. This fact did eventually impress itself upon the consciousness of the stockholders of the Metropolitan Opera house, but when it found lodgment there it created a notion—a natural one, and easily understood—that their predilections, and theirs alone, ought to be humored in the character of the entertainment. I have displayed a disposition to quarrel with the artistic attitude of the directors, but I would not be an honest chronicler of the operatic occurrences of the last twenty-five years if I did not so do. The facts in the case were flagrant, the situation anomalous. The stockholders created an art spirit which was big with promise while rich in fulfilment, and then killed it because its manifestation bored them. An institution which seemed about to become permanent and a fit and adequate national expression in an admired form of art, was set afloat again upon the sea of impermanency and speculation.

Krehbiel's long view—the view of the historian—told him that opera in the vernacular would become the necessary basis for an American opera: an American canon, American singers, a distinctive American vocal style based in language. This had been the norm in Italy, Germany, France, and Russia. In those countries, everything was sung in the language of the audience, and native works girded a national art. Krehbiel well knew that. He also contended (a wishful thought) that German opera—because it represented the future of opera; because it prioritized opera as drama— could be a stepping-stone to comparable works composed in English by Americans. Finally, Krehbiel believed that the boxholders' expectation that opera on a grand scale could pay for itself was a delusion. He was right about that. If he was wrong about opera in English—its time never came—his analysis was correct: absent a sustained exercise presenting opera with understandable words, an American canon did not materialize; opera did not become an American "national art."

Henry Krehbiel was never reconciled to the influence of individual wealth on American institutions of high culture. He had no use for noblesse oblige. He cherished the Met's German seasons as a possible seedbed for a people's opera. He suffered a second whiff of hope in 1906 when a populist impresario of genius—the same redoubtable Oscar Hammerstein* who composed an opera in forty-eight hours—created a Manhattan Opera that eschewed the influence of fashion. Having amassed a personal fortune in the cigar trade, Hammerstein himself bankrolled the enterprise. A self-made immigrant, he distanced himself from others of high affluence and disdained a board of directors. He scheduled five weekly performances in direct conflict with the Met. His Saturday nights were popularly priced. He landed a master conductor: Cleofonte Campanini. His casts were stellar. Krehbiel marveled at the Manhattan Opera's "freedom from art-cant and affectation." But the Met fought back with greater resources. In 1910, it bought out Oscar Hammerstein for $1.25 million and a pledge to refrain from producing opera in New York, Chicago, Philadelphia, or Boston for ten years. Hammerstein died nine years later.

From Krebhiel's perspective, this defeat further sealed the 1891 debacle and doomed American opera as an "exotic." This view may be debated but cannot be ignored. And yet such is the state of historical knowledge that cartoons of the Gilded Age prove impossible to dislodge. As we will see, Virgil Thomson in 1971 thought the Met began with its German seasons and got the dates wrong. The most recent history of the Metropolitan Opera, by Charles and Mirella Jona Affron, makes nothing of the Seidl chapter or of its terminus. The early Met was a hotbed of class and ethnic warfare. Only after World War I did it fulfill something like Edith Wharton's imagery of an aloof, elitist playground for the very rich.

---

* His grandson was the famous lyricist of the same name.

Henry Edward Krehbiel and "Negro Melodies"

Henry Krehbiel's memory, weighted with retrospection, imprinted on 1891. Wagner was for him the bellwether of contemporary cultural experience. The Met's Wagner ensemble comprised valued friends and acquaintances. And—although Krehbiel was not unaccustomed to his own importance—Anton Seidl was a paragon he felt privileged to know and observe.

A year and half later, Antonín Dvořák fortuitously arrived in Manhattan. He quickly discovered in Seidl a kindred Central European spirit. They met daily at Fleischmann's Café to sit in near silence, the one consuming beers, the other cigars.

Following Dvořák's lead, both Seidl and Krehbiel now intensified their ongoing efforts to support an American musical art. Dvořák was a butcher's son, an instinctive democrat. He attended the Metropolitan Opera once, for *Siegfried*, and never again—the tiaras and tuxedos made him fidget and retreat. He preferred the company of young Harry Burleigh, of his six children underfoot, of the birds he kept uncaged in his East 17th Street apartment: a facsimile of nature. Though Krehbiel kept no birds, he seconded Dvořák in his devotion to "negro melodies"—a natural music.

The topic was not new. For some time, an "American school" exploring Black roots had been an obvious musical option. As early as 1878, a Black writer, James Monroe Trotter, had published *Music and Some Highly Musical People*, surveying the activities of Black musicians in a wide range of genres. Some dozen years later, a white composer trained in Weimar, Henry Schoenefeld, began composing vignettes of "Southern Negro Life." But it took an eminent foreigner from Prague to pedigree the Black vernacular, and apply it, with overwhelming results. With Dvořák's music in play, Krehbiel's American school campaign gained a new focus: that American composers should pursue an American sound not incidentally, but consciously and purposefully. This cause proved fraught with facile claims and counterclaims. Philip Hale of the *Home*

Journal, Krehbiel's opposite number in Boston, declared "the negro is not inherently musical," as had been discerned "by all close observers in Africa." Hale maintained that the plantation songs of the South were more the offspring of the white man's parlor and campground than of the Black man's cotton field. He ridiculed the notion that American composers should draw inspiration from "Congo, North American Indian, Creole, Greaser, and Cowboy ditties, whinings, yawps, and whoopings."

As Hale was a Boston Brahmin, Krehbiel the son of a German-born Methodist circuit preacher, their instincts diverged. Previously dedicated to Wagner, the scholar/historian in Krehbiel now undertook a series of studies of music and race beginning in 1899—four years after Dvořák's return to Europe. These initially comprised seven dense *Tribune* articles, replete with musical examples and bibliographies, on the music of Hebrews, Orientals, Russians, Scandinavians, Magyars, African Americans, and American Indians. There followed *Tribune* pieces on Indian music (1902), Florida song games (1902), and Russian music (1905). These pathbreaking efforts are remarkable for their even-handed enthusiasms. Krehbiel is not wholly immune to notions of racial hierarchy: he did not stand outside his time and place. But he admires every strain. He does not play one against another. His spirit is ecumenical.

Huneker, in 1915, wrote:

> In Europe there is room for race prejudice, but not in America. Here it is self-stultifying, self-contradicting, and utterly abhorrent to democratic principles. We freed the Black race, we must free ourselves of all race prejudice. We need the Jewish blood as spiritual leaven; the race is art-loving and will prove a barrier to the rapidly growing wave of fanatical puritanism.

W. J. Henderson was clarion in declaring America's folk song Black. But it was Krehbiel, the historian, who wrote the book: *Afro-American Folksongs: A Study in Racial and National Music* (1914). Studying *Die Meistersinger,* he had traveled to Nuremberg to scrutinize that opera's historic sixteenth-century setting. In Chicago at the World's Columbian Exposition, he had studied the Dahomians and Kwakiutls. For his 176-page inquiry into Afro-American folksongs, he did not venture to Africa or even to the Deep South. But he scoured the existing literature in English, German, and French. And he closely studied a sampling of 527 songs.

The "songs created by the negroes while they were slaves on the plantations of the South," Krehbiel wrote, "have cried out in vain for scientific study." Rather, it was the poetry of the songs that had been acclaimed and analyzed by such writers as Thomas Wentworth Higginson and W. E. B. Du Bois as well as the foreigners Julien Tiersot and Albert Friedenthal. No one before Krehbiel had undertaken so detailed an exploration of rhythm, structure, and scales, of syncopation and pentatonicism. This inquiry led Krehbiel to an incipient study of African music, about which he lamented:

It is a pity that students are without adequate material . . . a pity and a wrong. Governments and scientific societies backed by beneficent wealth are spending enormous sums in making shows out of our museums. For these shows men go to Africa actuated by the savage propensity to kill, and call its gratification scientific research. Who has gone to Africa to capture a melody? No one. Yet a few scores or hundreds of phonographic records of music would be worth more to science and art to-day than a thousand stuffed skins of animals robbed of life by the bullets of a Roosevelt.

Krehbiel's book produced three central claims. The first was that African music was both remarkable and pertinent. Unburdened by ethnocentric bias, he marveled at the native musical resources of Black Americans, however subliminally acquired. Of "the art of drum talk," he wrote: "The most refined effects of the modern timpanist seem to be put in the shade by the devices used by African drummers in varying the sound of their instruments so as to make them convey meaning . . . by actual imitation of words."

Krehbiel's second claim was to "disprove the theory which has been frequently advanced that the songs are not original creations of the slaves, but only the fruit of the negro's innate faculty for imitation. . . . Some of the melodies have peculiarities of scale and structure which could not possibly have been copied from the music which the blacks were privileged to hear on the plantations or anywhere else during the period of slavery."

Krehbiel's third claim was that whatever ingredients may be traced to Africa, plantation songs are "American." "They contain idioms which were translated hither from Africa, but as songs they are the product of American institutions; of the social, political and geographical environment within which their creators were placed in America; of the influences to which they were subjected in America." And Krehbiel answered the charge that Black Americans were not "native" to America: "[They] are Americans in the same sense that any other elements of our population is American—every element except the aboriginal. But is there an aboriginal element? Are the red men autochthones? Science seems to have answered that they are not. Then they, too, are American only because they have come to live in America."

The polemical overtones of Krehbiel's book are unignorable and honorable. Without resorting to phony history or succumbing to cliché, it aims to inspire and instruct. It targets "ungenerous and illiberal attitudes toward a body of American citizens." Krehbiel endorses Du Bois's *The Souls of Black Folk* as "the most eloquent English book ever written by any one of African blood." He cites and painfully embraces the pathos of Du Bois's historic cry: "Your country? How came it yours? . . . Our song, our toil, our cheer and warning have been given to this nation in blood brotherhood. Are not these gifts worth giving? Is not this work and striving? Would America have been America without her negro people?"

While the whole of *Afro-American Folksongs* may be read as a rebuke to the cozy Boston of Philip Hale, imbued with "foolish pride . . . of more or less remote English ancestry," it must be added that Hale—who in later years would endorse jazz—is today too easy a target. Even abolitionists had assumed that African Americans were racially inferior in intellect. Frederick Douglass notwithstanding, countervailing evidence seemed scant. A colonialist mindset, however odious to us, did not in Krehbiel's day necessarily connote hostility toward people of color.

Are the humane views expressed in *Afro-American Folksongs* therefore anomalous for their time and place? To be sure, the New York of Dvořák and Krehbiel was a bad time and place to be Black. Nevertheless, not until Madison Grant's *The Passing of the Great White Race* (1916) did a poisonous ideology of racism—stressing heredity and physiology, preaching racial purity—supplant the more benign racial impressions embedded in the romantic nationalism of an earlier era. Another milestone in racial bigotry was the patrician Committee of Fourteen (1905–1932), which, beginning in 1917—after Dvořák's American sojourn, after Huneker's dismissal of "race prejudice," after *Afro-American Folk Songs*—snuffed out biracial dining and dancing in New York's public sphere. Afterward, the city became "more racially and musically segregated," fundamentally changing "the ways American music was made, heard, and appreciated."

History simplifies and generalizes, organizes and classifies—but does not move in straight lines.

The Fragmentation of Culture

Henry Krehbiel's traumatic encounter with Richard Strauss's *Salome*—its American premiere at the Metropolitan Opera on January 22, 1907—was decisive for his terminal nostalgic mode: it clinched his estrangement from the music of the new century. Krehbiel's 4,000-word review began:

> A reviewer ought to be equipped with a dual nature, both intellectually and morally, in order to pronounce fully and fairly upon the qualities of this drama by Oscar Wilde and Richard Strauss. He should be an embodied conscience stung into righteous fury

by the moral stench exhaled by the decadent and pestiferous work, but, though it make him retch, he should be sufficiently judicial in his temperament calmly to look at the drama in all its aspects and determine whether or not as a whole it is an instructive note on the life and culture of the time and whether or not this exudation from the diseased and polluted will and imagination of the authors makes a real advance in artistic expression, irrespective of its contents or their fitness for dramatic representation.

"Is it art?" Krehbiel asked. Though he ostensibly reserved judgment, the evidence he furiously amassed—of a meretricious "sensationalist" whose "business sense is large"—condemned Strauss to hellfire and damnation.

W. J. Henderson proved a relatively less severe critic of modernism. He made allowances for Schoenberg's *Pierrot lunaire* ("to deny that [it] has force and delineative quality is futile") and for Stravinsky's *Apollo* ("chaste, dignified, restful . . . genuinely beautiful"). But his repudiation of Strauss was final: "I challenge any living man to say honestly that he ever came away from the performance of a [Strauss] symphonic poem . . . with a finer impulse of his nature quickened, with any high emotion warmed, or with any sweeter sensibility touched." If Krehbiel and Henderson rejected twentieth-century music on principle—it failed the moral criterion—James Gibbons Huneker's limited sympathies were a matter of taste: he enjoyed Richard Strauss; he tried to like Schoenberg and Stravinsky and could not.

The bigger picture was of estrangement from the new century itself. Surveying operatic affairs between 1908 and 1918, Krehbiel recorded his intolerance for new techniques of mass arousal:

> Even in journals of dignity and scholarly repute the gossip of the foyer and the dressing rooms of the chorus and ballet stood in higher esteem with the news editors than the comments of conscientious critics. . . . If in this [the newspapers] reflect the taste of

their readers, it is a taste which they have instilled and cultivated, for it did not exist before the days of photo-engraving, illustrated supplements and press agents.

Krehbiel's swan song, in 1922, was titled "The Curse and Affectation of Modernism in Music." Its objects of opprobrium included traffic and machine noises, and Einstein's view that there was "no such thing as a straight line in the universe."

Virgil Thomson and Van Wyck Brooks would look back and see the Great War (in which Thomson served); repelled, they gazed toward the future. The Old Guard looked back at the Great War (in which they were too old to have served) and beyond—and saw a better past. They had lived through decades of hope, aspiration, and achievement. For Krehbiel, Henderson, and many another, Antonín Dvořák offered a galvanizing ecumenical vision of a future American art. Decades before the Harlem Renaissance, they foresaw that Black America would become a defining feature of American cultural accomplishment. Without shutting their eyes to prejudice, they propagated a resilient New World vision. Concurrently, they understood the arts as an instrument for individual self-knowledge and growth, and for national self-understanding and betterment.

The mindless duration of the Great War, its mechanized mass destruction, its unprecedented misinformational campaigns, igniting feverish national bigotries—all this advertised disturbing propensities of science and technology, of expanded literacy and tools of communication.

The Old Guard had long proselytized for great music. But Krehbiel and Henderson, though authors of music-education manuals, were not popularizers. They endeavored to expand the circle of culture without blurring the edges; as gatekeepers, they charged steep admission. Henderson's *What Is Good Music?* (1898) plotted a "path of musical salvation" prescribing months of active study; his discussions of musical structure and aesthetics sampled the writings of Immanuel Kant and

Eduard Hanslick. Krehbiel's *How to Listen to Music*, reprinted thirty times between 1896 and 1924, complained of "the majority of hearers in our concert-rooms":

> They are there to adventure a journey into a realm whose beauties do not disclose themselves to the senses alone, but whose perception requires a cooperation of all the finer faculties; yet of this they seem to know nothing, and even of that sense to which the first appeal is made it may be said with profound truth that "hearing they hear not, neither do they understand."

Huneker, who wrote no guidebooks for laymen, winced at "the glaring badge of 'popularity.'" He advised would-be critics: "be charitable, be broad—in a word, be cosmopolitan."

During World War I, George Creel's Committee on Public Information headed the United States government's first large-scale propaganda campaign. CPI advertisements, lectures, films, and expositions denounced the "wanton murder" of Belgian babies by Prussian Huns. "The Hohenzollern fang strikes at every element of decency and culture and taste," read an ad in New York University's *Alumni News*. A *Saturday Evening Post* notice titled "Spies and Lies" warned: "German agents are everywhere, eager to gather scraps of news about our men, our ships, our munitions." The ubiquity of mass arousal fed postwar isolation. It also corrupted cultural discourse and reception. Like Krehbiel, Henderson had discerned a new populist ambience around the turn of the century. Unlike Krehbiel, he lived long enough to witness its fruition. When in 1926 Arturo Toscanini first led the New York Philharmonic, other New York reviewers adopted a tone of hushed sanctimony; Lawrence Gilman—Virgil Thomson's predecessor at the *Herald Tribune*—actually likened Toscanini to Christ. Henderson took a long look back and dourly recorded:

> The concert of the Philharmonic Society last night in Carnegie Hall was one of those musical events which might well be turned

over to the star descriptive reporter. It was not a concert at all; it was the return of the hero, a Roman triumph staged in New York and modern dress. . . .

For these are days when the plain workaday utterance of music will not suffice for a populace incessantly demanding new ways of saying old truths and read to sink into apathy unless mental stimulants are liberally administered.

Huneker and Krehbiel were already dead. Of the other Old Guardsmen, Henry Finck of the *Post* died in 1926, Richard Aldrich, long of the *Times*, in 1937. Three days after Aldrich's demise, Henderson took a revolver out of his desk drawer and put an end to his life. His suicide marked the passing of an era—and he knew it.

By then the Old Guard, if remembered at all, was dimly recalled as a Victorian encumbrance—obtuse, pretentious, elitist. There is no doubt some truth to that cartoon. When I first read Krehbiel's "The Curse and Affectation of Modern Music"—which preceded his death by one month—I winced at its sour description of a *Pierrot lunaire* performance acclaimed by a self-appointed coterie. *Pierrot* does not make me wince. But neither, now, does Krehbiel's article. The Old Guard inhabited a consolidated circle of culture. The circle's expansion was regarded as desirable and yet controllable. The minority that embraced modernism shunned that circle in favor of a much smaller circle of its own. Meanwhile, a sudden infusion of newcomers inflated the first circle and blurred its contents. These were the new middle classes, pursuing a diluted yet high-toned culture product Dwight Macdonald would dub "midcult." In music, Arturo Toscanini was the star attraction. The earnest music-education volumes of earlier times were supplanted by "music appreciation" bibles flaunting a closed canon of European masterworks anointed by celebrated European performers. The commercial dividends of this compact marketing strategy were best exploited by the National Broadcasting Company and by RCA Victor's records and hortatory books. The result, overall, was a new relationship between culture and society—a seismic shift—that the Old Guard foresaw and forswore. Modernism and midcult were incompatible components of a skewed system.*

Then came the twenty-first century of social media impatient with the narrative—lovingly preserved, cautiously extended—that buoyed what culture had been. Krehbiel, reviewing *Salome*, asked "Is it art?" and had a ready answer. What is "art" today? On television, I once discovered Charlie Rose interviewing an expert in artificial intelligence. What can robots *not* do? he asked. "Housework" was the answer; the subtleties of the human hand cannot be mechanically reproduced. What about the creative act? Charlie Rose inquired. Oh, that's easy, came the response. A robot can paint a picture even experts cannot distinguish from a first-rate human product.

Jackson Lears, defending nostalgia, discovered "legitimate efforts to make sense of experience," a "respect for the pastness of the past," a refusal to be "steamrolled by the forces of progress." The Old Guard writers of America's *fin-de-siècle* illustrate that a considered nostalgic mindset may be compatible both with understanding the past, and with framing an enlightened social vision. Reading Huneker, Henderson, and Krehbiel today, absorbing their anxieties about upheavals they acutely sensed, I discover an act of prescience. In the prophecies of Dvořák, echoed by Henderson and Krehbiel, by Harry Burleigh, W. E. B. Du Bois, and other advocates of "negro melodies" as a fundament for American classical music, I discover a stream of inspiration soon to be redirected, dismissed, or forgotten.

---

* This is the central subject matter of my *Understanding Toscanini: How He Became an American Culture-God and Helped Create a New Audience for Old Music* (1987).

Chapter Three

Nostalgic Subversions

*Using the Vernacular: Mark Twain and Charles Ives—Race
and the Moral Core—The Transcendentalist Past*

Using the Vernacular:
Mark Twain and Charles Ives

In the half-century preceding World War I, the most iconic American novelist and the most iconic American symphonist were rebellious spirits. They violate stereotypes of Gilded Age tidiness and of turn-of-the-century restraints contradicting Europe's edgy *fin-de-siècle*. And yet they were steeped in the past—a warmly remembered milieu both personal and national. This was the very engine of their originality. I would call them agents of subversive nostalgia.

Ernest Hemingway famously quipped in 1935 that "all modern American literature comes from one book by Mark Twain called *Adventures of Huckleberry Finn.*" Huck's idiom is a southern dialect inspired in part by African-American voices.[*]

> You don't know about me, without you have read a book by the name of "The Adventures of Tom Sawyer," but that ain't no matter.

Charles Ives's Symphony No. 2, begun (perhaps) in 1899 and finished (we

* Cf. Shelley Fisher Fishkin, *Was Huck Black? Mark Twain and Afro-American Voices* (1994). See page 63.

think) in 1909 (some twenty-four years after *Huck* was published), is a comparable New World landmark, ingeniously transforming a hallowed Old World genre through recourse to vernacular American speech. An amalgam of parlor songs, patriotic airs, and church hymns, it begins with themes adapting Stephen Foster's "Massa's in de Cold Ground" and the fiddle tune "Pigtown Fling." Singularly (even for Ives), the entire five-movement, thirty-five-minute symphony contains not a single wholly original melody. No less than Huck, it speaks a saturated American language remembered from childhood.

The lineage of Mark Twain's novel combines rambunctious frontier humor and subdued New England fiction. Its "adventures" remember the anecdotage of Twain's San Francisco buddies Bret Harte and Artemus Ward. Its wholesome core absorbs the "genteel tradition" embodied by Twain's literary friend William Dean Howells. It abjures the complex urbanity of Twain's great contemporary Henry James—of whose novels he once observed: "You put one down, you simply can't pick it up."

The contradictions lacing Twain's creative personality could be self-defeating. *A Connecticut Yankee in King Arthur's Court* (1889) incoherently mingles Victorian notions of progress and propriety with gusts of invasive bitterness. Hank Morgan awakes in sixth-century England. He decries the profanity of language and manners, the injustice of rank and caste, the technological impoverishment of primitive lives. A paragon of Yankee ingenuity, he implements a program of reform including the abolition of slavery, the democratization of the law, and the invention of the telegraph, telephone, typewriter, sewing machine, and steamboat. The showman and entrepreneur in Hank are pure Mark Twain. But Twain/Morgan is also at war with himself. The fledgling stock exchange proves corrupt. The ingenious inventions include devastating weaponry. Resistance to Hank's agenda ignites a war. Twenty-five thousand men are killed by landmines, Gatling guns, and electrified fences. Rotting corpses spread disease and death. Hank returns to nineteenth-century Connecticut only to expire remembering Arthurian times. *Adventures of Huckleberry Finn* is Twain's pinnacle achievement in reconciling his double nature. His savagery of ridicule was never sharper or timelier. Its essence is a morality tale equally acute.

In Ives's case, the pertinent lineage is a corpus of previous symphonies by Americans barely remembered: John Knowles Paine, George Chadwick, and George Templeton Strong, among others remembered even less. These works are by no means as negligible as their obscurity implies. But with notable exceptions they candidly echo and re-echo with Beethoven, Schumann, Brahms, and Wagner. Ives's Second, by comparison, is equally Germanic in structure and scope. Its sonata forms are shrewdly made. Its passages of turmoil and anguish yield plateaus of uplift and serenity. But no listener, on either side of the Atlantic, could possibly mistake it for a European product.

In American classical music, the tensions afflicting a cultural colony naturally produced ambivalence toward the parent culture. The symphonies preceding Ives are to varying degrees imitative, deferent, or tentative. Ives alone brusquely levels the playing field. His paradoxical methodology is to burrow deep within the genteel tradition—its Germanic templates, suffused with striving; its hymns and parlor songs, remembered from his Danbury childhood. No less than Mark Twain's pivotal American novel, Ives's pivotal American symphony is the handiwork of a cocky subversive, a master practitioner of the inside job.

IT BEARS MENTIONING that—a fact as little-observed as the other connections I here extrapolate—Charles Ives and Mark Twain met one another.

The intermediary was the Reverend Joseph Twichell, whose dates are 1838 to 1918. Twichell presided for five decades at Hartford's Asylum Hill Congregational Church. He was a gregarious man with an exuberant sense of humor. He preached a nondogmatic "muscular Christianity" predisposed to social service. His congregants included Charles Dudley Warner and Harriett Beecher Stowe. His literary circle included John Greenleaf Whittier.

Twichell was for forty years Mark Twain's closest friend. Twain consulted him in matters personal and artistic. In 1870, with Thomas Beecher, Twichell married Twain to Olivia Langdon. In 1878, he accompanied Twain on an abortive walking excursion to Boston (they hitched a ride to the nearest railroad station twenty-eight miles later). In 1878 he accompanied Twain to Europe and became "Harris" in *A Tramp Abroad* (1880). In 1909 he married Twain's daughter Clara to the pianist Ossip Gabrilowitsch. In 1910 he gave the benediction at Mark Twain's funeral.

Of the nine Twichell children, the third daughter, born in 1876, was named Harmony. Soft-featured, with luminous eyes, she was a model of soothing self-possession. Her husband, as of 1908, was a young man as mercurial as Harmony was calm. Charlie Ives, age thirty-four, doubtless found the Twichell household anchoring and consoling. And he was there introduced to "Uncle Mark."

Did Mark Twain influence Charles Ives? I am not aware of any direct evidence. But it bears mentioning that in later life Harmony Ives was president of the Mark Twain Society. And if, as was likely, Ives had occasion to observe the interdependence of Samuel and Olivia Clemens, he would have absorbed an obvious model for his own lifelong marital happiness. Like Livy's, Harmony's fortitude would balance her husband's instability and lovingly buoy his artistic calling.

Twain's birthplace was Florida, Missouri, in 1835. He was raised in Hannibal—a port town—beginning in 1840. Ives was born in Danbury, Connecticut, in 1874. In Twain's fictions, in Ives's music, Hannibal and Danbury came to embody a lost America—a distant source of wholeness and inspiration; a rebuke to the harried present.

Hannibal was a playground for capers and pranks. It was also adorned with majestic steamboats, and with a mighty and inscrutable river. And it was split by a system of racial bifurcation: a nation's curse. Twain worked as a riverboat pilot before heading west to Nevada, where he failed as a miner but succeeded as a droll journalist. He moved on to San Francisco in 1864. "The Celebrated Jumping Frog of Calaveras County" brought him national attention a year later. His marriage to Olivia—the daughter of a New York State coal and iron mogul—made him socially distinguished. Though he would fantasize about a second lifetime piloting the Mississippi, the mature Mark Twain craved respectability in the cultural citadels of the Northeast.

With Livy, Twain eventually settled in Hartford—per capita, America's most affluent city. Their three-story mansion of nineteen rooms featured indoor plumbing, furnishings and mantelpieces opulently inlaid and carved, and a semicircular glass conservatory fronting. The downstairs was Livy's genteel domain; her duties included safeguarding her husband's prose against violations of good taste. The top floor was reserved for billiards, whiskey, and cigars. Twain's fictions likewise inhabit two worlds. They look fondly backward toward childhood and early adulthood, toward the river and the West; they equally limn an unknown future, a gathering storm.

In Charles Ives's Danbury, the bandstand was what the river was for Hannibal. "All Danbury loves music," the *New York Herald* reported. "Wherever you may go, no matter with whom you talk, ten chances to one music will become the topic of conversation. There are no less than a dozen regularly organized societies, embracing nearly all of the best vocalists, and about as many orchestras and bands. There are besides a Salvation Army band and drum corps innumerable." The charismatic local bandmaster, whose band was considered one of the best in the state, was Ives's father and first teacher. A Yankee renegade, George Edward Ives made Charlie sing "Old Folks at Home" in E-flat while accompanying himself in C. The boy thrilled to bumptious wrong notes and late entrances in the theater pit, to bands crowding and contradicting one another on Main Street. At Yale, Ives had a second teacher as staid as his first was experimental: Horatio Parker, who had studied with Josef Rheinberger in Munich. Ives was equally absorbent and rebellious—and sought no further formal training.

In New York in 1898, he was placed by relatives in a job with the Mutual Life Insurance Company. He cofounded a life insurance agency, Ives & Myrick, in 1909. It thrived. Meanwhile, more or less in secret, he prolifically composed music so heretical it could not possibly find an audience in its own time. Ill health curtailed both professions. By 1930, Ives had quit composing or selling insurance. He and Harmony stayed put in Redding, Connecticut—not fifty miles from Twain's Hartford. He was mainly known to a handful of musical free spirits including Henry Cowell, Lou Harrison, Bernard Herrmann, and Nicolas Slonimsky.

No part of Charles Ives craved respectability. His marriage had nothing to do with social mobility. His rural home was comfortable but private. Ives feared complicity in the genteel parlor world of Livy Clemens's downstairs rooms. A warm-hearted, compassionate man, he cloaked his softness with a bristling demeanor. His music, over time, mutually acquired new depth of feeling and an ever-sharper edge. His physical decline coincided with an ascendant reputation. For decades, nothing as formidably self-made as a musical Whitman or Melville had appeared. It now transpired that an autonomous American genius had long composed in necessary seclusion, undistracted by precedent or fashion. The landmark discovery took place in 1939, when John Kirkpatrick performed Ives's *Concord* Piano Sonata for a tiny audience at New York's Town Hall. Lawrence Gilman wrote in the *Herald Tribune*: "[Ives's] sonata is exceptionally great music—it is, indeed, the greatest music composed by an American, and the most deeply and essentially American in impulse and implication."

In 1947, Ives was awarded a Pulitzer Prize. In 1951 Leonard Bernstein premiered Ives's Second Symphony with the New York Philharmonic. Ives declined Bernstein's invitation to travel to New York. As he did not own a radio, he listened to a broadcast in a neighbor's kitchen. When it was over, he spit in the fireplace and walked home. Harmony Ives wrote Bernstein an appreciative note. She added that Ives had found the fast movements "too slow." Ives died of a stroke three years later.

∽

THE BOYHOOD NAUGHTINESS of Mark Twain and Charles Ives became a cherished object of nostalgic self-regard. One outcome was an irreverent man-boy act—a life-long defining attribute for both men.

If in Hartford Samuel Clemens transformed himself into a Victorian paterfamilias, as Mark Twain he remained, if not the lubricated buffoon of his San Francisco saloon days, a rude and unpredictable interloper in salons. Mark Twain the novelist was notably reticent about sex; his need to blaspheme was nonetheless lifelong and chronic. In hell-raising Nevada, he reported that proceeds from a Carson City charity ball would secretly "aid a Miscegenation Society somewhere in the East"—a drunken hoax for which he refused to apologize. Engaged to address a banquet for the Ancient and Honorable Artillery Corps of Massachusetts, he celebrated his own brief military history as a Civil War deserter. A connoisseur of dirty jokes, he once gave a lecture in praise of the high antiquity of masturbation.

In Ives, the need to blaspheme was even more unbridled. Today the best-known, best-loved image of Ives is that of the subversive hell-raiser. In *fin-de-siècle* Vienna, fistfights would break out between supporters and opponents of the new music of Mahler and Schoenberg. In *fin-de-siècle* America, Ives was said to shout "Sissy!" and "Listen like a man!" at timid concertgoers. His writings bristle with disdain for parlor "pansies," "lily-pads," "old ladies," "soft ears," and "pussy-boys." A typical 1930s tirade thundered:

> When I think of some music that I liked to hear and play 35 or 40 years ago—if I hear some of it now, I feel like saying, "Rollo, how did you fall for that sop, those 'ta tas' and greasy ringlets?" In this I would include the *Preislied*, *The Rosary*,* a certain amount of Mozart, Mendelssohn, a small amount of early Beethoven, the easy-made Haydn, a large amount of Massenet, Sibelius, Tchaikovsky, etc. (to say nothing of Gounod), most Italian operas (not exactly most of the operas, but most of each opera), some of Chopin (pretty soft, but you don't mind it in him so much, because one just naturally thinks of him with a skirt on, but one which he made himself).

---

* The Prize Song from Wagner's *Die Meistersinger*; "The Rosary" by Ethelbert Nevin.

Inflicted upon Old World musical monuments, the man-boy act was a source of comedy for both Twain and Ives. At the Wagner festival at Bayreuth in 1891, Twain was (as ever) an upstart Yankee, at once proud and insecure. His innocence was half-feigned, half-authentic. He admired the Festspielhaus as a model of functional simplicity. He "browsed" its "front yard." He approvingly observed that its patrons dressed "as they please." He disapproved of the deference paid a German prince arriving casually at the last minute. Twain's vernacular humor subversively appoints the New World the measure of all things.

In *Huckleberry Finn*, Huck's drawl tweaks great moral and existential themes. In his Second Symphony, Ives's vernacular humor—using the past—tweaks Bach, Brahms, and Wagner, all of whom he quotes. Significantly, these borrowings—unlike those of tunes native to the United States—are always tangential. When, for instance, Bach pokes his nose into movement five (measure 147), the E minor Fugue from the *Well-Tempered Clavier*, Book 1, becomes a straight man for slapstick, submerged by "Camptown Races." Vernacular musical humor takes a different twist in movement two, whose second subject appropriates a purposely inane college song (itself a parody of David Walker's hymn tune "The Hebrew Children"), now forgotten: "Where O Where Are the Verdant Freshmen?"

Where o where are the verdant freshmen?
Where o where are the verdant freshmen?
Where o where are the verdant freshmen?
Safe now in the soph'more class.

That Ives's version (measure 72),* for paired flutes and oboes, is as mellifluous as its unlikely source is boisterously brisk is a whimsical felicity

---

* That Leonard Bernstein eventually performed and filmed Ives's Symphony No. 2 with the Bavarian Radio Symphony Orchestra (1987) clinches Ives's mating of New and Old Worlds. For "Where O Where Are the Verdant Freshmen?" in Bernstein's performance, go to 9:36 at https://www.youtube.com/watch?v=d0OpTJlXdko.

an early-twentieth-century audience (had one existed for anything by Ives) would have appreciated. Elsewhere in the Second Symphony, Ives is as playfully naughty as Tom Sawyer in the later chapters of *Huckleberry Finn*. The pertinent imagery is of bands, picnics, childhood delights. The pertinent tunes include "Camptown Races," "Reveille," "Turkey in the Straw," and "Pigtown Fling." The symphony closes with a raucous guffaw.*

Race and the Moral Core

The man-boy in Mark Twain and Charles Ives inflamed their mutual alienation from the new century—a pendant to nostalgia.

Long preoccupied with issues of good and evil, long a double observer of Mississippi River vastness and of moral confinements bred by slavery, Twain in old age became a dark existential moralist: a nihilist. He was prone to excoriate democracy, universal suffrage, and the jury system. He frequently lampooned the vulgarity of great wealth and the venality of great power. The passing of the frontier famously observed by Frederick Jackson Turner in 1893 was the more keenly and wistfully felt by one who had known young Nevada and California. He observed the St. Louis levee nearly bereft of steamboats. He denounced the "triple curse" of the railroad, the telegraph, and the newspaper. "The twentieth century is a stranger to me," he wrote. "I wish it well but my heart is for my own century. I took 65 years of it, just on a risk, but if I had known as much about it as I know now I would have taken the whole of it."

Ives pursued a chimerical and eccentric faith in democratic ideals. He shared Woodrow Wilson's dream of reforming the world. In 1918 he conceived a People's World Union embracing universal disarmament, free trade, and an international police force. In 1920 he drafted a Twentieth Amendment implementing direct democracy; bypassing

---

* Sometime around 1950, Ives decided the ending of the symphony was too decorous and composed the ending we now hear.

politicians, the public would initiate legislation. The collapse of the Progressive movement produced in Ives a cranky resilience conditioned by estrangement and denial. He remained stoic in the face of illness and obscurity, immune to self-pity and depression. But he raged against what the world had become. He hated the telephone, would not use a phonograph, shook his fist at airplanes. He disapproved of FDR and the welfare state. He shielded himself against news of a terrible conflict overseas. He revisited Danbury and moaned aloud, head in hands, that it had so changed.

If Ives, in seclusion, remained devoted to a lost childhood world of innocence, Twain at least maintained contact—via Huck—with one boy's susceptibility to unsullied goodness. The profundity of *Huckleberry Finn*, and its most profound similarity to Ives's Symphony No. 2, ultimately resides in a moral component grounded in the American conundrum of race. Twain's obsession with the divided self took increasingly corrosive forms—and his moral compass fractured: Satan, in *The Mysterious Stranger*, preaches that only animals are benign. In such company, *Adventures of Huckleberry Finn* is supremely high and low, light and dark. Its vignettes of squalor, meanness, and bigotry retain pertinence and power. But the heart of Huck Finn's story—its enduring message and the signature of its artistic significance—is a moral epiphany.

Huck has run away and so has the slave Jim. They wind up together on a raft, sailing north on the Mississippi River toward Cairo, where Jim will be free. The linchpin is Chapter 15. Tom, in a canoe, is separated from Jim and the raft in dense nocturnal fog. Their mutual disappearance, aggravated by swift currents, strikes fear in both boy and man. Only sporadically do they hear one another's "whoops." When they fortunately reunite, Huck plays a trick: he tells Jim he has been "dreaming":

". . . I've been here all the time."

Jim didn't say nothing for about five minutes, but set there studying over it. Then he says:

"Well, den, I reck'n I did dream it, Huck; but dog my cats ef it ain't de powerfullest dream I ever see. En I hain't ever had no dream b'fo' dat's tired me like dis one."

"Oh, well, that all right, because a dream does tire a body like everything, sometimes. But this one was a staving dream—tell me all about it, Jim."

So Jim went to work and told me the whole thing right through, just as it happened, only he painted it up considerable. Then he said he must start in and "'terpret" it, because it was sent for a warning. He said the first tow-head* stood for a man that would try to do us some good, but the current was another man that would get us away from him. The whoops was warnings that would come to us every now and then, and if we didn't try hard to make out to understand them they'd just take us into bad luck, 'stead of keeping us out of it. The lot of tow-heads was troubles we was going to get into with quarrelsome people and all kinds of mean folks, but if we minded our business and didn't talk back and aggravate them, we would pull through and get out of the fog and into the big clear river, which was the free States, and wouldn't have no more trouble.

Jim's dream interpretation is of course a sanguine life metaphor, ending in redemption. Huck now cites evidence that Jim's dream was no fantasy: leaves and rubbish on the raft, and a smashed oar. When Jim understands he has been deceived, he eyes Huck "without ever smiling" and says of the debris:

"What do dey stan' for? I's gwyne to tell you. When I got all wore out wid work, en wid de callin' for you, en went to sleep, my heart wuz mos' broke bekase you wuz los', and I didn't k'yer no mo' what become er me en de raf'. En when I wake up en fine you back agin',

---

* A sandbar or other obstruction making ripples in a body of water.

all safe en soun', de tears come en I could a got down on my knees en kiss' yo' foot I's so thankful. En all you wuz thinkin' 'bout wuz how you could make a fool uv old Jim wid a lie. Dat truck dah is *trash*; en trash is what people is dat puts dirt on de head er dey fren's en makes 'em ashamed."

Huck reflects:

It was fifteen minutes before I could work myself up to go and humble myself to a nigger—but I done it, and I warn't ever sorry for it afterwards, neither. I didn't do him no more mean tricks, and I wouldn't done that one if I'd a knowed it would make him feel that way.

And so Huck's precocious early manhood is clinched by a dawning realization that laws of the heart trump human laws such as those dictating that Black men may be enslaved, and that slaves who escape be returned to their "masters." Also, Jim is revealed as a moral beacon— a source of wisdom; his existential metaphor, negating the fog, uplifts Huck and the reader both.

When *Adventures of Huckleberry Finn* was banned as "trash" by the Concord (Massachusetts) Public Library, Twain commended the library for its "generous action," certain to impel people to buy the book and read it. The greater irony is that Huck's "trashy" vernacular and the novel's ethical core are bound as one. His faulty speech and crude vocabulary ultimately register an innocence combating the artifice of "conscience" and "civilization." In this boldest of his fictions, applying Mississippi flotsam and jetsam to the vagaries of universal human experience, Mark Twain is like Huck and Jim on the river: afloat, unmoored—and therefore whole. "Other places do seem so cramped up and smothery, but a raft don't," Huck says. He also says: "We was always naked, day and night." But the shore, with its thieves and slaves, was "enough to make a body ashamed of the human race."

Mark Twain was by no means the first American writer of fiction to mine the vernacular, Black or white. But no previous American novelist had nearly so privileged a vernacular speaker. Huck's language is not only expressive and entertaining; it embodies human values that prove triumphant. The authenticity of vernacular speech thus conveyed was married to a belief in the authenticity of vernacular song. As I have observed, of his many musical affinities, Twain held in highest esteem the Fisk Jubilee Singers. And assuredly for Twain, Huck's speech was musical. In the 1990s, Shelley Fisher Fishkin ascertained that Huck's voice was partly based upon the dialect and discourse of two African Americans. One was a slave named Jerry, recalled from Twain's childhood as "the greatest orator in the United States." The other was a ten-year-old Black child named Jimmy who had impressed Twain as "the most artless, sociable, exhaustless talker" he had ever come across, someone to whom he had listened "as one who received a revelation." Huck's "negro melodies" have their counterpart in Dvořák and Gershwin—and also, metaphorically, among the people's tunes Ives so readily deployed, flaunting their rough edges.

It bears mentioning that the makers of *Porgy and Bess* closely studied the speech of the Carolina Gullahs (a dialect coach was employed for the 1927 play *Porgy*). And it bears stressing that Mark Twain's recourse to Black vernacular speech embraced not mere words or phrases. "A True Story, Repeated Word for Word as I Heard It" (1874) reproduces verbatim the words of Mary Ann Cord, an ex-slave who worked as a servant at the Clemenses' summer home in Elmira, New York. This "curiously strong piece of literary work," issuing "unpremeditated from lips untrained in literary art," was told so artfully that Twain did not retouch it. Just as he admired the Fisk Jubilee Singers for never "artificializing" their songs, Twain embraced Mary Ann Cord's improvisational narrative. Nothing could be further from the compositional refinements that Aaron Copland and Leonard Bernstein endorsed when appropriating jazz. Enshrined in *Huck Finn* or *Porgy*, this unadulterated "America" is susceptible to a litany of learned complaints: it is "unfinished," "immature," rough around the edges. But these qualities are veritably ours.

∽

EXTRAMUSICAL CONTENT IN a symphonic composition—events,
personalities, ideas—is most typically purveyed by a "program": a
tacit scenario. The most popular practitioner of symphonic program
music may be Richard Strauss (*Till Eulenspiegel's Merry Pranks, Don
Juan, Don Quixote, A Hero's Life, Thus Spake Zarathustra*, the *Alpine
Symphony*, etc.—all of them stories in music). Less commonly, a composer will add words to a symphony in order to specify meaning. The
best-known example is Beethoven's Ninth; setting Schiller's "Ode to
Joy," it is the very prototype of symphonic uplift. And then there are
composers—not so many—who resort to encoded "messages in a bot-
tle," the best-known case being Dmitri Shostakovich. When Shostakovich quotes Wagner's *Götterdämmerung* in his Fifteenth Symphony,
we realize he is referencing doom. When he quotes his initials DSCH,*
we know he is musically describing some aspect of himself. There are
also instances in which Shostakovich quotes well-known Russian
songs—say, "Exhausted by the Hardships of Prison," in the Eighth
String Quartet—in order to impart meanings beyond the notes.

The reason we know Ives's Second Symphony anticipates this Shostakovich procedure is a 1943 letter to the conductor Artur Rodzinski. Ives
here links his symphony with the "fret and storm and stress for liberty"
of the Civil War. Where the marches and dances of the symphony's
finale abate for a plaintive horn theme citing Stephen Foster's "Old Black
Joe," Ives (according to his letter) finds inspiration in Foster's "sadness
for the slaves."

The passage in question—a lyric high point—is the second subject
of the fifth movement (Meno allegro, cantabile, measure 58). When the
tune returns in the recapitulation (measure 189), it is assigned to a solo

---

* In German, Dmitri Shostakovich is "Schostakovich." The notes D, E-flat, C, B translate
in German as D-S-C-H.

cello*—the horn and cello being instruments that strikingly evoke the male human singing voice. Foster's tune, wordlessly sung by Ives, sets these words (which Ives assumes we know):

> Gone are the days when my heart was young and gay
> Gone are the toils of the cotton fields away
> Gone to the fields of a better land I know
> I hear those gentle voices calling, "Old Black Joe."
> I'm comin', I'm comin'
> Though my head is bendin' low
> I hear those gentle voices calling, "Old Black Joe."†

Ultimately, this culminating movement of Ives's Second takes a patriotic "victory" turn, climaxing with "Columbia, the Gem of the Ocean." The closing measures add a bugle call: "Reveille." And so Ives's recourse to the vernacular not only secures an American flavor; it enables him to use the past, citing specific elements of the American experience.

These pregnant references are by no means unique to the Second Symphony. The "Black March" (1911) beginning Ives's *Three Places in New England* memorializes Colonel Robert Gould Shaw's legendary Black Civil War regiment as famously depicted by Augustus Saint-Gaudens's Boston Common bas-relief, with its proud Black faces and striding Black bodies. Shaw's regiment perished heroically at Fort Wagner. Ives's ghost-dirge is suffused with weary echoes of Civil War songs, plantation songs, minstrel songs: a fog of memory, a dream

---

* For Leonard Bernstein's gorgeously distended rendition of "Old Black Joe" in his 1987 Munich performance, go to 4:28 at https://www.youtube.com/watch?v=LlUQRNRFEkQ.

† Foster's minstrel songs were sung by whites in blackface—an abhorrent practice. That they are nonetheless expressions of compassion for the slave cannot be doubted (see pages 8–9). It bears mentioning that Ives's father (whom Ives so revered) knew Foster in New York (according to Lucille Fletcher's unpublished *New Yorker* profile of Charles Ives, which may be read in typescript at the New York Public Library for the Performing Arts).

distillation whose hypnotic tread and consecrating "Amen" close celebrate an act of stoic fortitude. Like Saint-Gaudens's sculpture, Ives's "The 'St. Gaudens' in Boston Common," with its song shards, less describes than memorializes a remembered event. The Black vernacular is here not appropriated, but retrospectively observed with admiration and respect. At the same time, snatches of ragtime look forward to Black music to come.

In fact, Ives pioneered in incorporating ragtime in composed concert music. Though Aaron Copland wrote that "serious composers became aware of the polyrhythmic nature of Afro-American music only in its jazz phases," ragtime-inspired polyrhythms animate such bracing theater-orchestra concoctions as Ives's *Ragtime Dances* (1902–3), *Set of Nine Ragtime Pieces* (1902), and *Set of Four Ragtime Pieces* (1902–4). His piano sonatas, too, crackle with ragtime eruptions. The jerky rhythmic vocabulary of ragtime was actually an Ivesian staple. "Ragtime may be nature's way of giving art raw material," he once wrote. Ever the Victorian meliorist, he added: "Time will throw its vices away and weld its virtues into the fabric of our music."

Like Mark Twain's Missouri childhood, Ives's Connecticut childhood brought him into close contact with African-American experience. During the Civil War, Ives's father befriended a Black boy, Anderson Brooks, whom he taught to read and write. Afterward, Ives's abolitionist grandmother took in Anderson Brooks and raised him. At Yale, Ives played rag piano with the Hyperion Orchestra and frequented a tavern where he occasionally substituted for the pianist. Later, he was no stranger to New York music halls. These were years when ragtime first achieved national popularity. No less than Mark Twain's America, Charles Ives's America embraced the sounds of Black Americans, and also the tragedy and turmoil of slavery and race.

∽

The Transcendentalist Past

In the 1920s, a generation of American thinkers went looking for a usable past. Wholly unbeknownst to them, Charles Ives was already there. This element of Ives's nostalgia, a tidal reprise of the Transcendentalists, has no parallel in Mark Twain.

Of the Alcott house in Concord, Ives wrote in his *Essays Before a Sonata* (1920): "It seems to bear a consciousness that its past *is living.*" The living past—a quivering ether of ambient memory—is a signature of Ives's sonic world. Of the early deceased George Edward Ives he confided that he "talked to father every day." (Ives's text for his tiny song "Remembrance" reads: "A sound of a distant horn,/O'er shadowed lake is borne,/my father's song.") Ives also notably inhabited the persona of— another charged alter ego—Ralph Waldo Emerson. A kind of supernostalgia powered his highest flights of genius.

Huckleberry Finn was Mark Twain's peak achievement. He ventured no further in refashioning the novel as a New World genre. His later, estranged writings were increasingly fragmentary. Charles Ives looked back upon his Second Symphony as a mild early effort. He ventured quickly toward more radical appropriations of the European genres. His Sonata—*Concord, Mass., 1845* (1916–19) retains in spirit the sonata as developed by Beethoven and his successors. But it dispenses with sonata form and other structural templates the Germans deployed. Rather, it fixes on what Ives once termed the "ever-flowing stream partly biological, partly cosmic, ever going on in ourselves, in nature, in all life."

It was William James who coined "stream of consciousness" in his *Principles of Psychology* (1890). James's fascination with the evolutionary flow of mental attention owes something to the Transcendentalism of Emerson and Henry David Thoreau—itself rooted in German Romanticism and Eastern mysticism. Ever mining his American inheritance, Ives was a devotee of the Transcendentalists. The four movements of his *Concord* Sonata extol the Concord bards. Movement one, "Emerson," is dense, dissonant, striving. In *Essays Before a Sonata,* Ives writes: "We see him standing on a summit, at the door of the infinite ... peering into the mysteries of life, contemplating the eternities, hurling back whatever he discovers there." "Hawthorne," coming next, is presented as a poet of the supernatural. Ives conceives a cinematic phantasmagoria ranging from haunted churchyard strains to a demonic circus parade. "The Alcotts," a nostalgic hymn to better times and ordinary things, records Beth Alcott at the parlor piano, transmuting Beethoven's Fifth into a hymn. "Thoreau" is a contemplative nature poem culminating with the shudder of tolling bells heard at a distance over Walden Pond—a vibratory ecstasy. Here the four-note Beethoven motto, pervasive throughout, sublimates as a "human faith melody."

Ives's kinship to Beethoven in the *Concord* Sonata takes other forms. The spirit of heroic adventure is Beethoven's. The sonata's ethereal close, its way of dematerializing, evokes Beethoven's late piano sonatas Op. 109 and 111. For Beethoven, however, the Fifth Symphony's pounding motto is "fate knocking at the door." For Ives, the motto conveys a sanguine moral imperative: "the soul of humanity knocking at the door of the Divine mysteries, radiant in the faith it *will* be opened—and the human become the Divine!" Ives' four-movement plan may somewhat resemble a traditional sonata format, with "The Alcotts" in the slow-movement slot. But the whole German machinery of key relations and developmental argument, retained in Ives's Second Symphony, is here overturned. There are no key signatures or metered rhythms. There is no regularity of bar lines. Stream of consciousness is the intended impression. Rather than Beethoven's big works, the symphonies of Gustav Mahler—whose music Ives did not know—are the Old World equivalent, a product of a charged *fin-de-siècle* moment. In Mahler's Ninth Symphony (1909), sonata form is abandoned in favor of a tidal ebb and flow of music both quotidian and sublime. Nothing could be more Ivesian.[*]

---

[*] I pursue the topic of Ives and Mahler in *Moral Fire: Musical Portraits from America's Fin de Siècle* (2012).

If a New England ether recalled from earlier times binds Ives's multifarious sonata, in his songs—tremendous in variety—his many uses of the act of memory are surveyed in microcosm. He equally recaptures a father lost ("Remembrance") and a suppressed national memory ("The Indians"—"their children go to die"). Recalling a placid river, he is stirred to invoke, by way of restless contradiction, the elemental sea ("The Housatonic at Stockbridge"). A residue of church bells evokes a vision of eternity ("Serenity"). His Fourth Symphony (1912–25) is a final grand exercise in charting an "ever-flowing stream" both personal and cosmic, a lonely valedictory serenely out of touch with modernity. As in Beethoven's Ninth, a sung text—"Watchman, tell us of the night"—interpolates the sacred. Movement two—a raucous Fourth of July—is a final Danbury-like vignette. The finale's gathering current is oceanic: an upward wave.

WHILE *HUCKLEBERRY FINN* begets "all modern American literature," and Ives's Second is the first fully realized "American symphony," there is no such pioneer figure in American visual art of the late Gilded Age or *fin-de-siècle*. But there happens to be a master practitioner of nostalgia: Winslow Homer (1836–1910).

In fact, Homer shares many traits with Twain and Ives. Self-made, virtually self-taught as a painter, he apprenticed to a commercial lithographer at nineteen and became a frequent illustrator for *Harper's Weekly* and *Ballou's Pictorial*. A vernacular ingredient inflects Homer's style: the clean outlines and realistic tone, the stark contrasts of light and dark fields betray a homemade magazine lineage conducive to American subject matter. Homer is America's best Civil War painter. He also memorably inscribes the African American. Such closely observed canvases as *Visit from the Old Mistress* (1876) are humanizing because they are reportorial, not rhetorical. The same toughness distinguishes Homer's late paintings of Maine sailors and seascapes. It connects directly to a quality of hardness and self-reliance in Charles Ives.

But the clinching resemblance to Ives and Mark Twain in Winslow

Homer is his warm regard for the American past, conveyed by countless tableaux of boyhood. Henry James recoiled (of course) from Homer's "little barefoot urchins and little girls in calico sun-bonnets"; they were "almost barbarously simple" and "horribly ugly." But James also wrote of Homer: "He has chosen the least pictorial features of the least pictorial range of scenery and civilization; he has resolutely treated them as if they were pictorial, as if they were every inch as good as Capri or Tangiers; and, to reward his audacity, he has incontestably succeeded." *Snap the Whip* (1872) and *Breezing Up* (1876) are images of boyhood delight as vigorously cheerful as Tom Sawyer. That there are, however, no embattled Huck Finns among Homer's urchins help us to locate the subversive charge that immunizes Twain and Ives from sentimental retrospection.

In *Adventures of Huckleberry Finn* and Ives's Symphony No. 2 nostalgia feeds rebellion. The reckless energy of these works is barely controlled. They parody Old World conventions of behavior and expression. If their creators seem to us American originals, it is partly because by instinct we seek a particle of rawness, of pioneer self-sufficiency—something akin to the character type famously limned by Frederick Jackson Turner's "frontier thesis" of 1893. "Coarseness and strength combined," "restless nervous energy," "dominant individualism" are among the attributes Turner lists. They suit Mark Twain and Charles Ives. They also fit—a point of origin—Ralph Waldo Emerson.

Emerson's poem "Music" reads:

'Tis not in the high stars alone,
Nor in the cups of budding flowers,
Nor in the redbreast's mellow tone,
Nor in the bow that smiles in showers,
But in the mud and scum of things
There alway, alway something sings.

Emerson also wrote, in praise of the vernacular: "The language of the street is always strong. . . . I confess to some pleasure from the stinging rhetoric of a rattling oath in the mouth of truckmen and teamsters. How laconic and brisk it is by the side of a page of the North American Review." Charles Ives surely knew these Emerson writings. They inspired such passages in Ives's *Essays Before a Sonata* as:

> Like all courageous souls, the higher Emerson soars, the more lowly he becomes. . . . To think hard and deeply and to say what is thought, regardless of consequences, may produce a first impression, either of great translucence, or of great muddiness, but in the latter there may be hidden possibilities. . . . The mud may be a form of sincerity. . . . A clearer scoring might have lowered the thought.

Emerson "wrings the neck of any law," writes Ives. His "messages are all vital, as much by reason of his indefiniteness, as in spite of it." There is no "mud" in Ives's Symphony No. 2. But the *Concord* Sonata and Fourth Symphony wade in mud and "the scum of things." Striving mightily for "sincerity," both these great works forgo "translucence" in favor of a pregnant "indefiniteness."

IN HIS 1986 essay collection *Going to the Territory*, Ralph Ellison, one of the keen African-American voices of his generation, pondered the conundrum of American national identity—of synthesizing, however fitfully and incompletely, a young nation's tangled European, American, and African influences, of promises made and broken.

The American creative artist, Ellison wrote, is—or should be—possessed of "an imagination perennially engaged by the problem of national type." He expressed disappointment in American novelists disengaged with the puzzle of America—those who were "morally diffident" and consumed with "technical experimentation" in pursuit of a "morality of craftsmanship."

Ellison added this proposition: "It seems to me that our most characteristic American style is that of the vernacular," by which he means "the high styles of the past are democratized." Referencing *Adventures of Huckleberry Finn*, he continued:

> It was Mark Twain who transformed elements of regional vernacular speech into a medium of uniquely American literary expression and thus taught us how to capture that which is essentially American in our folkways and manners. For indeed the vernacular process is a way of establishing and discovering our national identity.

Long before Shelley Fisher Fishkin's research into Twain's linguistic sources, Ellison recognized that "the black man" is "co-creator of the language that Mark Twain raised to the level of literary eloquence" in *Huckleberry Finn*. The "tragic knowledge which we try ceaselessly to evade," he wrote, is "that the true subject of democracy is not simply material well-being but the extension of the democratic process in the direction of perfection itself. And . . . the most obvious test and clue to that perfection is the inclusion—*not* assimilation—of the black man."

Ellison also had something to say about the "supposedly unresolvable conflict between elitist and populist values"—the very conflict we will shortly observe distancing Virgil Thomson, Aaron Copland, and Leonard Bernstein from jazz: a preference for assimilation over inclusion. Ellison continued: "But this assumes that the vernacular process destroys the so-called elitist styles, when in truth past standards of excellence remain to be used again and again. . . . Let me say that although jazz musicians are practitioners of a vernacular style, they are also unreconstructed elitists when it comes to maintaining the highest standards of the music which expresses their sense of the American experience."

Early on an aspiring classical musician, Ellison became a music-lover of catholic and discerning taste. He admired Dvořák's *New World* Symphony and appreciated Dvořák's moral pursuit of an ecumenical American national type. I have no idea whether Ellison knew the Second Symphony of Charles Ives—certainly it, too, addresses his expectations of what American artists should strive to compass. The modernist composers who came after, however, were in many cases "morally diffident." Many prioritized technical innovation. Ostensibly looking for a usable past, they overlooked the vernacular American past, or held it at arm's length as exogenous to art.

Chapter Four

Oedipal Revolt

*The Useless Past: Van Wyck Brooks and the Myth of the
"Gilded Age"—The Useless Past: Virgil Thomson, Aaron
Copland, and the Standard Narrative—Leonard Bernstein
and the Ives Case—Copland and Mexico—Postscript: The
Standard Narrative and the CIA*

The Useless Past: Van Wyck Brooks and the Myth of the "Gilded Age"

What a social setting it was, that little world into which Mark Twain was born! It was drab, it was tragic. . . . That weary, discouraged father struggling against conditions amid which . . . a man can do nothing but rot away, that kind, worn, wan, desperately optimistic, fanatically energetic mother, those ragged, wretched little children, sprawling on the floor . . .—it is the epic not only of Mark Twain's infancy but of a whole phase of American civilization.

—from The Ordeal of Mark Twain
(1920) by Van Wyck Brooks

James Gibbons Huneker, looking backward, remembered habits more communal and considered, men more vigorous, lives less hurried and materialistic. Charles Ives remembered "a generation or so ago," in which camp meeting hymns, "simple but acute," conveyed

a vigor, a depth of feeling, a natural-soil rhythm, a sincerity, emphatic but inartistic, which, in spite of a vociferous sentimentality, carries . . . nearer the "Christ of the people" than does the Te Deum of the great cathedral. . . . If the Yankee can reflect the fervency with which "his gospels" were sung—the fervency of "Aunt Sarah," who scrubbed her life away for her brother's ten orphans, the fervency with which this woman, after a fourteen-hour work day on the farm, would hitch up and drive five miles, through the mud and rain to "prayer meeting"—her one articulate outlet for the fullness of her unselfish soul—if he can reflect the fervency of such a spirit, he may find there a local color that will do all the world good.

Mark Twain testified:

After all these years I can picture that old time to myself, now, just as it was then: the white town drowsing in the sunshine of a summer's morning; the streets empty, or pretty nearly so; one or two clerks sitting in front of the Water Street stores, with their splint-bottomed chairs tilted back against the wall, chins on breasts, hats slouched over their faces, asleep . . . Presently a film of dark smoke appears . . . instantly a negro drayman, famous for his quick eye and prodigious voice, lifts up the cry, "S-t-e-a-m-b-o-a-t a-comin'!" and the scene changes! The town drunkard stirs, the clerks wake up, a furious clatter of drays follows, every house and store pours out a human contribution, and all in a twinkling the dead town is alive and moving . . . people fasten their eye upon the coming boat as upon a wonder they are seeing for the first time. . . . She is long and sharp and trim and pretty; she has two tall, fancy-topped chimneys, . . . the paddle-boxes are gorgeous with a picture or with gilded rays above the boat's name . . . there is a flag gallantly flying from the jack-staff; the furnace doors are open and the fires glaring bravely; the upper decks are black with passengers; the captain stands by the big bell, calm, imposing, the envy of all.

Sometime around 1910, an impatience with the past, a brash distaste toward forebears, impelled a new generation. "Young Americans" harbored no memories such as those of Huneker, Ives, and Mark Twain. They attended to brisk currents of socialism and modernism from abroad. They equally drew upon a residue of native Progressivism. They gravitated to Greenwich Village and kept company with Mabel Dodge Luhan, John Reed, Isadora Duncan, and Eugene O'Neill. They consumed the 1913 Armory Show, with its onslaught of Picasso, Matisse, and Duchamp.

Then came the first modern mass war. It introduced poison gas and machine guns and a system of trench warfare as meaningless as it was lethal. The *New Republic* observed "a bankruptcy of ideas, systems, society" as complete as the French Revolution. Civilization, Henry James opined, had plunged into "an abyss of blood and darkness." American arts and scholarship had invested mightily in Germanic traditions. George Creel's Committee on Public Information had made *Kultur* a vulgar epithet. Verily, the war poisoned the act of memory. And yet the forward march of the Young Americans continued. They would simply spurn the past.

Their oracle was a literary critic of irresistible panache: Van Wyck Brooks. Brooks's *America's Coming-of-Age*, published in 1915 when he was all of twenty-nine years old, portrayed a material nation hostile to art, split between "lowbrow" and "highbrow": philistine entrepreneurs and hyperrefined intellectuals. It documented a quest for a "usable [literary] past" that led nowhere: come-of-age Americans would have to begin anew. Five years later, in *The Ordeal of Mark Twain*, Brooks produced a case study in futility.

Twain had started out with a native endowment "more extraordinary than that of any other American writer." A victim of "arrested development," he grew embittered by "a certain miscarriage in his creative life, a balked personality." "The spirit of the artist in him . . . overspread in a gloomy vapor the mind it had never quite been able to possess." Twain the writer lacked "inner control"; he was incapable of "sustained creative activity." The trouble was "the world into which he was born, and to which he succumbed." Compared to "the fertile human soil of any spot in Europe," Twain's Middle West was "dry, old, barren, horizonless." Its

inhabitants were obsessed with material gain and social status, shackled by conformist norms of behavior. Twain's Calvinist mother equated
creativity with sin. His well-born wife censored and corrected his every
lurch toward art. Seeking respectability and success, he acquired a Hartford mansion and poured aspiration into the notoriously imperfect Paige
typesetter and other ill-conceived commercial ventures.

Brooks adduced that Mark Twain was poorly read. "He never thought
of literature as art." Abroad, he found European civilization as "empty
and absurd" as did any other American man of business. "In his lack of
pride, of sustained interest, in his work, of artistic self-betterment and
self-control, in his laziness and loose extravagance one finds all the signs
of the impatient novice who becomes gradually the unwilling novice
without ever growing up to the art of letters at all." Late in life, turning
philosophical, Twain's ever-waning energies were "concentrated almost
exclusively in attacks of one kind or another." His "one masterpiece,"
Adventures of Huckleberry Finn, was fitfully composed over eight years,
finished "only by a sort of chance."

> Through the character of Huck, that disreputable, illiterate little
> boy, as Mrs. Clemens no doubt thought him, he was licensed to
> let himself go. . . . Huck's illiteracy, Huck's disreputableness and
> general outrageousness are so many shields behind which Mark
> Twain can let all the cats out of the bag with impunity. . . . He
> must . . . have appreciated the license that little vagabond, like the
> puppet on the lap of a ventriloquist, afforded him. . . . His whole
> unconscious life, the pent-up river of his own soul, had burst its
> bonds and rushed forth, a joyous torrent! Do we need any other
> explanation of the abandon, the beauty, the eternal freshness of
> *Huckleberry Finn*?

Brooks was the first to forcibly extrapolate the "dual personality" so
ubiquitous in Twain's fictions. It materialized Twain's embattled wish
to be an artist, so repressed and suppressed. It imposed a condition of

"moral infancy." It fostered the self-contempt so rampant in Twain's personal reflections. In sum: Mark Twain is

> the saddest, the most ironical figure in all the history of this
> Western continent. . . . He was the supreme victim of an epoch in
> American history, an epoch that has closed. . . . Read, writers of
> America, the driven, disenchanted, anxious faces of your sensitive
> countrymen; remember the splendid parts your confreres have
> played in the human drama of other times and other peoples, and
> ask yourselves whether the hour has not come to put away childish
> things and walk the stage as poets do.

∽

THE BACKDROP TO Van Wyck Brooks's polemic—and its true topic—is the "Gilded Age." Mark Twain may have coined the term when he coauthored *The Gilded Age: A Tale of Today* (1873) with Charles Dudley Warner. But it was Brooks, in Chapter 3 of *The Ordeal of Mark Twain* (itself titled "The Gilded Age"), who more than anyone propagated this pejorative labeling of a swath of postbellum American history.

The Gilded Age combined Victorian inhibition with political aggrandizement. Wealth and power were flaunted. In such an environment, ideals of culture were superficial or meretricious. Brooks translated his highbrow/lowbrow bifurcation into the "genteel tradition" (a term originated by George Santayana in 1911) and the "pioneer." Genteel intellectuals were stiff and complacent. Pioneers were dirty and greedy. Evoking Mark Twain in the gold fields of Nevada, Brooks envisioned "a sort of furnace in which all the elements of human nature were transmuted into a single white flame, an incandescence of the passion of avarice." The big picture—"the whole country"—was "a vast crusade that required an absolute homogeneity of feeling; almost every American family had some sort of stake in the West and acquiesced naturally, therefore, in that worship of success, that instinctive belief that there was something sacred in the pursuit of wealth without which the pioneers themselves could hardly have survived."

Brooks' Young America acquired a scathing disciple in Lewis Mumford, whose *Sticks and Stones* (1924) and *The Golden Day* (1926) were summarized by the author himself as "a bit of preliminary house-cleaning and rubbish removal" discarding "the barbarism of the Gilded Age." Meanwhile, Gilded Age imagery fed Vernon Parrington's "Great Barbecue" of 1927, serving up the nation's resources in gargantuan portions to "leading bankers and promoters and business men." Matthew Josephson's popular histories of *The Robber Barons* (1934) and *The Politicos* (1938) ensued.

It is perfectly possible to agree with Brooks's assessment of Mark Twain without scapegoating Gilded Age America. Many others (I include myself) find Twain an unfinished novelist; a prolix stylist working piecemeal; a riddle of conflicting aspirations. Brooks's ostensible starting point—Twain's extraordinary "endowment"—is an undeveloped inference required to impugn Twain's America. The very man-boy act in Twain that Brooks finds submissive powered the sustained dissidence of Charles Ives. Both Ives and Twain extracted moral fire from genteel canons of aesthetic worth, with their emphasis on uplift. If Twain was a compromised product of Gilded Age America, Ives was an artist whose Gilded Age beginnings catalyzed continued growth. If Twain and Ives succumbed to terminal despair, it was because the Gilded Age was over, replaced by a twentieth century they disavowed. As for Gilded Age inhibitions, they cut two ways. That ladies swooned when Albert Niemann, the Metropolitan Opera's peerless first Tristan, tore his bandages from his wound documents a degree of emotional engagement no longer to be found at the opera house.

In fact, Van Wyck Brooks' Gilded Age was a utilitarian myth. He expertly used the past—and used Mark Twain in the process. Were the actual pioneers dominated by avarice? Or did they rather embody decades animated by the rough, infectious vigor of a young and rapidly growing society? Was the Gilded Age actually inimical to the arts? A short list of high achievers would necessarily include Twain, Emily Dickinson, Edith Wharton, Henry Adams, and Henry James in literature and letters; Winslow Homer, Thomas Eakins, John Singer Sargent, and Louis Sullivan in art and architecture; Ives and the American Dvořák in concert music. When the Young Americans rejected a shackling past, they did not really imagine that a *tabula rasa* engenders creative inspiration. Brooks eventually recanted and so did Mumford—who in 1957 had occasion to observe with relief that they both had "purged" the "negative" and "querulous" tone of their earlier writings.

Ultimately, Brooks's "Gilded Age" was not an obstacle to new artistic flights; rather, it was a synthetic catalyst, a shrewd psychological spur serving an Oedipal need to escape the immediate past. That is why, revisited today, *The Ordeal of Mark Twain* seems shrill and redundant. Though it masquerades as literary criticism, its vital function was purely ephemeral. It heralded a new aesthetic epoch that would cherish originality as a necessary criterion of worth. The writers, painters, and composers of the Gilded Age decades more favored a moral criterion.

Alfred Kazin, in his seminal 1942 retrospection *On Native Grounds: An Interpretation of Modern American Prose Literature*, wrote of the early Van Wyck Brooks: "As a historian his dramatic misanthropy furnished a dangerous model for those emotional followers who were eager to lament the past, never to study it." Though Kazin was thinking of his literary colleagues, his admonition better fits a post–World War I coterie of Oedipal American composers whose purported quest for a usable past was as mythic as the useless past they adduced.

The Useless Past: Virgil Thomson, Aaron Copland, and the Standard Narrative

Though the impact of wartime Germanophobia on American culture and institutions of culture was pervasive, classical music was hit hardest. The United States had been a Germanic musical colony. Populating the cities of the Northeast, fast penetrating the interior, beaver-like Germans had amassed a fledgling network of orchestras and choral societies. A German-born conductor, Theodore Thomas, had preached that the "symphony orchestra"—itself a German-American coinage originating with Leopold Damrosch in New York—"shows the culture of the community." By World War I, orchestras in Chicago, Cincinnati, Minneapolis, Philadelphia, and St. Louis were already civic bulwarks. Their conductors were mainly German. They mainly played Germanic music. By 1900, even American opera was predominantly German: a Wagner fever gripped the nation.

Boston's German conductor was the imperious Karl Muck, whose tenure ended abruptly on March 25, 1918, when U.S. marshals appeared at Symphony Hall to arrest him as an enemy alien. Though charges of espionage were never proved, that Muck's sympathies lay with the kaiser was not in doubt. Jailed and deported, he never returned. His eventual successor, Serge Koussevitzky, was a cosmopolitan Russian whose quest for the Great American Symphony, presuming a useless American past, aligned with that of the American symphonists he championed—including Samuel Barber, Aaron Copland, Roy Harris, Howard Hanson, Walter Piston, and William Schuman.

The Boston Symphony's pre–World War I espousal of Boston's own considerable *fin-de-siècle* composers was now abandoned. Those local composers, most notably George Chadwick (about whom more later), were (and remained) Germanic. But Copland and other "come-of-age" Americans were Francophiles schooled in France by Nadia Boulanger, whose godhead was Stravinsky. The new American symphonic aesthetic they proposed was modernist: lean, precise, poised, cleansed of murky angst and *Innerlichkeit*.

Though Copland proved the iconic come-of-age embodiment, its patriarchal Moses, the movement's polemical Aaron was a lesser composer with a waspish tongue. No less than Van Wyck Brooks, Virgil Thomson extrapolated a New World cultural narrative spurning recent decades. No less than Brooks, he took no prisoners. His swift, sardonic prose limned freshly minted understandings. Without apparent effort, eschewing strain, he believed what he wished others to believe.

Born in 1896, he was a hybrid product of Kansas City and Harvard, then Paris, where he lived from 1925 to 1940. He studied with Boulanger (whom he remembered with uncharacteristic tenderness) and kept company with Gertrude Stein. He ultimately settled in Manhattan's Chelsea Hotel. The resulting juxtaposition—of New World whimsy interfused with the refinements of Old World high art—textured his gadfly persona; he himself traced his obstreperousness to "the Booth Tarkington-George Ade-Mark Twain connection."

Beginning in the twenties, Thomson wrote about music for the *Boston Evening Transcript*, *Vanity Fair*, and *Modern Music*. His *New York Herald Tribune* reviews, from 1940 to 1954, made him widely notorious and influential. If rereading Thomson's feuilletons today remains a bracing experience, his larger efforts are compromised by know-it-all slapdash judgments and chronic aesthetic biases more forgivable and delectable in a daily newspaper balanced by others' accounts. There are also insouciant howlers innumerable. Recalling the inception of the Metropolitan Opera on page one of *American Music Since 1910* (1971), Thomson recorded that "for its first seven years, from 1882 to '89, [it] gave everything, including Bizet's *Carmen*, in German." Yet the Met began in 1883 as an Italian house, ambushed by Germans from 1884 to 1891 before the boxholders took it back. Another: writing for the *Times* in 1962, Thomson called *Porgy and Bess* an "*opéra comique*, like *Carmen*, consisting of musical numbers separated by spoken dialogue." But Gershwin wrote sung recitatives. The dialogue one sometimes encounters in *Porgy* was added after Gershwin's death. Thomson himself loudly reviewed *Porgy* at its 1935 premiere.

As the Francophile in Thomson identified the Copland milieu—i.e., Thomson's own—as the starting point of American concert music, the useless past he inferred spanned the Gilded Age and *fin-de-siècle* both: a broader swath of condemnation than with Brooks or Mumford. In fact, Thomson discovered no "mature" forebears. His narrative began with Germanic "grandfathers" inhabiting a "state of adolescence"—Chadwick, Horatio Parker, Edward MacDowell.

> For all the charm and competence of their music, it is a pale copy
> of its continental models. Its thin perfume is of another time and
> place than twentieth century America. . . . And for all that Chad-
> wick and MacDowell had aspired . . . to depict their country, they
> did so as European travelers might have done and no whit more
> convincingly than Dvořák . . . in his *New World* Symphony. . . .

In Thomson's view, the ostensible ascendance of French models after
1900 improved the situation enough that "beginning about 1910" an
"adult" "twentieth century show" could begin. Copland appeared and
endured. So did Randall Thompson, Walter Piston, Roy Harris, William
Schuman, and Roger Sessions—all "older masters." Harris's Third Symphony of 1939 was "America's most convincing product in that form."

Thomson's version of the European narrative contextualizes this
American music-history lesson. The "most original" twentieth-century
composer was Claude Debussy. The Germans, by comparison, thought
"in simplified alternatives—black or white, right or wrong, our team
against all the others in the world." For them, "a certain degree of introversion was esteemed man's highest expressive state." But what seemed
to Thomson Germanic hot air for others conveys a moral afflatus in
Bruckner, Mahler, Sibelius, and Shostakovich—all on Thomson's list of
windbag composers.

Whatever merit one may find in Thomson's formidable eccentricities
of feeling and opinion, his mode of inquiry and espousal was fundamentally different from that of Van Wyck Brooks. Brooks closely studied the past he deemed useless. *America's Coming of Age* dedicates eight
densely argued pages to the thesis that James Russell Lowell was "a siz-
able figure, but one that has curiously gone blank." Thomson undertook
no comparable inquiries. Is Chadwick's music really "a pale copy of its
continental models"? The many Chadwick recordings we have today (a
poor substitute for public performance) postdate Thomson's verdict.
Might Thomson have scrutinized the score of Chadwick's big Fourth
String Quartet, with its potent echoes of Dvořák's American style? The

sly, casual scherzos of Chadwick's Second and Third Symphonies, which tweak their earnest Germanic models? It is more than doubtful.

Brooks evinces a hunger for the past. Thomson's attitude, by comparison, is one of blasé indifference. But his verdict serves the same Oedipal purpose: he cuts the umbilical cord to the parent culture abroad. In retrospect, he is more a guide to his own time and place than a sage chronicler of truths more timeless. If his influence was nonetheless centrist, it was not least because the false history he preached was buttressed by other, less querulous voices.

THE LONGTIME "DEAN" of American composers, Aaron Copland, was a more honest, more credible witness to the American musical experience—but was no better informed.

Copland's pivotal Piano Variations (1930), a clarion wake-up call for come-of-age compatriots, declaims a kind of pastlessness. Though its skittish rhythms sublimate jazz, the main affect is one of skyscraper music of steel and concrete, vibrating with the nervous energy of the city. Roots in the soil are eschewed. This clean "American" sound subsequently acquired a folkloric social conscience spurred by the Depression and World War II. But Copland's modernist methodology canceled any residue of nostalgia.

Copland's 1952 Norton lectures recount a "search for what Van Wyck Brooks calls a usable past." Copland also wrote, in 1941: "The great young American composer will not appear suddenly. . . . He will come out of a long line of lesser men." In 1968 he regretted: "Composers nowadays seem to have no sense of history whatsoever and practically no interest in where they came from. . . . You can't imagine how distressing to me that is." But Copland's own quest, recalled in decades of writings and lectures endeavoring to educate listeners and buoy colleagues, proved remarkably futile. As of 1941, he experienced the American composers of his generation as "only just out of our teens, musically speaking." Eleven years later, his Norton lectures reported: "By the late twenties, our search

for musical ancestors had been abandoned or forgotten, partly, I suppose, because we became convinced that there were none—that we had
none. We were on our own, and something of the exhilaration that goes
with being on one's own accompanied our very action."

In Copland's American musical topography, the entirety of the
Gilded Age and *fin-de-siècle* comprises a featureless wasteland. There is
no music of lasting consequence. There is not even a place for composers.

> Some idea of the [historic] difficulties encountered by [Amer-
> ican] composers, no matter how gifted, can be gained from an
> examination of the ten years prior to 1920.... The composer of
> that period was dependent on a local orchestra that occasionally
> "tried out" the work of a native son or on a personal acquaintance
> among concert artists.... [More recently] public opinion ... has
> remained comparatively unformed in regard to the relative merits
> of [contemporary] composers. We badly need critical works on the
> failures and achievements of recent composers, based on intimate
> knowledge of the composer's work. This kind of knowledge few of
> our critics possess.

Copland was the victim of an American memory hole, itself a casualty
of the ruptured American cultural narrative inflicted by World War I.
Only in recent decades have music historians begun to reconstruct the
vibrant cultural community once recorded by James Gibbons Huneker.
In no subsequent period was contemporary American concert music
more performed or more knowledgeably discussed than in the two
decades before 1900. The charged reception of Dvořák's *New World* sup-
plies a microcosm. Dozens of notable writers debated the question: "Is
it American?" In New York, a city of immigrants, the answer was yes—
Dvořák's self-evident absorption of "negro melodies" was embraced as a
notable acknowledgment of America's most potent, most pervasive "folk
music." In Boston, the answer was no; Dvořák was shunned as a med-
dling naïf.

The preamble was an American Composers' Concerts movement which by 1884 sponsored symphonic concerts exclusively presenting American works—a protectionist surge so powerful that it spilled into American Composers' Concerts in Germany, Austria, and France between 1889 and 1892, and in 1890 provoked one of its staunchest advocates, Henry Krehbiel, to write: "The American composer . . . after long suffering neglect, now seems to be in imminent danger of being coddled to death." Among the most noticed American works presented abroad by the conductor F. X. Arens in 1891–92 was a picture of "Southern Negro Life" scored for strings, tambourine, triangle, and tam-tam; this was "Marcio-fantastico" from the *Suite caractéristique* of Henry Schoenefeld, a Milwaukee-born composer who mined African American and Native American materials. In 1892, Schoenefeld's *Rural* Symphony won a prize awarded by the National Conservatory and praise from Dvořák himself. In the wake of Dvořák's 1893 symphony, Krehbiel took the lead in espousing compositional strategies favoring homegrown vernacular elements. Of the participating American Composers' Concerts conductors, Anton Seidl vigorously promoted Edward MacDowell (whom he considered "greater than Brahms") and Victor Herbert (whom he engaged as his frequent assistant); he also excitedly discovered, in George Templeton Strong's *Sintram* Symphony (1893), a Wagnerian American program-symphony of formidable caliber. Meanwhile, Henry Higginson's Boston Symphony routinely performed the leading Boston composers, whose progress was followed with enthusiasm and discernment. When Chadwick proved susceptible to "negro melodies," Philip Hale of the *Journal* felt impelled to decry Dvořák's obvious influence as "baneful."

In short, the late Gilded Age boasted a fractious, articulate musical community of the kind Aaron Copland presumed had never existed in the United States. Its chief topic was the emergence of an "American school" of composers that would one day ground American classical music. Of Copland's disappointed assessment of the music itself, it may be said that his search for a usable past, if feeble, was indubitably sincere. He appreciatively examined some of Chadwick's scores at

Harvard in 1952. He acknowledged in MacDowell an "individual poetic gift" and "special turn of harmony." He came to regard Charles Griffes as "a name that deserves to be remembered." But these were composers inimical to the Boulangerie. Chadwick and MacDowell were too Germanic. Griffes's vertiginous Piano Sonata (1918), upon which Scriabin exerted a necessary influence, was too exotic. Although limited knowledge did not permit him to realize it, Copland's problem with America's musical past was primarily aesthetic.

Might any of the pre–World War I American composers Thomson and Copland found useless have otherwise proven usable? Suppose the Germanic thread had never been severed? I will return to this interesting question after considering a third influential chronicler—who happened to be Copland's most famous protégé.

Leonard Bernstein and the Ives Case

"The Absorption of Race Elements into American Music"—Leonard Bernstein's 1939 Harvard University bachelor's thesis—begins with yet another invocation of the useless past. That Bernstein took sufficient pride in this precocious effort to sanction its publication in his 1982 collection *Findings* is understandable not merely because its author was only twenty-one years old, but because it told a tale he never wholly disavowed. Its crux is the advent of jazz after World War I. Jazz is "the really universal basis of American composition," the "ultimate common denominator." Before that, American concert music was ersatz. All the prejazz composers "sound more or less similar."

Bernstein's most striking conceit is a two-part treatment of the infiltration of jazz into concert idioms. An initial phase, epitomized by George Gershwin, is too literal: a fledgling composer, Gershwin "did not try to reconcile a 'modern' idiom with the diatonic Negro scale. He simply remained steeped in nineteenth-century methods and made the most of them." It was Copland, a schooled practitioner, who was able to merge jazz with "his own advanced style." That is: the jazz elements are abstracted and creatively manipulated, subsumed into "an independent idiom." Bernstein also cites Roger Sessions and Roy Harris as composers whose rhythmic ingenuities are traceable to African-American influences. The result is "mature" American classical music.

That Bernstein's entire exercise is actually a 20,000-word hunch is evident from a letter he wrote to Copland early on. It reads in part:

> The thesis tries to show how the stuff that the old boys turned out . . . failed utterly to develop an American style or school of music at all. . . . Now how to go about it? It means going through recent American things, finding those that sound, for some reason, American, and translate that American sound into musical terms. I feel convinced that there is such a thing. . . . This is where you can help, if you would. . . . You see, I know and hear so little American stuff.

Copland replied with encouragement but added: "Don't try to prove too much. Composing in this country is still pretty young no matter how you look at it."

The inquiry at hand—what is American classical music?—was a chronic Bernstein preoccupation. Classical music was born abroad. Bernstein was born in Massachusetts and did not hear an orchestra until the age of fourteen. As Lenny Amber, he had supported himself arranging popular songs and transcribing jazz improvisations. Upon taking over the New York Philharmonic in 1958, he was best known as a Broadway composer. Bernstein was determined that the Philharmonic would serve important American music—and that he would compose some himself. Finding his way, he focused his first Philharmonic season on "a survey of American Music from the earliest generation of American composers to the present," the earliest composers sampled being George Chadwick, Arthur Foote, and Edward MacDowell. Did Bernstein realize that the *Melpomene* Overture—a gloss on Wagner's *Tristan* Prelude—was atypical Chadwick? That Chadwick's truer métier was comedy? It is impossible to say. When Bernstein turned his Philharmonic survey into his second Young People's Concert—"What is American Music?" (February 1, 1958)—*Melpomene* was an easy target: "straight European stuff." This was "the kindergarten period" of American music. MacDowell was "grade school." With the introduction of jazz, "high school" commenced with Gershwin and Copland. The Sessions Chorale Prelude of his Harvard thesis, with its syncopations, was "college." "Mature" American music, Bernstein concluded, embraced five personality traits: "youth," "pioneer energy," "a kind of loneliness" evoking open space, and two varieties of sentimentality deriving from hymns and popular songs.

Bernstein's Young People's Concert omitted the wild-card composer who would complicate every telling of the useless-past thesis: Charles Edward Ives. And I have so far omitted Ives, as well, from my accounts of America's musical past as purveyed by Copland and Virgil Thomson. That is because the discomfiture caused by the belated discovery of Ives's genius deserves separate consideration as a study in cognitive dissonance.

As the reader may remember, it was Bernstein himself who premiered Ives's Symphony No. 2 with the New York Philharmonic in 1951. Seven years later, he led the Philharmonic in the first prominent recording. I am just old enough to have experienced the shockwaves. Had the manuscript of *Huckleberry Finn* been posthumously discovered in a drawer of unpublished Mark Twain writings, the impact would scarcely have been greater. A Great American Symphony had been forever awaited. As of 1951, the Harris Third was long considered the most likely candidate, endorsed by Copland and Thomson both. Ives's symphony was self-evidently more capacious, more protean, more universal. And this was the second such Ives earthquake, the first having been John Kirkpatrick's 1939 Town Hall performance of the *Concord* Sonata—the occasion of Lawrence Gilman's far-resounding testimony that he had just encountered "the greatest music composed by an American." * That had been like finding *Moby-Dick* in a closet.

* See page 56.

Did Aaron Copland's generation really confront a useless past? Ives's Second was believed to date from around 1900, the *Concord* Sonata from 1910–15.* Ives's catalogue remained an immense terra incognita, beginning with any number of precocious songs composed at Yale—i.e., before 1899. And Ives had mysteriously stopped composing sometime in the 1920s—before the 1930 modernist wake-up call of Copland's Piano Variations. Could Ives's rough round peg be somehow massaged into the useless square hole of the late Gilded Age? Of America's *fin-de-siècle*?

Though sounding Teutonic was allegedly incompatible with sounding American, Ives was as Germanic as any American symphonist of his day. His teacher, Horatio Parker, had studied in Munich. Ives wrote symphonies and sonatas. Until he tired of it, he practiced sonata form. He cherished interior feeling. Virgil Thomson predictably experienced another windbag. "Where will be the 'substance' [Ives] wrote so eloquently about and desired so urgently" in his "larger works?" asks Thomson in "The Ives Case"—Chapter 3 of *American Music Since 1910*. Thomson's answer: "For all their breadth of concept and their gusto, I have no faith in them." Of Ives's songs, Thomson (himself a song composer) opined that "they do not, will not, as we say, come off"—a verdict that cannot be taken seriously (ask any American concert singer). Thomson's risible prediction that Edward MacDowell "may well survive" Ives is driven by the central premise that, his undeniable talent notwithstanding, Ives was more "a homespun Yankee tinkerer" than a full professional. (MacDowell trained in Paris and Frankfurt.)

Copland, a musician of wider sympathies, absorbed the late advent of Charles Ives more favorably. He first encountered Ives in the 1930s, via the *114 Songs* Ives published in 1922. He later recalled: "There we were in the twenties searching for a composer from the older generation with an 'American sound' and here was Charles Ives composing this incredible music—totally unknown to us!" Copland subsequently programed and performed an assortment of favorite Ives songs. Of the entire collection,

---

* These datings are now somewhat later.

he offered a mixed assessment as of 1941: "despite many a serious short-coming ... a unique and memorable contribution." Of Ives generally, Copland ventured: "Even with our smattering of information concerning his extensive list of works, it seems safe to say that Ives was far more originally gifted than any other member of his generation. . . . [He] had the vision of a true pioneer, but he could not organize his material, particularly in his larger works, so that we come away with a unified impression." In 1952, Copland admonished: "Don't think for an instant that [Ives] was a mere provincial. . . . No, Ives was an intellectual. . . . Nevertheless Ives had a major problem in attempting to achieve formal coherence in the midst of so varied a musical material." Sixteen years later, Copland declared himself guilty of a "misapprehension"—Ives's complexities "don't always add up, but when they do, a richness of experience is suggested that is unobtainable in any other way." Taken as a whole, Copland's Ives's verdicts narrate a conscientious evolution of opinion that does not wholly erase a basic posture of skepticism. Ives was Germanic, Copland Francophile. Copland was meticulous, Ives experimental.

With Leonard Bernstein, the festering "Ives case" was processed by a composer/conductor of catholic taste and temperament—but the outcome remained unsettled. Already in Bernstein's 1939 Harvard thesis, Ives makes a substantive appearance: the *Concord* Sonata is "American," "worthy of respect"—if also "tiring, overlong, and a fierce challenge to any pianist." Bernstein's premiere performances of the Second Symphony came eleven years later. His 1958 Young Peoples' Concert tracing the history of identifiably American music omitted Ives. In 1967, however, Ives got a Young People's Concert of his own. The longest selections in this one-hour show were *Washington's Birthday* and *The Unanswered Question*. Bernstein's eventual Ives repertoire also included *Decoration Day, Central Park in the Dark*, the Symphony No. 3, and some shorter works—a relatively modest list. He considered conducting the Fourth Symphony but changed his mind. He returned repeatedly to the Symphony No. 2 and took it abroad.

In Munich in 1987, Bernstein prefaced Ives's Second with a fifteen-

minute lecture—reproduced as a note to his 1987 New York Philharmonic recording—extolling Ives as "an authentic primitive—a country
boy at heart." This odd designation is traceable to the Ives discourse
of Copland, Thomson, Elliott Carter, and many others who thought
they detected a whiff of the dilettante. But no primitive could possibly
have composed "Feldeinsamkeit," the Lied Ives produced for Parker
in 1898—it is a song both consummate and inimitable. And such Ives
endings as the dissipating sonic aureole concluding "The Housatonic at
Stockbridge" (never conducted by Bernstein) demonstrate an aesthetic
sophistication as genuine as any to be found within the Boulangerie.
When Bernstein's 1987 Ives encomium extols "all the freshness of a naïve
American wandering in the grand palaces of Europe like one of Henry
James's Americans abroad, or better still like Mark Twain's innocents
abroad," he could not possibly be referring to the Fourth Symphony or
Concord Sonata; the usable past traversed by these pieces is far more of
the New World than the Old. As for the Second Symphony, is it "naïve,"
or knowing? Bernstein's is the same suspect skepticism that Van Wyck
Brooks visited upon Mark Twain's ordeal in 1920.

Ultimately, Bernstein's Ives verdict retains the imagery of an incom-
plete composer challenged or shackled by the past he inhabited. Ives's
"health gave out under the strain" of having to live "a double life" as
composer and businessman (1967). He "lived in a country . . . where
being a musician was considered vaguely reprehensible" (1987). Ives
offered his own memorable riposte upon reading Copland's 1941 critique of his ostensible "'glorification' of the business-composer working in isolation." "I was paying my respects to the average man (there is
one) in the ordinary business of life, from the ashman down [sic] to the
president—among whom, it seems to me, there was more openminded-
ness and fair-fighting than among musicians—particularly of my age
and generation." Such was Ives's strategy for healing the schism between
lowbrow and highbrow that Brooks had decried.

The first American composer of consequence to endorse Ives without
reservation was Henry Cowell, who from the vantage point of Copland

and Thomson was a placeless iconoclast: an "ultra-modern." A product of the West Coast, he grew up hearing more Chinese, Japanese, and Indonesian than Western classical music. He never acquired complete familiarity with the Western canon. He first made his name in the twenties as an experimental pianist, pummeling the keys with his fists or stroking the strings under the lid. Cowell did not care that Ives was a part-time businessman. He had no qualms about Ives's failure to study abroad. Rather, he viewed Ives' heterodoxies as inspired by the rural fiddling and singing of American folk songs. If Copland and Thomson vaguely contextualized Ives as victim of a cartoon Gilded Age invented by Van Wyck Brooks, for Cowell Ives was a wondrous apparition, a clairvoyant musical inventor of nontonal harmonies and labyrinthine polyrhythms years ahead of Schoenberg and Stravinsky. Cowell was in fact the inveterate "tinkerer" Thomson thought Ives to be. He read Ives as a futurist like himself.

Only in recent decades has it become commonplace to recognize that Charles Ives was both buoyed and challenged by the complexly transitional period of American history to which he belonged. Whatever his eccentricities, he partook in the project of Germanic uplift anchoring what we still misleadingly label the "genteel tradition." Unlike Stravinsky or Copland, he retained Beethoven as his lodestar. He lovingly and fervently embraced the moral criterion. No less than Mark Twain, he rejected the future he foresaw. It is barely an exaggeration to suggest that Ives remained a stranger to the modernists incongruously fated to discover him. The result was a reclamation project that did not reclaim as usable either Ives or the America of which he was part.

The past remained impugned.

Copland and Mexico

Aaron Copland's modernist misgivings about Charles Ives—and also (as we shall see) about George Gershwin—were recapitulated in Mexico by Carlos Chávez in relation to Silvestre Revueltas.

In his lifetime, Chávez (1899–1978) was Mexico's leading composer of classical music and the spokesperson for Mexico's composers. He was also a prominent conductor and educator. Aesthetically, Chávez was a modernist akin to Copland, albeit more intransigently dissonant. They were colleagues and friends.

Revueltas, the outsider, was born in a village in 1899. Trained in Austin and Chicago as a violinist, he disdained formal instruction as a composer. Instead, the local *banda*, with its shrill clarinets and trumpets and booming tuba, tutored his ear. He absorbed other influences as he saw fit. Though he partook of modernism and nationalism, his core affinity was political: like the Mexican muralists, he cherished the arts as instruments for social and political change. He spurned tradition in pursuit of idiosyncratic forms imparting impassioned spontaneity. He drank hard and died young, in 1940. The poet Octavio Paz wrote: "All his music seems preceded by something that is not simply joy and exhilaration, as some believe, or satire and irony, as others believe. That element, better and more pure, . . . is his profound empathy with his surroundings. . . . His music occupies a place in our hearts above that of the grandiose Mexican murals, that seem to know all except pity."

In fact, Revueltas vividly embodies the trope of the unfinished genius. There is even something Ivesian about his sound mosaics, with their shards of street cries and splintered songs. Ivesian, too, is his rapscallion enjoyment of the wrong notes and missed entrances of vernacular musical entertainments.

Like Ives, like Gershwin, Revueltas was widely regarded as a gifted amateur by his putative superiors. Copland expressed wary admiration for his native gift. Chávez, who chose to patronize Revueltas as a fallen disciple, followed suit. If Copland mainly neglected Ives and Gershwin, he increasingly appreciated ingredients of incipient greatness. Chávez, by comparison, actively suppressed the inclusion of Revueltas in the many Mexican programs he influentially curated in Mexico and the United States. The writer/editor Herbert Weinstock, a Chávez friend and supporter, felt impelled to write to him on November 25, 1940, to beg an explanation: "Time and again, [I find] myself in the position of having to defend you against the charge of being jealous of Revueltas, of deliberately trying to smother his reputation by ignoring him." Revueltas, who had just died, seemed to Weinstock "a musician of something approaching genius." Citing Goddard Lieberson, for decades a key American advocate of twentieth-century composers, Weinstock reported that "many musical people here" struggled with the perception that Chávez "spitefully failed to do justice to his most important compatriot." Thirty-one years later, on October 8, 1971, Chávez delivered a lecture on Revueltas at a Mexico City conference about "La Música en México." He complained that the "construction" of Revueltas's compositions, "instead of showing development, was repetitive." He continued:

> Although he showed great talent in the beginning, abrupt and impressive, his creative capacities never managed to mature, his metier was not perfected, and his style did not evolve. All his compositions are essentially similar in procedure, in expression and in style. Once or twice, after he started composing, I warned him, in conversation, about the issue of renewing oneself—renew yourself or die—and he understood this in theory. But it was easier for him to repeat his early works, the unending ostinati, the explosive contrasts, the piangendo melodies, etc, etc.

The Revueltas scholar Roberto Kolb (to whom I am indebted for the Weinstock letter and Chávez lecture) comments: "Revueltas tends to base his compositions on the principle of montage and collage, dialectic or symbolic. This is linked to political goals. I find it extraordinary that this did not even occur to Chávez. He only evaluates Revueltas's music from a formal point of view."

Absent symphony, concerto, and opera, the Revueltas catalogue bristles with seeming bits and pieces. Among his peak achievements is the score for the 1935 film *Redes,* an uneasy partnership with Paul Strand and Fred Zinnemann. The former—like Copland, like John Steinbeck and Langston Hughes—sought inspiration from Mexico's artists on the left. The latter—later the Hollywood director of *High Noon*—was in flight from Hitler's Europe. The "nets" of the title ensnare both fish and poor fishermen. The resulting film is as epic and iconic, flawed and unfinished, as the Mexican Revolution itself. *

Revueltas's score—a peak achievement in music for the cinema—throbs with pathos and majesty. Its admirers have included the conductor Erich Kleiber, who resettled in Buenos Aires in flight from Hitler; Kleiber created a *Redes* concert suite. Copland wrote of *Redes*: "Revueltas is the type of inspired composer in the sense that Schubert was the inspired composer. That is to say, his music is a spontaneous outpouring, a strong expression of his inner emotions. There is nothing premeditated . . . His music is above all vibrant and colorful. . . . The score that Revueltas has written for [*Redes*] has very many of the qualities characteristic of Revueltas's art." When in 1937 these words wound up in the *New York Times*, Copland felt the need to explain to Chávez: "I suppose you must have wondered how I happened to write that piece for the N.Y. Times on Silvestre. As a matter of fact I had no idea the Times would use it . . . I did it rather hastily. . . ."

Aaron Copland wielded singular influence among his American composer colleagues, and was by far the American composer who most shaped public awareness and consideration of contemporary American classical music. In this role, he was notably unselfish. But he was hardly without prejudice. The sui generis pianist Oscar Levant, an intimate of George Gershwin, was the rare musician who interacted productively with Copland and Gershwin both. (He also studied composition with Arnold Schoenberg.) In his inimitable memoir *A Smattering of Ignorance* (1939), Levant recalls Copland's encouraging interest in his fledgling compositions, including a performance at Copland's Yaddo festival. Levant also writes that Copland's circle manifested "an atmosphere

---

* I am the producer of a Naxos DVD combining *Redes* with a newly recorded soundtrack. The original soundtrack, conducted by Revueltas, was hurriedly and inadequately recorded.

whose preciosity exceeded anything in my experience. The air was full of jeer for everything and everyone outside the closed shop of those present. This startled me somewhat, and I was at a further disadvantage because I was the only one present who had not either studied in Paris with Boulanger or D'Indy or was not scheduled to leave for France as soon as the festival was over." Levant adds: "Considering that I am a person who lacks no possible human failing, I have been constantly amazed by Copland's generosity." If other American composers fared less well, that Copland's generosity had its limits was merely human.

Latin America was of special interest to Copland; it was Mexico, in the 1930s, that turned him into a populist. In Copland's *Our New Music* (1941), Chávez is allotted a full chapter. Revueltas is here acknowledged in six sentences, two of which read: "[His] music is colorful, picturesque, and gay. Unfortunately, he never was able to break away from a certain dilettantism that makes even his best compositions suffer from sketchy workmanship." A second, 1968 edition repeats these two generalizations, both of which suffer from limited acquaintance with Revueltas's catalogue. Silvestre Revueltas is a composer whose time will come.

Copland's arms-length relationship to jazz, in *Our New Music*, is pertinent here—because, in addition to Ives, a composer to whom Revueltas may be likened is Duke Ellington. Both were masters of the short form. Both mediate, ingeniously and unpredictably, between vernacular, popular, and art-music influences. Both use color and timbre to memorably imprint ethnic identity. Both showcase spectacular instrumental virtuosity. Both eschew sonata form, developing variation, and other learned means to organize musical structure. Both equally eschew complexity or originality for their own sake. And both succumb to the modernist critique—not least because of the fatal whiff of the nightclub and cocktail lounge in Ellington, and the dusty streets of Durango in Revueltas. And yet, more than Copland, both fulfill Copland's own ideal of a music for both "us and them"—something for everyone, including the cognoscenti.

Postscript: The Standard Narrative and the CIA

Beginning in 1966, the *New York Times, Ramparts* magazine, and other publications revealed that the sixteen-year-old Congress for Cultural Freedom—which had prominently hosted festivals and conferences abroad celebrating American cultural achievements—had been covertly created and funded by the Central Intelligence Agency. In effect, the CCR was the chief cultural propaganda arm of the United States Government, waging a cultural cold war with the Soviet Union.

The music specialist for the CCR was Nicolas Nabokov, a minor composer of great personal charm. Nabokov was a White Russian expatriate closely associated with Igor Stravinsky, whom he regarded as the dominant figure in twentieth-century classical music. Like Stravinsky, Nabokov viewed Soviet music with contempt; his campaign tarring Dmitri Shostakovich as a Soviet tool was relentless.

The most ambitious and widely noticed CCR music festival took place in Paris in 1952. Curated by Nabokov, it was called "L'Oeuvre du XXe siècle"—the English version being "Masterpieces of the Twentieth Century." No fewer than twenty-five concerts with orchestra were given at exorbitant expense. The participating ensembles included the Boston Symphony, the New York City Ballet Orchestra (with the entire company), the Orchestre des Concerts Lamoureux, the Orchestre de la Suisse Romande, the Orchestra National de la Radiodiffusion Française, the Orchestre de la Société des Concerts du Conservatoire, the RIAS Orchestra of West Berlin, the Royal Opera Orchestra (a staged performance of Benjamin Britten's *Billy Budd*), the Santa Cecilia Orchestra, and the Vienna Philharmonic (a staged performance of Alban Berg's *Wozzeck*). The conductors included Karl Böhm, Britten, Ferenc Fricsay, Pierre Monteux, Igor Markevitch, Charles Munch, and Bruno Walter. The dominant composer, by far, was Stravinsky, who also participated as a conductor. Stravinsky's Neoclassical period—which included his move to the United States—was overwhelmingly stressed.

It was merely predictable that Nabokov's programs included not a note of Charles Ives, George Gershwin, or Silvestre Revueltas.* But Aaron Copland was represented with three works. The entirety of Virgil Thomson's *Four Saints in Three Acts* was also given. The other American composers performed were Samuel Barber, Walter Piston, and William Schuman. Of these five Americans, all but Schuman had studied with Nadia Boulanger at her American School in Fontainebleau. Boulanger's godhead was Stravinsky. In Paris in 1952, she served as the main point of contact for Nabokov and Stravinsky both.

Though the festival was more controversial and less impactful than Nabokov had anticipated, he was nothing if not a formidable cultural powerbroker. Willi Brandt made him a Commander of the Grand Cross of Merit of the German Federal Republic. Through his friendship with Arthur Schlesinger, Jr., he arranged for the Kennedy White House to host Stravinsky on the occasion of his eightieth birthday in 1962.

This nexus of influence further documents the exaggerated pedigree of a musical standard narrative favoring modernist abstractions over vernacular resources, overlooking a usable past, and marginalizing America's two foremost concert composers.

---

* But Ives's *Concord* Sonata was performed on an ancillary program (not chosen by Nabokov) of chamber and solo works.

Chapter Five

The Bifurcation of American Music

*Why American Classical Music Stayed White—Was There
a Usable Musical Past?—Using Whitman and Melville—
Confluence—The Souls of Black Folk*

Why American Classical Music Stayed White

R esponding to Jeannette Thurber's challenge, Antonin Dvořák
identified "negro melodies" as the motherlode for American
composers to come. Though his *New World* Symphony was for
decades misapprehended as "typical Dvořák," we now realize that its
songs and dramaturgy are saturated with the imagery of Longfellow's
Hiawatha, and with the ambience and inflections of plantation song.
This beloved work—called "hackneyed" by Virgil Thomson—retains
its allure because, however subliminally, listeners experience an act of
empathy. Leonard Bernstein's notion that the Largo, because pentatonic,
would with Chinese words "sound Chinese" is an act of denial; William
Arms Fisher was able to adapt this pregnant English horn melody as a
synthetic spiritual—"Goin' Home"—because Dvořák apprehended the
heartbreak of the African-American slave.

If the American accent of Dvořák's New York symphony of 1893
remains remarkably little acknowledged, even less is his subsequent
American style of 1894 noticed or appreciated. This was the year of his
G-flat Humoresque, a tune mainly familiar to Americans who have
never heard of Antonín Dvořák. Its tripping dotted rhythms, its aura of

nostalgia, its amazing bluesy cadences add up to a New World concoc-
tion as distant from "Dvořák" as Scott Joplin. Joplin is in fact the composer that the third movement of Dvořák's *American* Suite (also 1894),
with its stride-piano left-hand skips, most evokes. Another of his 1894
Humoresques, in F major, begins with a refrain that sounds spun off
from *Porgy and Bess*, composed by Gershwin forty years later. Dvořák
was now no longer a Bohemian composer with a New World accent; as
surely as Domenico Scarlatti became Spanish, or Kurt Weill American,
the Dvořák of 1894–95 deserves to be counted an American composer.*

As such, he assembled a coterie and exerted an influence. Of his
pupils, Harry Burleigh—as I have earlier observed—was the composer/
singer who translated spirituals into art songs. Both directly and via his
adherents, Dvořák galvanized a movement to integrate "negro melodies"
into the Western concert tradition. However much challenged, ignored,
or forgotten, however little used, a straight line runs from Dvořák to
Joplin's rags and his opera *Treemonisha*, to the keyboard and symphonic
works of Samuel Coleridge-Taylor, to the *Negro Folk Symphony* of William Dawson, and to George Gershwin's hybrid opera. The no-man's-
land between classical and jazz, shunned by Copland and Thomson, is
where the American Dvořák resides. He is far closer than they would
ever be to James Reese Europe, and to the Black Broadway of *Clorindy*
and *In Dahomey*.

Dvořák was musically catholic: a sponge. Gustav Mahler, in New York,
could not possibly have composed a *New World* Symphony. Dvořák, a
dozen years earlier, could not have failed to do so. Throughout his creative odyssey, he organically absorbed his environs, high and low. In
Manhattan, he counseled the American composer to at all times "prick
his ear." By 1895, he was advising American colleagues to heed whatever
vernacular strains the New World melting pot afforded. Uncomfortable

---

* When I lecture on the history of American music, I typically begin at the keyboard
with the opening of Dvořák's F major Humoresque and ask people to guess the composer;
the usual guess is Gershwin. Then the opening of movement three of Dvořák's *American*
Suite; the usual guess is Joplin.

at the Metropolitan Opera, Dvořák doubtless patronized minstrel shows. He admired the songs of Stephen Foster. He attended Buffalo Bill's Wild West and in Iowa fraternized with Native American entertainers. He acknowledged Louis Moreau Gottschalk's Creole concoctions as a precursor to his own American project. He influenced George Chadwick's recourse to homegrown sources. The raucous ragtime snatches in Ives's piano and symphonic works embody the same easy, unprejudiced access to folk and popular strains that Dvořák exemplifies.

Though composers and music historians have long conjectured about Ives's possible influence had he been discovered earlier, a more plausible prospect is the influence Dvořák would have exerted had the Panic of 1893 not bankrupted Jeannette Thurber's husband and sent Dvořák back to Bohemia in 1895. What if Dvořák had stayed on in New York? What if there had been no Great War against the kaiser? Dvořák's American style, which he (characteristically) dropped upon returning to Prague, had been rapidly evolving. He had already produced what would become his most popular symphony and string quartet, among other irresistible American-sounding works. His allusions to American sights and sounds—to African and Native Americans, to a vast and elegiac West, to rustic fiddlers and dancers—were increasingly bold and varied. He aspired to compose a Hiawatha opera or cantata. He exerted a profound influence both on his pupils and the American musical public. In Manhattan, his ecumenical attitude toward race and equality was acclaimed by Henry Krehbiel and W. J. Henderson. However briefly, he actually embodied a formidable national movement, a New World quest. All these factors might have generated a sustained legacy—a usable past.

Dvořák had famously and influentially extolled "negro melodies" as "pathetic, tender, passionate, melancholy, solemn, religious, bold, merry, gay, or what you will . . . music that suits itself to any mood or any purpose." How much more circumscribed was Copland's endorsement of jazz half a century later. It had, he wrote in 1941, "only two expressions: the well-known 'blues' mood, and the wild, abandoned, almost hysterical and grotesque mood so dear to the youth of all ages. . . . Any serious composer who attempted to work within those two moods sooner or later became aware of their severe limitations." (Try applying this reductionist generalization to the compositions of Duke Ellington.) Rhythm, Copland added, was an aspect of jazz that had made a "real contribution" to the composer's art. And he expressed admiration for jazz experiments in timbre and instrumental virtuosity. At the same time, he was capable of inferring among African Americans "a conception of rhythm not as mental exercise but as something basic to the body's rhythmic impulse." He compared "interest in jazz" with "interest . . . in the primitive arts and crafts of aboriginal peoples." Listening to jazz as a stunted art music, Copland was more Eurocentric than such Europeans as Stravinsky, Bartók, Weill, Ravel, or Milhaud.

While this kind of racial analysis is merely symptomatic of another time, it remains ponderable that Copland's take on Black musical roots, compromising his quest for a usable musical past, is more cartoonish than any I have encountered in Dvořák's New York. And it is pertinent that Copland the man—unlike Dvořák or Ives or Twain—did not mingle easily with "common men." In the thirties, to be sure, he was a fellow traveler on the far left; he acquired a communal ethos that buoys his opera *The Tender Land* and also *Appalachian Spring* with its Shaker hymn. He vacationed in Minnesota and addressed Communist farmers at a picnic. His letters reveal the pleasure he took in this new activity— and also the incongruity of it all: "If they were a strange sight to me, I was no less of a one to them. . . . I was being gradually drawn, you see, into the political struggle with the peasantry!" Dvořák swigging his beer with inebriated Iowa farmers; Dvořák absorbing Burleigh's sorrow songs in his bird-infested Lower East Side apartment, his children underfoot; Twain among mischievous Black playmates and knowing Mississippi pilots and seedy Nevada gamblers; Ives on his Danbury porch, thrilling to the circus parade's "lady all in pink"; Ives banging out ragtime at some New Haven club; Ives in cleats, hurling his fastball for Yale; Gershwin "shouting" alongside transported Gullah congregants in a Carolina island church—all paint a different New World picture.

Copland was no snob. He explored jazz as an eager and appreciative interloper, intent on artfully appropriating ingredients of a neighbor art form. His youthful enthusiasm for such exercises, manifest in his *Music for the Theatre* (1925) and Piano Concerto (1926), afterward diminished—perhaps under the influence of such friends and colleagues as Roy Harris, who in 1926 counseled: "A word of warning to you—dear brother Aaron—the Jazz idiom is too easily assumed and projected . . . as a serious expression it has nearly burned out already I believe. . . . Don't disappoint us with jazz."[*] In fact, *Rodeo* and *Appalachian Spring* notwithstanding, Copland was no surrogate cowboy or Shaker. And his most prestigious New York adherent, the critic Paul Rosenfeld, was nothing if not a snobbish German-Jewish American. Certainly Rosenfeld was no friend of "negro melodies." Assessing *Rhapsody in Blue* in the *New Republic*, he detected in Gershwin the Russian Jew a "weakness of spirit, possibly as a consequence of the circumstance that the new world attracted the less stable types." In New York, Copland himself steered clear of Gershwin (and vice versa). Asked at a 1937 New York City Composers' Forum event how he would compare his music "to Mr. Gershwin's jazz," Copland replied: "Gershwin is serious up to a point. My idea was to intensify it. Not what you get in the dance hall but to use it cubistically—to make it more exciting than ordinary jazz."[†] Bernstein (notwithstanding his abiding admiration for Gershwin's gifts) took a similar view when in 1959 he wrote: "I don't think there has been such

---

[*] Cited by Beth Levy, "From Orient to Occident: Aaron Copland and the Sagas of the Prairie," in Carol Oja and Judith Tick, eds., *Aaron Copland and His World* (2005), p. 311. Here and in her *Frontier Figures: American Music and the Mythology of the American West* (2012), Levy speculates on the impact on Copland of feedback questioning his chosen sources of musical identity, directing him away from jazz and "Jewishness" toward distant prairie realms.

[†] Copland's appreciation of Gershwin subsequently deepened. And, subsequent to his *Music for the Theatre* and Piano Concerto, he composed a 1949 Clarinet Concerto on commission from Benny Goodman. It is significant that none of these three works, whatever their considerable merits, ever invited jazz renditions after the fashion of Gershwin's *Rhapsody*, Concerto, or *Porgy and Bess*.

an inspired melodist on this earth since Tchaikovsky . . . but if you want to speak of a *composer*, that's another matter."

The applicable modernist premise was once articulated by Copland like this: "A hymn tune represents a certain order of feeling: simplicity, plainness, sincerity, directness. It is the reflection of those qualities in a stylistically appropriate setting, imaginative and unconventional and not mere quotation, that gives the use of folk tunes reality and importance." What Copland has in mind is a "cubistic" Stravinskyan process abstracting and recombining molecular distillations of the vernacular. The composer Arthur Berger, who admired Stravinsky and Copland both, praised Copland's "exceptional degree of selectivity, transformation, and abstraction through which the essence of the material as well as a specific attitude, heightened emotion, ingenuity, and personality are conveyed." The result was an "indigenous substratum"—a synthetic American hybrid. But Stravinsky's predilection for the radical impersonality of the pianola (evoking the harshness of rustic ritualistic singing) and the rasp of the cimbalom (with its dissonant aureole) have no parallel in Copland's appropriations of the vernacular; rather, their affect of "authenticity" evokes a Bartók or Ives. And it is pertinent, as well, that Stravinsky knew the brutal pagan ceremonies of rural Russia.

Another frame of reference, more pertinent to Copland's American sources, was articulated by Maurice Ravel. A master of refined assimilation, Ravel created a sublime jazz/classical hybrid in the "Blues" movement of his 1925 Violin Sonata, about which he wrote: "Popular forms are but the materials of construction, and the work of art appears only on mature conception where no detail has been left to chance. Moreover, minute stylization in the manipulation of these materials is essential." Copland attempted a comparable classical/jazz fusion in his Piano Concerto. Is Copland's jazzy concerto more exciting and enduring than *Rhapsody in Blue* two years before? Rosenfeld thought so. As never in the "hash derivative" compositions of Gershwin, he opined, jazz had in Copland's treatment at last "borne music." But Copland lacks Ravel's gift for sublimation. His concerto's busily shifting meters cancel the intended illusion of improvisatory abandon; he also fails to come up with a good tune. In *El salón México*, the dissection and recombination of dance-hall songs is Copland's solution to what he considered a "formal problem"—that "most composers have found that there is little that can be done with such material except repeat it." For Rosenfeld, these tactics rescued vulgar materials transferred to the concert stage. For others, a work such as Gershwin's *Cuban* Overture, with its infectious danzón—or Dvořák's *American* Suite, with its catchy tributes to plantation and minstrel song—does just fine without them.

When Gershwin blithely embeds the thirty-two-bar song form into his concert works, the melodic distinction and harmonic subtlety of his actual songs divinely carry the day. And the popular energies never sound suppressed or denatured. By comparison, Copland's relative lack of enthusiasm for jazz, and for cowboy and dance-hall tunes, yields a self-consciously "composed" style of appropriation. No one could accuse Charles Ives of fashioning kitsch. But Copland's vernacular borrowings in such signature works as *El salón México*, *Rodeo*, and *Appalachian Spring*, scrupulously compacted, scrubbed clean of Emersonian "mud and scum,"* of American self-contradiction and travail, can seem antiseptic or cheap.

It speaks volumes that Virgil Thomson's recourse to American vernacular strains was—as Thomson and Copland mutually agreed—a crucial source of Copland's "American" style. Equally ponderable is that Thomson's American style began not with Americana, but with his 1928 operatic divertissement *Four Saints in Three Acts*, to a faux-naïve libretto by Gertrude Stein. The gnomic borrowings that Thomson inscrutably strings together, emulating Stein's "discipline of spontaneity," include Anglican chant, Baroque opera, Puccini—and American church hymns and banjo tunes. Then came Thomson's film scores for *The Plow that Broke the Plains* (1936) and *The River* (1937), and his opera *The Mother of Us All* (1947), in all of which the American vernacular nuggets predominate, creating a

* See page 70.

"white" (consonant, triadic, diatonic) Midwestern or New England pastiche. The American prairie, village, or street corner of Copland's *Rodeo*, *Billy the Kid*, and *The City* adopt Thomson's simplicities of citation and many of the same ingredients. His Kansas City roots notwithstanding, Thomson was an eccentric urban sophisticate whose common touch was more "about" than "of" the people. Copland followed suit. Compared to Dvořák, Ives, or Gershwin, both are synthetic populists.*

It comes as no surprise that Thomson endorsed the writings of George Pullen Jackson, who in the thirties and forties influentially maintained that American folk music was fundamentally Anglo and "white"; according to Jackson and Thomson both, Black spirituals arose from white spirituals. "The ethnic integrity of American folk music will be surprising news to many who have long held to the melting-pot theory of American life," Thomson informed readers of the *Herald Tri-*

---

* And both were gay, as were Leonard Bernstein, Samuel Barber, and countless others who defined "America" in music—a topic tackled by Nadine Hubbs in her estimable *The Queer Composition of America's Sound* (2004). Even if Hubbs lays too much stress on Stein and Thomson as prime movers (Copland's America has more flesh and blood, as well as a self-conscious complexity foreign to *Four Saints*), the point stands. Equally undeniable is the queer network of professional influence that Hubbs adduces; Thomson's music staff at the *New York Herald Tribune*, for instance, included his gay colleagues Paul Bowles and Lou Harrison—hardly mainstream picks. And Hubbs further adduces a queer musical aesthetic favoring a leaner, more accessible, more consonant style than the high modernism Copland initially embraced, not to mention such more "masculine" heterosexual nontonal composers as Roger Sessions, Ralph Shapey, and Leon Kirchner. From Hubbs's queer perspective, antipathy to Ives was merely predictable. The "unfinished" aesthetic I extrapolate in Ives and Gershwin is here pertinent as an alternative American trope linking to Mark Twain, Walt Whitman, and Herman Melville (of whom, as it happens, Whitman was queer and Melville betrayed queer affinities). Also doubtless pertinent is my own heterosexuality. Hubbs assumes the centrality of Copland's achievement. I vividly remember being taken aback, in the 1970s, by an encomium to Copland written by William Flanagan—one of the queer Americans corralled by Hubbs. Flanagan's assessment of Copland as a master composer of world stature seemed to me a fulsome verdict arising from a community of opinion to which I was an outsider. Hubbs's book ultimately proposes that America's queer composers comprise a "self-composing and –historicizing project," locating a queer past and inscribing a queer history (p. 13).

bune—and surprising it remains.* Thomson was writing in 1944, when the collection and study of rural American music—yet another quest for a usable past—marginalized the sorrow songs and jazz as contaminated transformations. A short list of composers appropriating these findings between 1936 and 1945 would include Thomson (*Four Saints in Three Acts, The Plow that Broke the Plains, The River, The Mother of Us All, Louisiana Story*), Copland (*Billy the Kid, Rodeo, Appalachian Spring*), Norman Dello Joio (*Prairie*), Eugene Goossens (*Cowboy Fantasy*), Lukas Foss (*The Prairie*), and Elie Siegmeister (*Prairie Legend* and *Western Suite*)—the pieces that most endure being Copland's ballets and Thomson's operas and film scores.

Abroad, Béla Bartók had famously appropriated rural songs to forge a complex modernist idiom as challenging and combustible as the faux folk strains of Copland and Thomson were friendly and bland. The tang of the Transylvanian vernacular, as preserved by Bartók, fed on performance practice: musical effusions heedlessly out of tune and out of synch, as rustic and spontaneous as the peasant performers themselves. The most obvious American equivalent may be found in the musical speech of Mark Twain or Charles Ives. But Gershwin is scarcely irrelevant: the trumpet snarls, clarinet wails, and piano licks of *Rhapsody in Blue* drive an explosive informality not to be found among the Paris-trained Americans of the Copland/Thomson generation. As for the cacophony of simultaneous spirituals in the hurricane scene of *Porgy and Bess*, and the communal response to Serena's "Doctor Jesus," it may truly be said that for American classical music, Gershwin's summer on

---

* Present-day scholarship traces the African-American spiritual both to West African music and ritual, and to the Anglo-American hymns cited by Jackson; i.e., this music is appropriative, not "essentialist"—Black or white. When Henry Krehbiel and others extolled "negro melodies" as America's folk music, they were not being naïve essentialists. Rather, they argued that, empirically, the African-American spiritual spoke to a greater number of Americans than any other native folk music. The Thomson/George Pullen Jackson view is dated today. But it would be rash to condemn it as "racist." If you are looking for allegedly anti-Semitic American composers, Carl Ruggles and Daniel Gregory Mason come to mind—neither one a modernist.

Folly Island produced more combustible results than did decades of musical research in rural white America.

∾

GEORGE GERSHWIN WAS not merely written out of the American classical music narrative by Thomson, Copland, and Bernstein; he was relegated to "pops" status by American orchestras: the *Rhapsody*, the Concerto, *An American in Paris* all lacked pedigree.* Gershwin's prominent admirers, among American classical musicians, were mainly foreign-born. Otto Klemperer, for whom Gershwin was the "important" American composer, performed his dirge-like transcription of Gershwin's Second Prelude at the Hollywood Bowl's Gershwin Memorial Concert. Arnold Schoenberg, who played tennis with Gershwin, felt compelled to contradict the "many musicians" who did not consider Gershwin "serious," named him an "innovator" and "great composer." Jascha Heifetz, who transcribed Gershwin's tunes and tried to get him to compose a vio-

---

* The performance history of the Concerto in F documents Gershwin's vexed reputation. Gershwin's own renditions attracted exceptionally large and enthusiastic audiences, but the critical response swirled with confusion over the work's pedigree. Walter Damrosch, at Carnegie Hall, gave the world premiere on a program with a symphony by Glazunov and a suite by Henri Rabaud. In St. Louis, Vladimir Golschmann (who had already conducted the concerto in Paris to resounding popular and critical acclaim) positioned it after Tchaikovsky's *Pathétique* Symphony. Fritz Reiner, in Cincinnati, presented it with Beethoven's Seventh Symphony, Strauss's *Till Eulenspiegel,* and *Rhapsody in Blue.* But during his later tenure as music director of the Chicago Symphony (1953 to 1963) Reiner conducted not a note of Gershwin—not even Robert Russell Bennett's ever-popular *Porgy and Bess* synthesis, which Reiner himself had commissioned and introduced. Not until 2000 did Daniel Barenboim become the first Chicago music director to lead the Concerto, *Rhapsody in Blue*, and *An American in Paris* on regular-season subscription concerts. The Boston Symphony first gave these works on subscription in 2005, 1997, and 2005, respectively. It seems that Gershwin most fell out of favor on mainstream American symphonic programs around midcentury. Then, in Pittsburgh in the 1980s, Lorin Maazel brought him back. More recently, Andrew Litton in Dallas and Michael Tilson Thomas in San Francisco conspicuously advocated Gershwin. Of the most prestigious American orchestras, the New York Philharmonic alone has never marginalized Gershwin. Artur Rodzinski, Dimitri Mitropoulos, Leonard Bernstein, Zubin Mehta, Kurt Masur, Maazel, and Alan Gilbert all conducted Gershwin for regular-season subscribers.

lin concerto, said when Gershwin died: "We should be ashamed that we did not appreciate this man more when he was in our midst."

In fact, antipathy to jazz within classical music after World War I resonated with American prejudice. The jazz threat was far less felt abroad. Visiting New York, Europe's leading composers would gravitate to Harlem, not Carnegie Hall. Ravel even felt impelled to lecture Americans about using their own past:

> I think you have too little realization of yourselves and that you still look too far away over the water. . . . I think you know that I greatly admire and value—more, I think than many American composers—American jazz. . . . I am waiting to see more Americans appear with the honesty and vision to realize the significance of their popular product, and the technique and imagination to base an original and creative art upon it.

Others speaking up for jazz included Bartók, Hindemith, Honegger, Milhaud, Poulenc, Roussel, Stravinsky, and Weill. But in the United States the race factor bluntly obtruded. Henry Ford's *Dearborn Independent* took note of "the organized eagerness of the Jew to make alliance with the Negro," of "monkey talk, jungle squeals, grunts and squeaks and gasps suggestive of cave love." Frank Damrosch of the Institute of Musical Art denounced the "outrage on beautiful music" perpetrated by musicians "stealing phrases from the classic composers and vulgarizing them." A Music Memory Contest in Cleveland aimed to "cultivate a distaste for jazz and other lower forms." The resulting bifurcation of American music* was more crippling to fastidious highbrows than to popular musicians. The pure pedigree they craved was a symptom of provincialism. †

---

* American musical theater also falls on the "white" side of things. The early success of "Black Broadway"—of such explosive all-Black hits as *In Dahomey* (1903) and *Shuffle Along* (1921), with their edgy minstrel-show stereotypes—could not endure.

† For the jazz threat, see my *Classical Music in America: A History of Its Rise and Fall* (2005).

In twentieth-century American music, modernism furnished a source of identity, prestige, and self-esteem. It set technical standards and charted a progressive direction. It did not preclude a conscious nationalism, even populism, among its New World adherents. But it was also a constraining factor for Americans in search of an indigenous musical identity. Copland's particular modernist aesthetic, greatly shaped by France and by Stravinsky, was thrifty. A child of immigrants, he was fired by a need to define himself as an American. A modernist, he equally needed to embrace the new. The wisdom of hindsight suggests that modernism, however necessary to Copland's "come-of-age" project, was also a sanitizing buffer against popular styles that the world today regards as a more notable twentieth-century American musical endowment. Hindsight likewise infers that the great hope for American classical music in Copland's time was not that a Copland or Roy Harris would compose a mighty symphony, but that a mighty interloper might synergistically connect Copland's world with the world of Ellington and Armstrong. Now that modernism has waned, now that American classical music has relaxed a bit, it becomes apparent that not Copland but Gershwin—mining a usable American past traceable to such *fin-de-siè-cle* interlopers as Joplin and Dvořák—embodied this lost hope.

The late Gunther Schuller—an American musician of rare catholicity whose two-volume history of jazz is a seminal study—considered the best concert appropriation of jazz to be a 1923 composition for chamber orchestra: Darius Milhaud's *La création du monde*. How was it possible that Milhaud and Ravel—not to mention Dvořák and Gershwin—could do more with "negro melodies" than Copland and his come-of-age colleagues? To be sure, in the United States African-American music had taken a turn away from the concert hall. But talent and disposition were hardly irrelevant. As assuredly as Dvořák, Ravel, and Gershwin were blithely promiscuous, Copland was not. They embraced a range of appropriation—past and present, high and low—he did not command.

Barnacled with history, the past can be encumbering: a trap. It can also be empowering. Purging the past can be a catalyst or therapy. It can also be devitalizing. Is it merely serendipitous that the music that first inspired Gershwin to compose was Dvořák's G-flat Humoresque, wafting down to the Brooklyn pavement from Maxie Rosenzweig's flat? Virgil Thomson's *The River*, its imagery of Mississippi wharves notwithstanding, is brisk and icy cold; is Mark Twain's capacious Mississippi therefore a watery cliché? Is the sweet nostalgia of Dvořák's Largo, or of Porgy's "Plenty o' Nuttin,'" a "hackneyed" convention? Is the "heavenly land" for which Porgy yearns a sentimental evasion? I would call it an authentic vision of redemption.

Todd Duncan, the first Porgy, cherished Gershwin's easy candor and accessibility, and (contradicting Virgil Thomson) the truthfulness of his opera. And Harry Burleigh revered the memory of Antonín Dvořák. That Dvořák was an unprejudiced European outsider to the American experience and its racial strife, a rustic Bohemian outsider to Hapsburg Vienna with its Germanic hegemony, a butcher's son, an open-eared traveler, are all factors contributing to the humility of his genius and its one-time New World impact.

Was There a Usable Musical Past?

Searching for usable forebears, Van Wyck Brooks threw a tangled lifeline to Nathaniel Hawthorne. "No other talent is of so shining a purity as Hawthorne's—scarcely one other so light, no inevitable, so refined, so much a perfectly achieved intention," writes Brooks in *America's Coming of Age*. "He models in mist as the Greeks modelled in marble; his beings take shape in the imagination with a sunlit perfection." Hawthorne's rude Puritanical New England environs, Brooks continues, forced him to inhabit a world of his own—he neither enriched society nor was enriched by it. Still, he evades the ruination of other New England talents, America's signature "highbrow" escape into cerebral fantasy: Transcendentalism. Brooks's most delicious pages accordingly skewer Ralph Waldo Emerson:

Consider Emerson's style—that strange fine ventriloquism, that attenuated voice coming from a great distance. If it is irritating, as many readers find it, if it is filled with assertions that fairly insist upon being contradicted, it is because so often Emerson . . . has so little natural sense of the relation between the abstract and the concrete. . . . A prose that violates the actual overmuch, a prose in which the poetic effect is more than a heightened version of the actual is, I think, a prose one is entitled to find irritating. . . .

. . . He never lingers in the bodily world, he is always busy to be off again; and if he takes two or three paces on the earth they only serve to warm him for a fresh aerial adventure. . . .

. . . [B]efore he was thirty-five he seems to have acquired that fixed, benignant, musing smile that implies the consciousness of having solved one's problem and which is usually accompanied by a closure of the five senses.

This assault is delectable because, rather than descending to casual sophistry, it arises from deep familiarity with its subject matter. By temperament and purpose Brooks is a heuristic polemicist; we do not expect from him a balanced account. Anyway, such is the nature of his ongoing engagement with the literary past that he returned to Emerson again and again, ultimately reaching a positive verdict. The past, for Brooks, exerts traction. In fact, the new appreciation of the Transcendentalists of which Brooks was part in the thirties contributed to the belated success of Charles Ives's *Concord* Sonata.

The active past animating Brooks, Lewis Mumford, and other investigators of pre–World War American literature, art, and architecture contrasts sharply with the dormant past overseen by Copland and Thomson. Theirs was a static purview that stranded the considerable composers I am about to extol. Had American classical music ever acquired an active past, the American Dvořák would have ignited discussion and debate beginning in the 1990s, when Michael Beckerman began publishing irrefutable evidence of the pervasive extramusical presence of *The Song of Hiawatha* in many pages of the *New World* Symphony. Here was a composition regularly performed by every American orchestra, whose genesis was demonstrably different than anyone remembered or supposed. There did not even any longer exist a widely read publication in which Beckerman's discoveries could be reported and examined. The *Musical Courier, Musical America,* and the *Etude,* once staples of the parlor, had long disappeared. The *High Fidelity* magazine of my childhood was never replaced. The conventional wisdom instilled nearly a century ago—that American classical music enjoyed no usable past—is conventional wisdom still. Finally: Is it generally just? Is Ives a single anomalous exception? Let me share a dozen musical snapshots.

Sometime in the 1850s, Louis Moreau Gottschalk composed a four-minute showpiece for piano. A rapid-fire simulation of plucking and strumming, *The Banjo* builds to a breathlessly cascading transmutation of Stephen Foster's "Camptown Races." Since its rediscovery in the 1950s, it has held a tenuous place in the American piano repertoire. I would call *The Banjo* the most irresistible keyboard étude composed by an American. Combining Foster's sassy minstrel tune with the salon pyrotechnics of Franz Liszt and Sigismond Thalberg (and Gottschalk had triumphed in French salons'), it encapsulates the seamless intermingling of "popular" and "classical," "high" and "low," predating twentieth century cultural schisms.

Gottschalk was not the only notable American original of his day. William Henry Fry was a rampaging New World eccentric who tirelessly lambasted obeisance to Old World masters. If his widely performed *Santa Claus* Symphony (1853) cannot equal in musical panache Gottschalk's "symphony" *Night in the Tropics,* its present-day obscurity

---

* Gottschalk's music subsequently influenced Claude Debussy via Debussy's teacher Ernest Guiraud (born in New Orleans in 1837). It was also known to Dvořák. Gottschalk, Debussy's "Golliwog's Cakewalk," and the third movement of Dvořák's *American* Suite are cousins. Steeped in Americana, Gottschalk (to my knowledge) exerted no comparable influence on any American composer of consequence. He was more esteemed in Paris than in the United States. Gershwin's reception would follow suit.

is unwarranted. Fry's tenacious Christmas narrative includes a baby falling asleep to the Lord's Prayer, chanted syllabically by high strings. A soprano saxophone (newly invented) sings "Rock-a-bye Baby." Santa Claus is a chortling high bassoon accompanied by sleigh bells. Though the idiom amalgamates French, Italian, and German influences, no European could so cheekily have disdained standard practice (Fry boasted he had achieved "the longest instrumental composition ever written on a single subject, with unbroken continuity"). If there is American lineage here, it begins with the Boston-born tanner William Billings, whose rugged and untutored "fuging music" broke the rules half a century before.

Dvořák's American example inspired George Chadwick to compose an eight-minute 1895 symphonic cameo he called *Jubilee*. A salty Yankee who ate in cafeterias and was known (to Charles Ives) to reek of beer, Chadwick was no Boston stuffed shirt. His métier was merriment. *Jubilee* exudes an archetypal American exuberance—the horns quote "Camptown Races"—alternating with a love song Oscar Hammerstein might have set. Its coda gorgeously forecasts the sunset clip-clop of Hollywood cowboys to come. An equally plausible point of reference is Winslow Homer's poetic boyhood romps. *Jubilee* deserves to be a staple of the American symphonic repertoire.

If Dvořák's *Carnival* Overture is an obvious influence on *Jubilee*, Arthur Farwell's early keyboard miniatures were undertaken in explicit response to "Dvořák's challenge." The Indianist movement Farwell spearheaded was mainly kitsch. But Farwell's fearlessly astringent *Navajo War Dance* No. 2 (1904) and *Pawnee Horses* (1905) may be the music closest to an American Bartók. In 1937, Farwell expanded *Pawnee Horses* as an eight-part a cappella choral work sung in Navajo: an American showpiece without precursors or progeny. (I will have more to say about Farwell, and certain obstacles impeding his recognition, in Chapter 6.)

Sometime in the 1960s, as the post–World War I rigidities of pedigreed classical music began to soften, it was discovered that Scott Joplin, the King of Ragtime, had not mainly composed for bars, brothels, and Charlie Chaplin movies. Rather, his concert rags were a distinctive compositional achievement, susceptible to harmonic subtleties and to exquisite shades of feeling not excluding sublimated dance passages of Schubertian innocence. Joplin also composed theater works, a piano concerto, and a symphony—music mainly lost as a function of bias and neglect. But his magnum opus, the 1911 opera *Treemonisha*, survived (if barely). Revived in the 1970s, it proved an enchanting period piece. Proper discovery of Joplin's stature, and of his place in a usable musical past, remain a work in progress.

The most original *fin-de-siècle* American compositional talent, after Ives, was Charles Tomlinson Griffes, who died young in 1920. Griffes's hallucinatory Piano Sonata (1918) marries Scriabin and Orientalism to a New World ferocity.

As for Dvořák, we take for granted the familiarity of his G-flat Humoresque without pausing to marvel that it long ago acquired the vernacular pedigree of a veritable American folk song. Any pianist who bothers to assay this piece as Dvořák wrote it, or the obscure "American" Humoresque in F, will discover on every page the imprint of a master composer, including piquant turns of phrase and harmony new to the Dvořák style. The concurrent *American* Suite (which exists both in keyboard and symphonic versions) surpasses in variety and originality such better-known specimens of the Bohemian Dvořák as the String Serenade and *Czech* Suite. If the *New World* Symphony intermingles Longfellow with echoes of Beethoven and Wagner, the *American* Suite is a deck of New World postcards. The finale begins with an Indian dance punctuated—like the *New World* Scherzo—by ankle bracelets (a triangle) and tom-toms (timpani). When this A minor dance modulates to A major, it becomes a minstrel song. The slow movement portrays the desolate Iowa prairie. There is also a scherzo that features in sequence a jaunty minstrel dance, an aching plantation song, and an elegiac "Indian" refrain redolent of the vanishing Noble Savage. The bleak, whispered reprise of this third motif over a drumming accompaniment, and the ensuing shattered reprise of the sorrow song, comprise a passage as indelible as any in the *New World* Symphony. The whole is framed by big skies and wide horizons.

You can hear something like Stephen Foster, Scott Joplin, and Jerome Kern's *Show Boat*. You can glean the lyric sweep of Mark Twain's Mississippi River animated with waterfront detail. The painters most exquisitely evoked include both landscapists like George Inness and the genre artists Eastman Johnson, Asher Durand, and George Caleb Bingham.

Can such charmed mementos of a useless past be sold today? I can testify to the following brief encounters. When in 2003 I was invited to curate a three-week "American Roots" festival for the New Jersey Symphony, I had occasion to introduce David Alan Miller to Gottschalk's *Night in the Tropics*. Though Miller is a conductor who has long specialized in American repertoire, the work was new to him. His performances made a stronger case for the languid sublimity of Gottschalk's Caribbean sunset, and for the Cuban exuberance of the ensuing fiesta, than any extant recording. He took *Night in the Tropics* back to his Albany Symphony and made it a house specialty.

At the same New Jersey festival, I had occasion to introduce Gerhardt Zimmermann to the *American* Suite. Zimmermann is a distinguished Dvořák interpreter, but had not realized the piece existed. He adopted it with alacrity.

In 2004, I oversaw a Dvořák festival at the University of Texas at Austin. I invited James Morrow, who conducts the superb UT Chamber Singers, to perform *Pawnee Horses*. Farwell's Indianist choruses were a surprise to this experienced American choral conductor. Morrow subsequently led the first recording. He is itching to record some more Farwell.

Gunther Schuller, who guest-conducted at the same Texas festival, commanded a singularly compendious purview of American repertoire. Though he ran the New England Conservatory and the Tanglewood Music Center, Schuller never acquired the orchestral music directorship he sought and deserved. His exceptional performance of *Jubilee* in Austin reflected long familiarity with Chadwick. Most Chadwick conductors, however, are not American. The Estonian Neeme Järvi and the Uruguayan José Serebrier have both copiously sampled Chadwick's orchestral output on CD. When Mstislav Rostropovich was music director of the National Symphony, he presented Chadwick's Second Symphony. Jarvi, Serebrier, and Rostropovich all came to this libeled American without prejudice. What they doubtless discovered was not "straight European stuff" from a "kindergarten period." Chadwick sounds like Chadwick.

I once encountered Garrick Ohlsson in Central Park. My head that day was full of Charles Griffes. Garrick is an inquisitive pianist. He wound up recording an hour of Griffes, including the Sonata, and widely performing it as well.

Another pianist of my acquaintance, Steven Mayer, long ago antagonized his conservatory teachers by acquiring the spectacular nightclub solos of Art Tatum (transcribed from recordings after Tatum's death). From there, Mayer moved on to James P. Johnson, Fats Waller, and Jelly Roll Morton. It was I who introduced him to the American Dvořák. The result was a program, "The Black Virtuoso Tradition," that we have jointly presented countless times. It argues for a formidable American concert piano repertoire long invisible because it transgresses the high/low divide; the other pertinent composers—Black and white, mutually inspired by the Black motherlode—include Louis Moreau Gottschalk and Scott Joplin, Nathaniel Dett and George Gershwin, Leonard Bernstein ("The Masque" from his *Age of Anxiety*) and William Bolcom.

For a decade I presided over "Dvořák and America" festivals supported by the National Endowment of the Humanities as exercises in cultural history. I accompanied the *New World* Symphony with a visual presentation extrapolating the *Hiawatha* imagery of the Largo and Scherzo.* To dramatize Dvořák's American accent, I sampled the First Symphony of John Knowles Paine (1875)—extolled by Chadwick as proof America "could have a great musician, and that he could get a hearing." Paine is an effective foil—he sounds like Schumann—but as I quickly

---

* To view the *New World* Symphony "visual presentation" that I cocreated with Peter Bogdanoff: https://vimeo.com/13524207. Accompanying live symphonic music with content projected on a screen is usually a bad idea. The goal here was to restore the cultural vocabulary of the symphony's first listeners.

discovered, he happens to make a stellar impression in live performance. At the Buffalo Philharmonic's Dvořák festival, JoAnn Falletta was sufficiently astonished that she wound up recording Paine's First with distinction. Schuller was always of the opinion that, had he been European, Paine would today be far better known; certainly he evinces the breadth of stride of a true symphonist.

Will any of these achievements ever attain the popularity and esteem they warrant? The two most recent recordings of the *American* Suite as of this writing, both outstanding, were made in Lucerne and Budapest. When in 2003 I invited the New Jersey Symphony musicians to spend a rehearsal break discussing the "new" American works they were performing, there were two takers.

If anything, interest in America's classical-music past is dissipating. Historians of American classical music mainly shun the pre-1920 decades they do not know. Dvořák—and Krehbiel and Henderson and Thurber—assumed that American orchestras and opera companies would eventually acquire a native canon. It never occurred to them that in the twenty-first century the repertoire of American orchestras and opera companies would remain overwhelmingly European. The result is a mutant musical high culture based in a "culture of performance"— American classical music is defined by orchestras, conductors, pianists, and violinists, not composers. This failure to use the past, if ever potentially reversible, today seems chronic.

Using Whitman and Melville

The landmark volume in sealing a usable American literary past was F. O. Matthiessen's 700-page *American Renaissance: Art and Expression in the Age of Emerson and Whitman* (1941). Born in the author's realization "of how great a number of our past masterpieces were produced in one extraordinarily concentrated moment of expression," *American Renaissance* identified five writers—Emerson, Thoreau, Hawthorne, Whitman, and Melville—and a half-decade—1850 to 1855—

comprising "our first great age." Matthiessen provided the antebellum lodestar toward which Brooks was now trending. Compared to Mumford, he amassed his five authors not as a club to beat the Gilded Age, but as an anchor to secure the future. He insisted that they were worthy of the same exhaustive consideration as their counterparts abroad. Citing George Santayana's claim that "the American mind does not oppose tradition, it forgets it," and also André Malraux's exhortation that "a heritage is not transmitted, it must be conquered," he consciously undertook to "extend the horizon of our cultural past."

The big picture that now emerged retained the Great War as a fault line. There was still a new beginning in the twenties. But forebears were permanently in place. Ernest Hemingway looked back to Mark Twain as a model of understatement, irony, and linguistic deflation. William Faulkner called *Moby-Dick* the one novel he wished he had written and named Twain "all our grandfather," the "father of American literature." In fact, Faulkner's authenticity of dialect and folk humor, the timeless sorrows and racial complexity of his tales, the lyric flux and musical structure of his prose all draw upon the legacy of the sorrow songs; no American composer so combines the cosmopolitan modernist and vernacular regionalist.

Of the two most recent writers of Matthiessen's "first great age," Walt Whitman was copiously dedicated to a range of personal experience. His language, however incongruously polystylistic, possessed (he said) "bases broad and low, close to the ground." His flights of intuition, however inchoate, embraced a "blending for all, the unlearned, the common, and the poor." But it was Herman Melville, especially, who was lionized by Matthiessen and others as a factor protean and capacious enough to power a lineage. Beyond Whitman, he processed an immense personal odyssey, populated by men of every race and stripe. Reliant on capricious wind and current, the sailor's vocation demanded formidable skill, trust, courage, patience, self-reliance. It invited a feast of metaphor. It sampled foreign shores and customs. In *Moby-Dick*, Ishmael's realization that Queequeg is "a human being just as I am" foretells Huck's epiphany that an escaped slave is his equal. Melville acknowledged "democratic dignity," a "democratic God," the "kingly commons." His heroes may be of any rank or station. He documented their solitary courage and travail, and the blackness to which they could succumb. He was a psychologist, a seer, a metaphysician. He could even be read as an experimental novelist, a protomodernist.

The same year as *American Renaissance*, Aaron Copland's *Our New Music* appeared with "Composers in America" taking up fully half its pages—and fundamentally commencing with Roy Harris and others of Copland's generation. Many extenuating factors could be adduced for Copland's failure here to reference a usable American past. American music got a later start than American literature. Copland was a composer first, not a critic or historian. The compositions of Americans before World War I were often hard to locate; absent performances, they had to be read in score. But it is simply stated that the world of interwar American music included no Brooks, no Mumford, no Matthiessen. Musical scholarship as we know it today did not even exist in the United States. In the press, the closest thing to a consequential historian of American music was Paul Rosenfeld, the apostle of modernism. But as Rosenfeld did not read music, the past was necessarily closed to him.

Had there been someone with the will and the time—not to mention a versatile aesthetic posture more likely to be found in a historian than in a composer—a modicum of research would have readily disclosed that Boston's *fin-de-siècle* composers did not all sound alike; that in New York Dvořák had been part of a formidable New World quest including plantation song and Indian chant, Longfellow and Catlin, Joplin and Farwell; that Charles Ives—could there possibly have been a more useful composer?—had connected to a cornucopia of Americana, including the very writers that Matthiessen so powerfully regathered: not merely to the Transcendentalists he acknowledged as precursors, but to Melville and Whitman as well.

A larger American trope here in play is the self-made imperfect genius. Emerson, bypassing logic and coherence, belongs to this honored species.

So does Whitman—a New World vagabond for whom Civil War service, not British or Parisian salons, afforded a necessary rite of passage. Emerson's "The American Scholar" famously preached: "Free should the scholar be—free and brave. . . . We have listened too long to the courtly muses of Europe. The spirit of the American freeman is already suspected to be timid, imitative, tame." No less than Emerson, Whitman called for an indigenous egalitarian American art, unbeholden to European sages. Anticipating Mark Twain's impassioned approbation of the Fisk Jubilee Singers, he adored the Hutchinson Family Singers for their winning artlessness—"clearness, simplicity, no twistified or foggy sentences." The Hutchinsons sang about ordinary lives: "they are democrats." Whitman's musical enthusiasms also included Stephen Foster (no less than Dvořák, he cherished "Old Folks at Home") and, ultimately, a New York Italian opera craze that markedly excited "the common crowd as well as the connoisseurs." Espousing an idiom based in the quotidian and the vernacular, he scribbled: "American opera—put three banjos, (or more?) in the orchestra—and let them accompany (at times exclusively,) the songs of the baritone or tenor." He called America a "teeming nation of nations." He cherished the working-class culture of immigrant Irishmen.

Melville's formative "education" included plying the South Seas; the variegated enormity of *Moby-Dick,* its reckless range of style and content, is mortared with the "mud and scum" of Emerson's "Music."* Melville himself said of it: "Small erections may be finished by their first architects; grand ones, true ones, ever leave the copestone to posterity. God keep me from ever completing anything." He also testified: "In history, the great moment is when the savage is just ceasing to be a savage . . . that moment of transition,—the foam hangs but a moment on the wave." In *Billy Budd* he restated: "Truth uncompromisingly told will always have its ragged edges." In his copy of Joshua Reynolds's *Discourses,* Melville marked the sentence: "If we examine with a critical view the manner of those painters whom we consider as patterns, we

---

* See page 70.

shall find that their great fame does not proceed from their works being more highly finished than those of other artists." Matthiessen, in *American Renaissance*, called Melville "unchecked by formal education." He also called *Moby-Dick* "more notable for abundance than control or lucidity." Had Melville better polished his art, he would have more lost than gained.

And so to Ives, who disdained formal tutelage beyond his studies with Parker at Yale; who considered his bandmaster father his truest teacher; who cautioned against the dangers of a "superimposed idiomatic [musical] education" that may not fit a composer's "constitution." The experimental Everyman of *Leaves of Grass*, the ecstatic highs and quotidian lows of *Moby-Dick*—its catalogues, its stream-of-consciousness surges, its susceptibility to both Victorian and modernist readings—all quite obviously correlate with Ives. The "common denominator" Matthiessen extrapolated from his American Renaissance masters—"devotion to the possibility of democracy"—could hardly be more Ivesian. But Matthiessen, two years after John Kirkpatrick's historic *Concord* Sonata performances, remained apparently innocent of Ives. As for Whitman and music—an unavoidable topic—Matthiessen made no mention of Frederick Delius's peerless 1909 setting of *Sea Drift*.* Excepting three excursions into visual art via W. S. Mount, Jean-François Millet, and Thomas Eakins, his was a siloed treatment, a critical purview as narrowly literary as James Gibbons Huneker's had been catholic mere decades before. Notwithstanding Whitman's own immersion in opera and song, notwithstanding Melville's affinities with Ives, Matthiessen secured a usable literary past that left American music as stranded as ever. One well may marvel at this missed opportunity, for which American classical music—its sluggish response to the Ives awakening; its institutional failure to engage with contemporary culture—was mainly to blame.

---

* Ives's song "Whitman" derives its text from *Leaves of Grass*. He planned an orchestral overture, *Whitman*, as one of a projected series of "Men of Literature Overtures."

Confluence

The most memorable sentences in Copland's *Our New Music* express isolation:

> Very often I get the impression that audiences seem to think that the endless repetition of a small body of entrenched masterworks is all that is required for a ripe musical culture. . . . Needless to say, I have no quarrel with masterpieces. I think I revere and enjoy them as well as the next fellow. But when they are used, unwittingly perhaps, to stifle contemporary effort in our own country, then I am almost tempted to take the most extreme view and say that we should be better off without them!

Copland was of course referencing the culture of performance. In 1941, the Toscanini cult was at its height: the iconic American classical musician was an Italian recycling the European warhorses. No previous classical music culture had anointed a noncomposer its figurehead; no previous conductor of comparable stature had been so divorced from the music of his time and place. And this Eurocentric mutation, boasting the "world's greatest" orchestras and performers, was a source of effusive pride and excitement. Vibrant it certainly was; but built on sand. The mutation had many causes. A "new audience," much pondered by Copland, was ready to acquire the classics. Commercial forces—led by David Sarnoff's RCA and NBC—were eager to teach what could be most readily packaged and marketed; what Virgil Thomson dubbed the "music appreciation racket" risked an infantilization of high culture unprecedented in strategic scope and effectiveness. The failure to discern a usable past—a failure shared by composers, performers, and institutions of performance alike—necessarily completes this picture. The fault line in literature marked by the Great War was in American classical music a chasm with no equivalent abroad. Today a lineage of fiction and poetry orients American literature, and

American painters and sculptors can trace their native parentage to the eighteenth century. Classical music in America, by comparison, comprises a series of stuttering beginnings.

When Copland wrote *Our New Music*, Roy Harris was the most popular, most performed American symphonic composer. Twenty-seven years later, Copland confessed: "My prognostication that [Harris] was writing music on which 'future American composers will build' now strikes me as downright naive. . . . As it has turned out, the young men [of today] show no signs of wishing to build on the work of the older American-born composers, the generation of the '20s and '30s." Who are the American concert composers who today loom largest abroad as prestigious or influential participants in the Western narrative? Probably Charles Ives and George Gershwin. Where are the shoulders in this picture?

Twenty-first-century American orchestras are sometimes likened to museums by those attempting to gauge and understand their marginality. But America's museums—no less than our novelists and poets—use the past. They connect to American and contemporary visual art. Their galleries narrate an American lineage beginning in the eighteenth century.

If using the past we are to re-ask Leonard Bernstein's question—"What defines American classical music?"—the best, most capacious answer might be: miscegenation—a confluence of New World and Old World influences incorporating American vernacular voices. That is a definition that reaches back and uses Dvořák and Ives and "negro melodies." In retrospect, the bifurcation of American music after World War I, signified by the jazz threat, was partly an unhappy bifurcation between Black and white; Roy Harris, born in Oklahoma, was actually called "the white hope" by adherents of a wholesome "Anglo-Saxon" America.* It

---

* Cf. John Tasker Howard's *Our Contemporary Composers* (1941): "When [Roy Harris] first appeared on the scene, . . . he seemed the answer to all our prayers. Here was a genuine American, . . . untouched by the artificial refinements of Europe or even the stultifying commercialism of cosmopolitan New York. . . . Small wonder that we called him the white

was not only they, however, who once widely extolled the Harris Third as a Great Symphony—a judgment that today should give us pause. The American experience is so impregnated with Black strains and stains that our classical-music culture after World War I must be considered not only inordinately Eurocentric, but also racially insensitive. It elevated a circumscribed modernist "America" of clean lines, fastidious detail, and ("elevating" jazz) complex syncopation. It was supposed to grow roots. But Gershwin sprang from another soil—and so, after their fashion, would such postmodernist composers as Lou Harrison, Steve Reich, Philip Glass, and John Adams.

Finally: another thought experiment. Dvořák returned to Prague in 1895, shortchanging the full potential of his American legacy. But what if Charles Ives had been powerfully espoused in the following decades? It is believed that during his New York Philharmonic tenure Gustav Mahler encountered Ives's Third Symphony in score, took an interest, and might have premiered it with the Philharmonic had he not died in 1911 at the age of fifty. Imagine that the score Mahler found was instead Ives's Second and that he led the premiere performances at Carnegie Hall sometime before the Great War. The discovery of Ives's songs and the *Concord* Sonata would have been accelerated. American classical music would have acquired a past linking to the vernacular, and to writers and painters of consequence. No interwar commentator—not even Virgil Thomson—could have claimed that all pre-1910 American composers were faceless European clones. The spasmodic odyssey of American classical music could have acquired a pertinent ongoing shape.

---

hope of American music." Harris's idiom was notably untouched by jazz. For "cosmopolitan New York" read "Blacks and Jews." Another writer for whom the Anglo-Saxon criterion overmattered was the ultraconservative Columbia University composer Daniel Gregory Mason, who decried the influence of immigrant Jewish musicians. The immigrant Jewish composer Lazare Saminsky, incredibly, was himself a prime practitioner of anti-Semitic stereotyping. See MacDonald Smith Moore, *Yankee Blues: Musical Culture and American Identity* (1985).

The Souls of Black Folk

No one could dispute the accuracy of Dvořák's prophecy that American music would be Black. But what accounts for the dominance of Black American music? And why was this foreknowledge less accessible to Aaron Copland three decades later?

Copland's insufficient reckoning with jazz was equally an insufficient reckoning with the sorrow songs that came first. This failure to make adequate use of the Black American past was not grounded in selfishness. Rather, his was a failure conditioned by aesthetic stricture and constraint: the formative Stravinsky influence of the twenties. One need only compare his jazz appropriations with those of Gershwin, or his absorption of church songs and rags with that of Ives, or his Latin swagger with that of Silvestre Revueltas to recognize that Copland the populist composer, however sincere, was more visitant than native.

Dvořák and Gershwin were readily capable of composing tunes as enduring—as archetypal—as "Swing Low" or "Old Folks at Home," and of wielding them without qualm or qualification. Ives's borrowings from the vernacular took many forms; he was as likely to seamlessly assimilate an allusion to "Old Black Joe" as the second subject of a sonata form as to slap "Columbia, the Gem of the Ocean" atop a roistering conglomerate of vernacular and "cultivated" strains, or interrupt a reverie with boisterous ragtime snatches. As we have seen, Copland—no tunesmith—objected to using jazz without "intensifying" it so as to "make it more exciting than ordinary jazz"; in his *El salón México*, the borrowed folk tunes are subject to compositional ingenuities, fractured or compressed. Bernstein considered Gershwin's borrowings "too literal"; he praised a Roger Sessions chorale prelude for abstracting jazz syncopations and applying them to an "advanced style" and "independent idiom."

Recall Ralph Ellison on the "supposedly unresolvable conflict between elitist and populist values"—the modernist preference for "assimilation" over mere "inclusion"; Ellison rejected "the assumption that the vernacular process destroys the so-called elitist styles, when in truth past standards of excellence remain to be used again and again."* He might have added that to ingeniously "assimilate" the vernacular risks denaturing its essence and canceling its timelessness.

Necessity powers the strongest art. In Western classical music, Bach's *St. Matthew* Passion, Beethoven's Fifth, Wagner's *Tristan*, Shostakovich's Eighth Symphony all convey peremptory impressions and experiences that we sense, as listeners, could not possibly have been diluted or suppressed. To my ears, the pathos of Dvořák's *New World* Symphony, and of Harry Burleigh's version of "Steal Away," is a necessary pathos, an irrepressible empathic surrender to "negro melodies" heard in something like vernacular form.

Whence the "wild notes" heard by Frederick Douglass near the Great House Farm? The "faith in the ultimate justice of things" discerned by W. E. B. Du Bois in the sorrow songs? The pulsating strains of America's Black music passed through a veritably biblical crucible.

ON MARCH 7, 1991, the *New York Times* ran an editorial titled "Dvořák Doesn't Live Here Anymore":

> Two years ago, Beth Israel Hospital in Manhattan bought a small row house on East 17th Street. It hoped to demolish the house and replace it with an AIDS hospice. If everything had gone according to plan, the hospice could by now have been caring for patients. But community residents objected. They and others asked the Landmarks Commission to save the house because Antonín Dvořák, the famous composer, lived in it for 3 of his 63 years.
>
> Last week, the commission did just that; it declared the building a landmark, thwarting Beth Israel's plans.
>
> The commission claims the Dvořák House is a cultural and historic site worth saving, but it's hard to see why. Dvořák did live at

---

* See page 72.

327 East 17th Street from 1892 to 1895, and wrote the "New World" Symphony there. But it's not as if people could visit the house and get a sense of how the composer lived. It's been changed radically inside and out.

The original stoop is gone. What was once the front door is now a kitchen window. A spiral staircase cuts the parlor floor in half and rooms have been partitioned and repartitioned.

The commission made the building a landmark not for its physical attributes but as a kind of historical memory bank. That raises the prospect of a city dotted with shrines because a celebrity passed through. New York City, which has always attracted the notable, cannot turn every site of sentimental interest into a landmark, protected from demolition and even most exterior changes. . . .

The Landmarks Commission weakens its own authority when it makes frivolous decisions. . . .

The campaign to save Dvořák's Manhattan residence was supported by Miloš Forman, Josef Suk, Rudolf Firkušný, Rafael Kubelík, Václav Havel, and the Archbishop of Prague. As Czechs, they well understood that Dvořák's three years in the United States were among the most fabled in the history of Western music.

The Dvořák house was demolished that August.

This story is both remarkable and unsurprising.

Chapter Six

Classical Music
Black and "Red"

Rediscovering William Levi Dawson—Rediscovering Florence Price—Rediscovering Nathaniel Dett—America's Forbidden Composer

Rediscovering William Levi Dawson

In 1926, Langston Hughes wrote "The Negro Artist and the Racial Mountain," a seminal Harlem Renaissance essay (which I earlier quoted, with reference to the concert spiritual). The mountain "standing in the way of any true Negro art in America," he declared, was an "urge toward whiteness," a "desire to pour racial individuality into the mold of American standardization, and to be as little Negro and as much American as possible." Hughes cited, as an antidote, "the eternal tom-tom beating in the Negro soul": jazz and the blues.

Truly, America's protean Black musical motherlode has found expression in popular genres of its own invention—not string quartets, symphonies, and operas. Nevertheless, a concurrent Black classical music was pursued—a buried history glimpsed earlier in this account and today being exhumed. The notable interwar Black symphonists comprise a short list of three: William Grant Still, Florence Price, and William Levi Dawson. Their failure to excite attention was partly a consequence of institutional bias: African Americans did not play in American orchestras, or conduct them, or perform concertos with them. And there was also a pertinent aesthetic bias: the reigning modernist idiom was streamlined and clean, inhospitable to vernacular grit.

However little performed, Still has long been acknowledged as "the dean" of the Black composers of his generation. But the buried treasure is Dawson's *Negro Folk Symphony*. As the music historian Gwynne Kuhner Brown pointed out eight years ago, the "tumultuous approbation the 'Negro Folk Symphony' received from critics and audiences alike set it apart—not only from contemporaneous works by African Americans, but also from most new classical music of the period." This was the result of a galvanizing 1934 premiere by Leopold Stokowski and his incomparable Philadelphia Orchestra. Speaking from the stage of the Philadelphia Academy of Music, Stokowski called Dawson's symphony "a wonderful development" in American music. He also broadcast the *Negro Folk Symphony* nationally and took it to Carnegie Hall. One reviewer of the Carnegie performance wrote that it "took the house by storm."

> The custom of no applause during a symphony gave way after the second movement to a spontaneous outburst that brought the orchestra to its feet, and at the end the enthusiasm was so great that Mr. Dawson was called to the stage repeatedly to bow his acknowledgements.
>
> It is easy enough to account for this commotion. The Negro themes chosen by the composer are striking in themselves and are employed with skill; the music is vivid with imagination, warmth, drama; and then there is the sumptuous orchestral dress.

Leonard Liebling of the *New York American*—a critic of consequence—went the distance and heralded "the most distinctive and promising American symphonic proclamation which has so far been achieved." The symphony's ardent admirers included W. E. B. Du Bois's future wife, the composer Shirley Graham, who wrote to Dawson of her "joy and pride." Harry Burleigh attended the Carnegie Hall performance and reportedly responded with excitement. Alain Locke, having previously called Dvořák's *New World* Symphony "a large, unheeded musical sign-post pointing the correct way to Parnassus," declared that Dawson's symphony had taken "the same path, only much further down the road to native and indigenous musical expression"; it was in fact "unimpeach-ably Negro." Dawson, too, saw Dvořák as a signpost and his own sym-phony as music "only a Negro could have written."

After that, the *Negro Folk Symphony* plunged into obscurity. Sto-kowski returned to the work in 1963, recording it with his American Symphony Orchestra—a spectacular performance hiding in plain site on YouTube. If you want to hear what all the excitement was about, sam-ple the ending of "Hope in the Night"—the central slow movement. The movement begins with a dolorous English horn tune not cradled by strings, as in Dvořák's Largo, but set atop a parched pizzicato accompa-niment: "a melody," Dawson writes in a program note, "that describes the characteristics, hopes, and longings of a Folk held in darkness." A weary journey into the light ensues. Its eventual climax is punctuated by a clamor of chimes: chains of servitude. Finally, three gong strokes that prefaced the movement—"the Trinity," says Dawson, "who guides forever the destiny of man"—are amplified by a seismic throb of chimes and timpani. This culminating threefold groundswell is the original inspiration that shocked audiences into a state of high arousal eight decades ago.

Elsewhere, Dawson quotes spirituals and deploys a heraldic horn call symbolically linking Africa and America. In terms of structure, this remarkable first symphony transcends prefabrication. Its light-ning physicality of gesture exudes spontaneity, even improvisation. If the symphony's governing mold is European and (as Langston Hughes put it) "standardized," Dawson retains proximity to the vernacular: he seizes the humor, pathos, and tragedy of the sorrow songs with an orac-ular vehemence. The best-known roughly contemporaneous American symphony—Copland's Third—is a leaner work favoring a modernist decorum. Dawson's symphony, in comparison, exudes a vernacular energy driven by an exigent cause. Wilfrid Mellers, in his indispensable *Music in a New Found Land* (1964), gamely defines "the essence of jazz": "it began as a freeing of the libido: was negatively a protest against persecution, positively a rediscovery of the earth-rooted vigour that urban man had lost. It was also a refinding of the forgotten relationship between flesh and spirit, in that the best jazz, through its physical excitement, led to a condition of ecstasy comparable with some aspects of religious or mystical experience." Dawson's starting point is more religious than secular; his symphony is not jazz-indebted, not "libidinal." That said, to my ears it exudes something like Mellers's jazz "essence"—and also fulfills Dvořák's prophecy.

The Philadelphia Orchestra repeated the *Negro Folk Symphony* in 1935 (under another conductor), the Birmingham Civic Symphony played it half a dozen times—and, notwithstanding expressions of interest from Pierre Monteux, Otto Klemperer, Artur Rodzinski, and the BBC, that was it. Lacking a publisher, Dawson had only two conductor's scores and a single set of parts for the musicians. He entered a composition competition at Juilliard that would have funded publication, and lost to music now forgotten by Albert Elkus. Only in 1963 (following a series of revisions) did Shawnee Press publish the *Negro Folk Symphony*—hence the Stokowski recording later the same year. There have been scattered hearings since, including performances by the orchestras of Atlanta, Baltimore, Detroit, Houston, and Kansas City. A 2020 Naxos recording was noticed, not least by National Public Radio. By then, Dawson was thirty years deceased. He had over his long lifetime become a leading arranger of Black spirituals, an honored *éminence grise*. His twenty-four years on the faculty of the Tuskegee Institute were not without frustrations imposed by limited funding and opportunity; on several occasions, he nearly resigned.

The obscurity of Dawson's symphony would be a mystery were it a Black artist's painting or novel. But American classical music is pastless. There is also, needless to say, a pertinent saga of cultural bigotry. During decades of neglect of Black compositions, American orchestras and opera companies were segregated. Highly trained Black vocalists, no matter how eminent, were unwelcome in white opera companies;

Black opera companies singing French and Italian opera, Black orchestras playing Beethoven and Brahms, were New World curiosities. White orchestras did not engage Black conductors or instrumental soloists. The first internationally prominent African-American symphonic conductor, Dean Dixon, left the United States in 1949 to pursue a distinguished career abroad. The first internationally prominent African-American instrumental soloist, the pianist André Watts, was introduced by Leonard Bernstein to a national television audience in 1963 (playing a Liszt concerto at the age of sixteen). Meanwhile, a seventy-one-year history of segregated musicians' unions within the American Federation of Musicians lasted until 1974. A landmark event was the engagement of Elayne Jones, a member of the New York City Opera Orchestra, as an extra percussionist by the New York Philharmonic in 1958—the first time an African American performed within that ensemble. Four years later, Sanford Allen became the first full-time Black member of the Philharmonic; he resigned fifteen years later saying he was "tired of being a symbol."

That in the 1930s Otto Klemperer was one of the few conductors to express interest in the *Negro Folk Symphony* is tantalizing. In Weimar Berlin, Klemperer had been an early champion of Kurt Weill and Igor Stravinsky—composers who fed off American popular styles. His political sympathies were on the far left; aesthetically, he was greatly influenced by Neue Sachlichkeit—the "new objectivity." In California, as music director of the Los Angeles Philharmonic (1933–39), the American composer he most admired was George Gershwin, whose Second Prelude he orchestrated in the dour style of *Dreigroschenoper*. His interest in a *Negro Folk Symphony* is therefore logical—but so would be his rejection of its Romantic afflatus. Whatever other obstacles it faced, the Black classical music of such post-Dvořák composers as Dawson and Florence Price—its vernacular grit and Romantic roots-in-the-soil mentality—was aesthetically out of step in the interwar United States.

William Dawson had hoped to write a series of symphonies. He had hoped to conduct orchestras (and his recordings document a formidable gift). Notwithstanding Langston Hughes's famous admonition, Dawson's symphony does not "pour racial individuality into the mold of American standardization." It is not "as little Negro and as much American as possible." The vital question becomes: What if its call had been heard?

Rediscovering Florence Price

Between 1931 and 1934, Dawson's was one of three symphonies by Black composers that were prominently premiered. The others were William Grant Still's *Afro-American*, with the Rochester Philharmonic under Howard Hanson in 1931, and Florence Price's Symphony in E minor by the Chicago Symphony under Frederick Stock in 1933. Of the three premieres, the Dawson was the most prominent, the most prestigious, and the most acclaimed. But while Dawson never wrote another symphony, Price's proved to be the first of four.

Price was born in 1887 in Arkansas. She attended the New England Conservatory directly after high school, graduating with honors in 1906. After returning south, she relocated north—part of the Great Migration—to escape Jim Crow. In Chicago, she established a strong local reputation as the first Black woman symphonist of note; her Chicago Symphony Orchestra performance came about after she won a local competition. Though she successfully arranged and adapted spirituals, Price did not, like Dawson, wind up ensconced in a Black musical milieu. Nevertheless, Chicago was effectively segregated: her local prominence was centered in the "Chicago Renaissance," which had succeeded the Harlem Renaissance as a bellwether for African-American cultural achievement. And Chicago hosted the annual convention of the National Association of Negro Musicians, which in 1940 honored Price alongside W. C. Handy for her lifelong commitment to Black music.

In Chicago, beginning in the late 1920s, Price composed prolifically in all the principal genres. Ultimately, her catalogue included four symphonies, three concertos, two string quartets, two piano quintets, and a variety of piano, choral, and organ pieces. Because she was a woman, because she was Black, her bigger pieces remained unpublished in her lifetime.

Her songs and spiritual arrangements were notably popular, admired by Harry Burleigh, sung by Marian Anderson, Roland Hayes, Abbie Mitchell, and Blanche Thebom (who was white). Two years before her death, in 1953, she was invited by Sir John Barbirolli to compose a concert overture for his Hallé Orchestra in Manchester, England. Barbirolli knew her music from his earlier tenure as conductor of the New York Philharmonic. This commission, writes Rae Linda Brown in her 2020 Price biography, signified "the personal and professional affirmation that had eluded her" in the United States. The overture, as yet unrecovered, was duly premiered in Spring 1951, but Price did not attend; Brown conjectures that her weak heart did not permit it.

The Third Symphony occupies a special place in Price's output. Though Price's style was not invariably "Black," she had in her First Symphony more firmly hugged the spirituals and dances that inspired her. "It is intended to be Negroid in character and expression," she wrote. "In it no attempt, however, has been made to project Negro music solely in the purely traditional manner. None of the themes are adaptations or derivations of folk songs. The intention was a not too deliberate attempt to picture a cross section of present-day Negro life and thought." The 1940 premiere was given by Valter Poole and the Michigan WPA Symphony Orchestra at the Detroit Institute of Arts. There was a standing ovation, with the composer repeatedly recalled. Eleanor Roosevelt was there and mentioned it in her syndicated column. A review in the *Detroit Free Press* read:

> Mrs. Price . . . spoke in the musical idiom of her own people, and spoke with authority. There was inherent . . . all the emotional warmth of the American Negro, so that the evening became one of profound melodic satisfaction. . . .
>
> Beautiful and emotionally satisfying the whole work was, and there were moments in which true greatness seemed within the grasp of the writer. . . . Certainly Mrs. Price has achieved what few women of any race are capable of doing when she made her invasion of the symphonic field.

But no less than William Dawson's *Negro Folk Symphony*, Florence Price's Third gathered dust despite the composer's persistent attempts to interest conductors in reviving it. She especially targeted Serge Koussevitzky, who with his Boston Symphony campaigned for contemporary Americans. Koussevitzky acknowledged looking at the score, but no performances resulted. However the novelty of a Black woman composer may have impressed him, his attention was mainly directed to Aaron Copland and kindred modernists. Price's symphony was more traditional in style, more intimately engaged by the vernacular—more Dvořákian. At the same time, within her oeuvre it represented a departure toward a bolder play of chromatic harmony and orchestral color—and this richness of palette is varied throughout the four movements. Concomitantly, the symphony consciously broaches a kaleidoscopic variety of mood. The outer movements build toward cumulative grandeur. The scherzo, a juba dance, is intermittently bluesy and jazzy; a xylophone solo over pizzicato strings evokes Gershwin's world.

Anyone with an ear for George Chadwick's sunshine mode will occasionally hear in Price's Third Symphony the voice of her distinguished New England Conservatory composition teacher; within a busy schedule—as the school's director, he was intent on professionalizing the curriculum without merely cloning German models—he had made time to instruct her privately on scholarship. The first movement's second theme, a trombone solo with harp accompaniment, remembers Chadwick's way of casually embedding a breezy song in a sonata-form structure. The significance of Chadwick as a mentor is twofold: he was America's most prominent late-nineteenth-century symphonist, and he was part of the Dvořák lineage. This is the same composer whose music we have heard mischaracterized by Virgil Thomson as "adolescent," "a pale copy of European models," by Leonard Bernstein as "kindergarten," "straight European stuff"—and whose witty symphonic scherzos are nose-thumbing responses to Old World decorum. Chadwick's enthralling (and absurdly neglected) Fourth String Quartet (1896), with its holiday minstrelsy and hymnody, and rustic pentatonics, unquestionably replies to Dvořák's *American* Quartet, premiered in Boston three years previous by the Kneisel Quartet and subsequently dubbed the "Nigger Quartet." That this is the work that provoked Philip Hale to regret the "baleful" influence of the "negrophile" Dvořák on Boston's most eminent composer says it all: Hale heard Chadwick's quartet as Black.

Price's Symphony No. 3 could not be mistaken for Chadwick. But the stylistic template is the same, with earthy Black roots substituting for Chadwick's Yankee salt. In her First Symphony, she had adopted the E minor key of Dvořák's *New World*: an homage. But Price's Third is a truer and riper successor to Dvořák and Chadwick both. Like Dawson, it answers Dvořák's prophecy—and travels a road not taken. *

Rediscovering Nathaniel Dett

At least one other exceptional African-American orchestral composition—not a symphony—was notably premiered in the thirties and forties. This is Nathaniel Dett's *The Ordering of Moses* for soloists, chorus, and orchestra, first performed in 1937 by the Cincinnati Symphony conducted by Eugene Goossens at Cincinnati's May Festival. A live national broadcast was prematurely terminated with an announcement: "We are sorry indeed, ladies and gentlemen, but due to previous commitments, we are unable to remain for the closing moments of this excellent performance."

The reason Dett was born in Canada, in 1882, is that his maternal grandmother elected to leave Washington, D.C., in the 1850s. His mother ran a rooming house, his father was a railroad porter, his uncle a law school graduate. The family moved across the border to New York State in 1893. He graduated from the Oberlin Conservatory in 1908 and embarked on a distinguished career as a teacher and choral director

* Chadwick was also an important composition teacher for William Grant Still, who in 1969 said: "It was [Chadwick] more than anyone else who inspired me to write American music." (Eileen Southern, "Conversation with William Grant Still," *Black Perspective on Music* 3, no. 2 [1975], p. 170.)

affiliated with Black colleges, most notably the Hampton Institute from 1913 to 1931. He toured his Hampton Choir to Carnegie Hall, to Boston's Symphony Hall, and to Europe. At Oberlin, he heard the Kneisel Quartet perform the same Dvořák *American* Quartet that had inspired George Chadwick. Of the lulling slow movement, Dett wrote: "Suddenly it seemed I heard again the frail voice of my long departed grandmother calling across the years; and in a rush of emotion which stirred my spirit to its very center, the meaning of the songs which had given her soul such peace was revealed to me."

A striking feature of Dett's odyssey was an intermittent sequence of advanced studies—at the Eastman School (where he earned a master's degree), at Nadia Boulanger's Fontainebleau school, at Columbia University, and at Harvard University, where he won the Bowdoin Prize for his four-part essay "Negro Music" as well as a composition prize for the choral "Don't Be Weary, Traveller." Dett documented his strivings in his writings. He called the spirituals "this wonderful store of folk materials, the melodies of enslaved people who poured out their longings, their griefs and their aspirations in one great, universal language." Of the singing of slave songs in rural churches: "I have felt that they become very sincerely the voice of a divine power, as wonderful as that which wakens the magnolias into their gorgeous bloom, hurls a Niagara over a thundering precipice, wakens the trill of the morning bird or paints the glories of a sunset sky." Of the uses to which such music could be put: "The Negro folk song is rich in elements which may be the inspiration of new creations, more or less invisibly related to their source even as before the song there was the wild cry and before the symphony was the choral ring."

Dett wished to create a body of work for African Americans "musically peculiarly their own and yet which would bear comparison with the nationalistic utterances of other people's work in art form." As of 1920, he identified, as obstacles, "the lack of proper musical and academic training among Negro composers" as well as "the general indifference of Americans, amounting almost to contempt for things of native origin, and a slavish admiration on the part of American composers, critics, and, to some extent, publishers, for European ideals in music and art." He added: "Only through the appreciation shown worthy Negro efforts by this great nation . . . will the Negro be able to raise his musical art up to those rare and worthy high places which have previously been occupied by the masterpieces created by the other peoples of the world."

Dett composed extensively for solo piano and for voice, including a body of choral works setting aside the transcriptions and arrangements associated with Burleigh and Dawson in favor of extended compositions original in form—"motets" or "anthems" incorporating vernacular influences. *Listen to the Lambs* (1914), today perhaps Dett's best-known composition, powerfully fulfills his intention to create "a form of song . . . which contained all the acceptable characteristics of Negro folk music and yet would compare favorably in poetic sentiment and musical expression with the best class of church music." *The Chariot Jubilee* (1919) for chorus and organ, thirteen minutes in length, incorporates "Swing Low" and other spirituals while tacitly absorbing the religious choral traditions of Handel and Mendelssohn.

Dett also wrote in 1920: "For nearly thirty years the development of Negro music was perhaps too dependent upon creations in the smaller forms. . . . Though one who makes pencil sketches on paper may achieve results every bit as perfect in their way as another who chisels similar figures from marble, there is little doubt as to which artist's name will be written higher in the hall of fame." Hence *The Ordering of Moses*, fifty-five minutes long, composed as Dett's 1932 Eastman thesis project and subsequently revised for publication in 1937. The Cincinnati premiere was followed by performances in New York City, Chicago, Washington, D.C., and elsewhere. Interest in the work waned prior to a 1956 revival, again by Cincinnati's May Festival, this time with Leontyne Price and William Warfield among the soloists. Eleven years later, William Dawson conducted *The Ordering of Moses* with the Mobile Symphony and Talladega College Choir. The 2014 revival by the Cincinnati Symphony was recorded in live performance at Carnegie Hall with James Conlon

conducting—a polished reading, but Dawson's, also recorded, is the one
that catches fire.

Dett created his own text, skillfully culled from scripture and folklore, to narrate the flight from Egypt. The musical setting is hot with
pathos and ecstasy, with the spirit of the sorrow song and of African
song and dance, all channeled via his concentrated Hampton milieu.
Of Manhattan's high-toned concerts and opera, of Hollywood's glamour and sheen, there is not a whiff. And yet evidence of Dett's musical
sophistication is omnipresent in the effortless counterpoint, the pungent
chromatic palette, the instrumental panache of the writing. The presence of spirituals that are—as he put it—"more or less invisibly related
to their source" is complemented by the invisibility of the other music
well known to him (his Hampton repertoire regularly featured Russian
liturgical numbers). The role of Moses is boldly assigned to a tenor, not
the accustomed baritone or bass—here "The Voice of God" and "The
Word." A four-note rhythm with the accented passing tone sometimes
called the "Scotch snap" (it happens to be identical to that of the lead
leitmotif in Dawson's *Negro Folk Symphony*) is pervasive, and implicitly
morphs into the four syllables of "Go Down, Moses"—another pervasive
presence. A central interlude describes the Israelites crossing the Red
Sea, then the calamity inflicted upon Pharaoh's chariots. The final rite of
triumph is shrewdly capped by a high C for a solo soprano (Miriam) in
rapturous duet with Moses.

We have heard Langston Hughes, in 1926, fearing an "urge toward
whiteness," a "desire to pour racial individuality into the mold of American standardization, and to be as little Negro and as much American as
possible." Dett wrote:

> It should be stated that controversies arising from the discussion
> as to whether or not one ought to try "to improve" the folk song . . .
> are absurd. One might as well talk of "improving" a full grown tree
> or a rose blossom. We try to preserve the tree or the rose because of
> its beauty and worth. Either one, through the skill of man, may be

made presently to disintegrate later to reappear in other creations of beauty and utility. Even so the folk song is rich in elements which may be the inspiration of new creations resembling the original as a desk resembles a tree—only in the nature of its material.

Like the folk strains of other lands, Dett believed, the Black vernacular could be powerfully embedded in concert genres—if the composer dug deeply enough into the past. In the case of *The Ordering of Moses*, the result—as with Dawson's symphony or Gershwin's opera—is an epic dimension. These "long-form" compositions, espousing uplift, notably resist modernist redefinitions of style and purpose.* They may in fact be regarded as a late manifestation of Romantic exaltation, an even-handed dialectical reconciliation of Black and white a la Du Bois. Whether other such examples will come to light as the repertoire of Black classical music is belatedly explored is impossible to say. My own impression is that in anointing William Grant Still the "dean" of African-American composers—the one invariably cited in histories, invariably anthologized by scholars for students—we have been looking in the wrong place.

In the post-Dvořák lineage, Florence Price's protégée Margaret Bonds (1913–1972) was a prolific composer commanding both originality and versatility. Her bigger pieces, requiring editorial attention, have barely begun to circulate. Her 1967 description of her style as "jazzy and bluesy and spiritual and Tchaikovsky all rolled up into one" is just—and suggests that she may ultimately become known as a polystylistic harbinger of postmodern things to come. The most prominent Black concert composer of Bonds's generation, George Walker, turned a page: in comparison to Bonds and her precursors, he was an impressive modernist who rarely treated Black sources as an overt stylistic feature.

* In *Racial Uplift and American Music, 1878–1943* (2012), Lawrence Schenbeck writes "[Black] composers like Dett avoided modernism . . . like the plague. . . . It is hardly surprising that Dett chose not to [feature] saxophones, syncopation and secularity. To have done so would have undermined his own central project, that of battling racism by eliminating the secular—and especially the erotic—in Negro music" (p. 145).

America's Forbidden Composer

We have tried four methods of approach to the Indian. First by fighting him; second by seeking to convert him; third by treating him as a scientific specimen; fourth, by offering him the hand of fellowship. By the first way we have received in turn wounds, torture, and death, and the material for a little superficial romance. Through the second method we have given him something he did not want and received nothing in return, being prevented by bigotry from receiving what he had to give us. . . . By the third process we have filled the shelves of great museums with rare and valuable objects, all carefully labeled. . . . It is wonderful work, but there is an aristocracy . . . about it all, that constitutes an almost impassible barrier between it and the American people.

Finally, in the fourth way, the only way wholly compatible with democratic ideals, we have gained that which is to bring—which brings—the American people as a whole into a sympathetic relation with the Indian. For through his . . . poetic expression, in ritual, story and song, which he is willing to communicate to one who approaches him as a fellow man, we are to recognize, once for all, his humanity and the wealth of interest and significance which it offers for the enrichment of our own lives.

Thus Arthur Farwell in 1904.

If Dawson, Price, Dett, and Bonds are already being rescued from oblivion, it seems likely that Farwell will remain America's forbidden composer. "Probably the most neglected composer in our history," opined the late composer/critic A. Walter Kramer in 1973. "At the turn of the century no one wrote music with greater seriousness of purpose or fought harder for American music. . . . He was an intellectual and spiritual giant." This assessment rings ever louder today; Farwell and his "Indianist" output have been deemed untouchable.

I first discovered Arthur Farwell via a New World Records "Indianists" LP twenty years ago. The Farwell pieces on that recording were not very good, but they were original. I was curious to know more about a composer who, inspired by Dvořák, thought Americans would one day become sufficiently enlightened to embrace Native America as an essential component of our national identity. I soon discovered, in score, Farwell compositions far more challenging both for performer and listener—forgotten music, once esteemed, and yet never recorded. Not long after my Farwell discovery, I encountered a prominent Native American ethnomusicologist who told me that she did not listen to Arthur Farwell's music as a matter of principle. This is the kind of challenge Farwell poses. Whether his time will come will depend upon political, not musical winds of change.

Charles Martin Loeffler called Arthur Farwell's *Pawnee Horses* for solo piano (1905) "the best composition yet written by an American." As Loeffler was for a time the most highly regarded American composer, a schooled aristocratic musical personality, a man who also grasped the importance of George Gershwin when others dismissed him as a gifted dilettante, his opinion means something. The piece itself, setting an Omaha song, is not even two minutes long. A downward-cascading chant is framed by galloping figurations. The pianistic layout, with multiple hand-crossings, is idiomatic and ingenious. Most memorably, Farwell deploys harmony and texture to create a fragrant aura of mystery; at the close, the gallop dissipates in the treble. Considered as a musical composition, without reference to source or inspiration, *Pawnee Horses* is indisputably top-notch. In 1937, Farwell created a second version for a cappella chorus; the closing ascent touches a pianissimo high C. Musically considered, *Pawnee Horses* is a choral tour de force.

Another early Farwell piano solo, *Navajo War Dance* No. 2, was championed by John Kirkpatrick—the same pianist who premiered Charles Ives's *Concord* Sonata. This 1904 Farwell miniature is brutally harsh, rhythmically and harmonically complex. It is also hard to play. Bartók is an obvious point of reference. But Farwell could not possibly have known pertinent Bartók keyboard music in 1904.

In the hidden world of Arthur Farwell, the two piano pieces I have just mentioned are relatively known. But his biggest Indianist composition, the *Hako* String Quartet of 1923, is certainly not. I had occasion to present it with student performers at the New England Conservatory in 1999. The late David MacAllester, an eminent authority on Native American music, was at hand to react. McAllester was stunned by the *Hako* Quartet; he emphasized that it evoked Native American ceremony without attempting "imitation." That is: the *Hako* claims no authenticity. Though its inspiration is a Great Plains ritual celebrating a symbolic union of Father and Son, though it incorporates passages evoking a processional, or an owl, or a lightning storm, it does not chart a programmatic narrative. Rather, it is a twenty-minute sonata form that documents the composer's enthralled subjective response to a gripping Native American ritual. It builds skillfully to an enraptured close, marked "with breadth and exaltation." It is Arthur Farwell's rapture that is here "authentic."

Other Farwell compositions are differently conceived. They more resemble transcriptions or adaptations of Native American song. *Pawnee Horses* attempts to evoke the complexity of Indian rhythms and tunes. But it would be glib to infer that it aspires to "authenticity."

So what was Farwell trying to do? He believed it was a democratic obligation of Americans of European descent to try to understand the indigenous Americans they had displaced and oppressed—to preserve something of their civilization; to find a path toward reconciliation. His Indianist compositions attempt to mediate between Native American ritual and the Western concert tradition. Like Bartók in Transylvania, like Stravinsky in rural Russia, he endeavored to fashion a concert idiom that would paradoxically project the integrity of unvarnished vernacular dance and song. He aspired to capture specific musical characteristics— but also something additional, something ineffable and elemental, "religious and legendary." He called it—a phrase belonging to another time and place—"race spirit."

As a young man, Farwell visited with Indians on Lake Superior. He hunted with Indian guides. He had out-of-body experiences. Later, in the

Southwest, he collaborated with the charismatic Charles Lummis, a pioneer ethnographer. For Lummis, Farwell transcribed hundreds of Indian and Hispanic melodies, using either a phonograph or local Indian singers. Even so, our present-day criterion of authenticity is a later construct, unknown in Farwell's day. If he was subject to criticism during his lifetime, it was for being naïve and irrelevant, not disrespectful or false. The music historian Beth Levy—a rare contemporary student of the Indianist movement in music—pithily summarizes that Farwell embodies a state of tension intermingling "a scientific emphasis on anthropological fact" with "a subjective identification bordering on rapture."

Other writings perpetuate misleading assumptions. John Troutman's *Indian Blues* (2009), a valuable treatment of "American Indians and the Politics of Music, 1879–1934," groups Farwell with other Indianists "dedicated to the production of Indian themes palatable to non-Indian ears . . . they seemed in the end to share much more in common with the imagery found in Tin Pan Alley numbers than with the performances as originally observed and recorded by the ethnologists." This verdict may fit Charles Wakefield Cadman, also mentioned by Troutman. But Farwell cannot credibly be dismissed in the same breath. Neither does the distinguished Native American ethnomusicologist Tara Browner, in a 1997 *American Music* article, undertake any concerted effort to assess the varied style and caliber of Farwell's Indianist output. Though she prefers him to Edward MacDowell (who lacked Farwell's passion for ethnology), Browner expresses regret that Farwell failed to "seek permission" to "incorporate" Native American music in his own. In 1905, when *Pawnee Horses* was conceived, no composer, writer, or painter adapting Native American music and ritual would have thought to do that. The only present-day Native American Farwell authority of whom I am aware is the pianist Lisa Cheryl Thomas, who admires and performs him.

Classical music lives in the concert hall and the opera house. But classical composers—many of them—crave the primal. It impels them to compose, no questions asked. Bartók in rural Transylvania, Falla in the gypsy caves of Granada, were galvanized by elemental songs and dances they proceeded to diligently research. Harry Burleigh was impelled to turn the sorrow songs once sung by his grandfather into tuxedoed concert songs. These transformations will always be genuinely controversial. Flamenco purists find *El amor brujo* denatured. Zora Neale Hurston found concert spirituals sanitized. But these are aesthetic, not moral judgments.

Some suggest applying a kind of bell curve, with respectful appropriation at one end and cultural theft at the other. But an aesthetic bell curve makes more sense to me. When appropriation makes us cringe, it becomes kitsch—dictionary-defined as "in poor taste because of excessive garishness or sentimentality." The most popular Indianist song was "From the Land of the Sky-Blue Waters," composed by Cadman in 1909. I would call that a specimen of tuneful kitsch. Though Cadman adapted an actual Native American tune, the relationship to source material is merely expedient, self-evidently casual. Cadman's song is as remote from *Pawnee Horses* as a balalaika orchestra playing "Dark Eyes" is remote from Stravinsky's *Les noces*.

Farwell explicitly declared himself an enemy of kitsch. He did not always succeed. To my ears, his *Navajo War Dance* No. 1 in its piano and choral versions is "in poor taste." Removed from the context of Farwell's better efforts, it suggests a nonchalant submission to cliché. Be that as it may, like the Black symphonists, Arthur Farwell is an essential component of the American musical odyssey. Like them, he drew inspiration from Dvořák. Like them, he spurned modernism and aspired to a capacious American idiom bristling with vernacular grit. He saw himself as a Whitmanesque apostle of an American music as yet unborn, singing a song in which "the Indian, the American, the European, the African, all, will live again in a universal expression which will be the collective voice of America's world-wide humanity." If today he is off limits, it is partly because of fear—of castigation by a neighbor. I know because I have seen it. *

* See pages 178–180.

Chapter Seven

Using History—
A Personal Quest

The Condition of Pastlessness—Culture and "Social Control"—
Trigger Warnings—Reencountering Harry Burleigh—
Reencountering John Singer Sargent—Reenncountering Arthur
Farwell—Porgy and Dvořák's Prophecy

The Condition of Pastlessness

Georg Wilhelm Friedrich Hegel's *Philosophy of History* influentially argued that world epochs succeed one another "dialectically," describing a pendulum of action and reaction. Whatever the merit of that claim, certainly the interpretation of history—historiography—is a dialectical study. We are well accustomed to perceiving a continuum of ebb and flow. When Van Wyck Brooks unfavorably characterized postbellum America as the "Gilded Age," the impetus of this reading provoked a revisionist wave of counterinterpretation. Brooks's disciple Lewis Mumford was himself instrumental in favorably revisiting the late Gilded Age as "The Brown Decades."

That history is malleable is easily understood. New times, new information, engender new perspectives. But a certain weight of retrospection is required to sustain the dialectic. In the realm of American classical music, as we have seen, a failure of retrospection stranded the past. There is no dialectical evolution in our understandings of Dvořák's America, or of musical Boston before World War I.

In classical music generally, a dead end is already observable. Dialectical periodization of the standard repertoire extrapolates Baroque, Classical, Romantic, Modern, and Postmodern epochs, each a response to its predecessor. As modernists once rejected Romantics—too sentimental and crazy, too chromatic and programmatic—postmodernists reject modernist aesthetic constraints. Concomitantly, a canon of exceptional composers materialized, beginning with Bach. The canonized Classical composers include Haydn, Mozart, and Beethoven, with Schubert falling between the cracks. The Romantic canon includes Brahms and Wagner, themselves antinomies. The modernists include Debussy, Stravinsky, Schoenberg. The postmodern present is harder to glean.

And yet the symphonic canon is not ongoing. It stops in 1953 with Shostakovich's Symphony No. 10; no subsequent composition for orchestra has entered the standard repertoire. This is a dialectic unlikely to be renewed.

What happened? Shostakovich labored in a Soviet hothouse—and it is well-known that exigent conditions can paradoxically stimulate great art. The hothouse, moreover, was walled by an Iron Curtain itself paradoxical in effect. The Shostakovich symphonies connect to a lineage including Beethoven and Mahler, both obvious influences—and also to a Russian symphonic tradition whose programmatic and autobiographical propensities (think of Tchaikovsky) Shostakovich honored. Shostakovich's Twenty-Four Preludes and Fugues for piano—arguably the terminus of the Western keyboard canon—honor Bach. The relative insularity of Soviet culture made these connections possible. In the West, channels of tradition—and especially of national tradition—were already blurred and dispersed. The Iron Curtain doubtless foreclosed myriad creative opportunities. But it also preserved a useful past.

As I have already had occasion to recall: during the Cold War, the CIA covertly funded a cultural Cold War of its own with a music division headed by Nicolas Nabokov. Nabokov extolled his friend Stravinsky as a progressive paragon and vilified Shostakovich as a retrograde Soviet stooge. Meanwhile, JFK read eloquent speeches claiming that the arts only flourish in "free societies." But no concert music being produced in Western Europe or the United States proved as durable as Shostakov-ich's post-1950 symphonies, string quartets, and preludes and fugues. A false god—twelve-tone serialism—had ensnared the free artists in Nabokov's camp. Arnold Schoenberg, who invented it, was a conscious historical actor who misread the past, extrapolating from spent Romanticism a "necessary" method of nontonal composition he prophesied would "insure the superiority of German music for the next hundred years." Schoenberg's mistake made Kennedy's claim risible. As creative seedbeds, free societies are less efficacious than usable pasts.

HEGEL GREATLY SHAPED notions of rise-and-fall historical trajectories. His understanding of history notably privileged culture. So it was, as well, with the German immigrants who implanted orchestras and *Singvereine* throughout the United States before World War I. Their allegiance to *Kultur* correlated with the late consolidation of a German political entity: the nation-state of 1871. In the absence of political unity, German music had long buttressed personal and national identity both. Its long and lucid evolutionary lineage, beginning with the Bach, Haydn, and Mozart that Germans sang and played, engendered a template for historical understanding. A later wave of Germans, fleeing Hitler, included legions of eminent conductors, instrumentalists, and composers brandishing a German cultural pantheon they were eager to propagate and share. The interwar immigrants also introduced Americans to musicology: an intellectual discipline that German-speakers had invented. The consequences for American classical music, given its tenuous and increasingly invisible past, were complex.*

Otto Kinkeldey, though born in New York, earned a doctorate in church music in Berlin and was named a Royal Prussian Professor in

---

* In my *Artists in Exile: How Refugees from Twentieth-Century War and Revolution Transformed the American Performing Arts* (2009), a central finding is that Germanic immigrants "remained German," whereas immigrants from Russia were substantially more assimilative.

Breslau. Beginning in 1930 at Cornell, Kinkeldey held the first chair in musicology in any American university. Four years later, the American Musicological Society was formed, with Kinkeldey as president. Antipathy to American music was an AMS signature. American musicologists, many of them German-trained, thought of American composers as clones or amateurs. Jazz was off the table.

To an extraordinary degree, these attitudes also typified American classical music—its institutions and practitioners, its "culture of performance." Not composers, but great American orchestras were celebrated, as were European masterworks and imported European conductors and instrumentalists. The jazz threat and the Gershwin threat, both of which we have observed, were symptoms of immaturity—of an obsession with pedigree, pedigrees being European. All this helps to explain why Virgil Thomson, Aaron Copland, and Leonard Bernstein became the makeshift historians of American music; there was no one else to do the job.

American musicology ripened after World War II. The first dissertations on Ives began to appear in the 1960s; in 1989, the *Journal of the American Musicological Society* published an article on Ives for the first time. By then, a group of AMS defectors had in 1975 formed the Sonneck Society—after Oscar Sonneck, the first critical scholar of American music—to promote and consolidate inquiry into American music in all its forms. The Sonneck Society renamed itself the Society for American Music in 1999. Richard Crawford, born in 1935, became the first prominent music historian to study American music and nothing else. The relative lateness of these developments bears stressing. Study of the early institutional history of American music was even more delayed, because the German founders of American musicology were not interested in that. There is still little enough: today's young American music historians shun nineteenth-century American classical music in favor of topics more familiar.

I myself began to research American music out of frustration. As a *New York Times* music critic in the 1970s, I found that most of the musical events to which I was sent seemed formulaic and redundant. In an

attempt to discover how American classical music had become so Eurocentric, so much less adventurous than American cinema, theater, or
visual art, I undertook to learn something about its present institutions
and performers—topics, as I discovered, about which little had been
written. There existed no biography of either of the individuals who
most shaped the symphonic culture that would define American classical music—these being Theodore Thomas and Henry Higginson, about
whom more in a moment. There were no first-rate histories of American
orchestras or opera companies with a single exception: Howard Shanet's
Philharmonic: A History of New York's Orchestra, published in 1975. The
story of Dvořák in America was still the province of European scholars
who knew little and cared less. Among American music historians, Gilbert Chase, who in 1955 authored the first notable scholarly history of
American music, simply ignored Dvořák's American sojourn; the name
Dvořák appears on three of the 713 pages of the 1987 "revised third edition" of his seminal *America's Music: From the Pilgrims to the Present*.
Not until Charles Hamm's *Music in the New World* of 1983 did Dvořák
begin to infiltrate the narrative to a degree remotely commensurate with
his onetime importance.

My *Wagner Nights: An American History* (1994) resurrected from
obscurity the dynamic institutional history of classical music during the
Gilded Age and *fin-de-siècle*; its charismatic central personality, the conductor Anton Seidl, had last been the subject of a book in 1899. Absorbing the unsuspected magnitude of American symphonic and operatic
activity preceding World War I, I wrote *Classical Music in America: A
History of Its Rise and Fall* (2005). A long view—a historical view—has,
I believe, helped me to account for a silo mentality I sought to escape.
The past I uncovered exposed and indicted the pastlessness I adumbrate
in this volume. I became equally cognizant that, during the Gilded Age
itself, silos were confined to farms.

The cultural breadth of James Gibbons Huneker was a common
aspiration. The defining cultural movement of the late Gilded Age—
Wagnerism—espoused synergies of thought, theater, music, and design.

Wagner was himself a conscious historical actor. Unlike Schoenberg, he did not misread the past. Pondering the history of music and theater, he inferred a teleological narrative proposing an artistic strategy for the future: the *Gesamtkunstwerk*. American Wagnerites accordingly embraced Schopenhauer and Nietzsche, theosophy and Christian socialism, Nordic myth and Greek theater, the *Parsifal* tocque and the incipient New Woman. They included Mabel Dodge Luhan and Isabella Stewart Gardner, Carl Schurz and Robert Ingersoll, Albert Ryder and John Singer Sargent, Kate Chopin, Willa Cather, and Upton Sinclair. Journals in general circulation—*Atlantic Monthly, Harper's New Monthly Magazine, Century Illustrated Monthly Magazine, Scribner's Magazine*—regularly published such articles as "Wagnerianism and the Italian Opera" "Wagner and Scenic Art," "Wagner from Behind the Scenes," "How Wagner Makes Operas," "Wagner in the Bowery," "Ruskin and Wagner," as well as informed reports from Wagner's Bayreuth Festival.

The world of symphonic music was no less widely significant to Gilded Age Americans. More than museums, universities, or libraries, it was the concert orchestra that signified civic cultural identity. In fact, the "symphony orchestra"—in contradistinction to the pit orchestras of Europe—is an American coinage, practically an American invention. A self-made conductor, Theodore Thomas, created the world-class Thomas Orchestra that, beginning in the 1860s, toured and retoured the nation. In his wake emerged fledgling musical organizations affirming his credo: "A symphony orchestra shows the culture of the community." In New England, the Boston Symphony Orchestra was invented fully formed by Henry Higginson in 1881. He hired the musicians, chose the conductor, and paid all the bills; there was no board. Its frequent concerts, its inspirational mission, its civic influence, embodied a New World institutional template pursued ever since (a longevity intimating not resilience but stagnation). Thomas and Higginson were Gilded Age visionaries from an epoch of heroic personal achievement; no other individual—no composer, no performer—ever impacted as mightily on American classical music as they did.

Thomas's orchestra doubtless found its way to Missouri. If Mark Twain never heard it, he surely heard of it. That Twain—whose aural acuity enabled him to absorb and retain the musical speech of a slave or frontier raconteur—was himself a music lover is hardly irrelevant to this pre-silo picture of New World cultural achievement. His affinities ranged far beyond savoring the Fisk Jubilee Singers.* He himself played the piano, banjo, and guitar. At the keyboard, he would sing "Go Down, Moses" or "Old Folks at Home" or "Die Lorelei." Late in life, he purchased an Aeolian Orchestrelle—a kind of player organ—that rendered Beethoven, Schubert, and Wagner. "I hate the very name of opera—partly because of the nights of suffering I have endured in its presence, and partly because I want to love it and can't," Twain recorded in his travel notebook in 1878. He also complained that *Lohengrin* "gave me a headache." And yet he had a favorite opera: *Tannhäuser*—whose hero, a blasphemous but repentant pariah, doubtless struck a personal chord. Twain's Bayreuth visit of 1891—during which he characteristically performed his man-boy act, feigning an innocence he half possessed†—was not merely fashionable, as in various biographical accounts. It was in fact the summer of the first Bayreuth *Tannhäuser.*

Twain had last encountered *Tannhäuser* at the Metropolitan Opera. Of the third act at Bayreuth, beginning with the pilgrims' chorus, he recorded: "From that moment until the closing of the curtain it was music, just music—music to make one drunk with pleasure, music to make one take a scrip and staff and beg his way round the globe to hear it." Leaving Bayreuth for Bohemia, Twain declared his "musical regeneration" to be "accomplished and perfect."

Some six years later, Mark Twain and family spent twenty months in Vienna. Countess Misa Wydenbruck-Esterhazy, whose close friends included Gustav and Alma Mahler, organized public readings of Twain's books; Twain's own lecture, titled "The Terror of the German Language,"

* See pages 3–4.

† See page 58.

was attended by Gustav Mahler, who had crossed paths with Twain in Manhattan. In Vienna, as well, Clara Clemens auditioned for Theodor Leschetizky, the city's preeminent piano pedagogue. Leschetizky agreed to take her on. A leading talent in Leschetizky's circle was the Russian-born pianist/conductor Ossip Gabrilowitsch, whom Clara had already met at a New York dinner party given by her father. Later, in New York again, Clara reencountered Gabrilowitsch. He was extricating himself from a long and inconvenient infatuation with Alma Mahler, whose husband he revered. Clara and Ossip eventually wed in Connecticut in 1909. Clara had by then given up piano in favor of vocal studies. According to the New York critic Henry Finck, she became "an artist of the front rank." When in 1911 Henry Krehbiel excoriated the dead Gustav Mahler in the *Tribune*, Mahler had no more vehement defender in the New York press than Mark Twain's Russian-American son-in-law.

But all this happened long ago—before Van Wyck Brooks and Virgil Thomson, before the culture of performance, before the stranding of American classical music. Today, penalized by its pastlessness, classical music does not much interest leading American novelists, or eminent historians of the American experience. Concomitantly, orchestras, unlike museums, do not engage distinguished scholars on staff, do not produce significant publications, do not engage with the intellectual life of the nation. Otherwise, the linkage I have proposed between Mark Twain and Charles Ives would have been clinched long ago, and Ives would inhabit the same pantheon as such kindred Americans as Emerson, Whitman, and Melville.

Culture and "Social Control"

Addressing the artistic output of the Gilded Age and the *fin-de-siècle,* the dialectical pendulum has by now long swung toward a more positive view, generally understood as a revisionist corrective to Oedipal modernists. The latest anthology of Gilded Age scholarship, edited by Christopher Nichols and Nancy Unger, is *A Companion to the Gilded Age and*

Progressive Era. The thirty-four chapters include "Decades of Upheaval and Reform" and "Why the Gilded Age and Progressive Era Still Matter." A 12,000-word treatment of "Art and Architecture" sympathetically considers dozens of painters, architects, and sculptors, ranging from Thomas Eakins and Henry Hobson Richardson to Edwin Blashfield and Lorado Taft. "Race, Sex and Gender"—topics more fashionable than the arts—account for no fewer than five chapters. A conspicuous omission from this compendious purview is classical music—as stranded, as ever, from the American past as from its own.

What Virgil Thomson wrote of the New York Philharmonic in 1940 has for some time been applicable to American classical music generally: it is not part of our intellectual life. In recent decades, only one prominent intellectual historian has even attempted to integrate classical music into a cross-disciplinary American portrait. This was the late Robert Crunden, who in his books *From Self to Society* (1971) and *Ministers of Reform: The Progressives' Achievement in American Civilization, 1889–1920* (1982) positioned Ives in the topmost echelons of Americana. Crunden's argument that Ives partook in a progressive "climate of opinion," however, led nowhere in particular. Otherwise, American cultural historians have concentrated on literature, film, theater, and the visual arts. Rarely is classical music even mentioned. I can think of only one greatly influential exception, crippled by plausible yet erroneous assumptions and impressions that, in the absence of a consolidated historical narrative, were subsequently more adopted than rebutted. That is Lawrence Levine's *Highbrow/Lowbrow: The Emergence of Cultural Hierarchy in America* (1988), itself belonging to a body of cultural inquiry stemming from a book even more influential and—at least with regard to music—misleading: Alan Trachtenberg's *The Incorporation of America: Culture and Society in the Gilded Age* (1982).

As both books vigorously illustrate, the "Gilded Age" of Van Wyck Brooks—with its rampant materialism, hegemonic millionaires, and effete, elitist "highbrows"—never wholly lost adherents. But their themes are fresh. Trachtenberg addresses the effects of "the corporate system" on American manners and beliefs. He discovers a "more tightly structured society with new hierarchies of control." An evolving Gilded Age consensus understood culture—here meaning "high culture"—as a "sphere of activity associated with class privilege and with the older Anglo-Saxon America, a sphere distinct from the crudeness and vulgarities of common life, of trade and labor." *The Incorporation of America* is distinguished by its scope of erudition and easy intimacy with topics in American literature and visual art. That American classical music passes unmentioned is as much a consequence of its own pastlessness and rootlessness as of the limitations of the author's purview—all familiar defects.

Trachtenberg's Chapter 5—"The Politics of Culture"—subsequently took on a life of its own, informing countless skewed case studies. A WASP elite, shackled by conservative taste and psychological need, by anxious disapproval of restless immigrant masses, is depicted creating universities, museums, concert halls, and libraries as instruments of "social control." This bold interpretive hunch is an extrapolation of ideology, historical perspective, and personal predisposition. No evidence is adduced. The closest approach to an empirical observation reads:

> Organized by the urban elite, dominated by ladies of high society, staffed by professionally trained personnel, housing classic works of European art donated by wealth private collectors, the museums subliminally associated art with wealth, and the power to donate and administer with social station and training. Their architecture reinforced the message: magnificent palaces with neoclassical fronts, marble columns, sweeping staircases, frescoed ceilings, and stained-glass windows. The splendor of the museums conveyed an idea of art . . . available in hushed corridors. . . .

Trachtenberg adds: "Culture was represented increasingly as the antidote to unruly feeling, to rebellious impulses." It offered "an alternative to class hostility."

Though concerts and operas are not similarly evoked, we know what sort of musical milieu Trachtenberg has in mind. Its defining embodiment is New York's Academy of Music as famously recalled by Edith Wharton in *The Age of Innocence*. Christine Nilsson is singing in Gounod's *Faust*. The world of fashion has assembled in the boxes to be seen and admired. The opera itself, in a foreign tongue, is an expensive backdrop to a social ceremony flaunting power and wealth. Wharton's description—arguably the single most familiar image of Gilded Age high culture—is no doubt just; it takes in the New York she knew. Here is an alternative view of the same Academy of Music from the *Evening Post*, surveying the basement "beer cavern":

> A long room . . . where, in a cloud of cigar smoke and amid the fumes of lager and liquor, the artists and their friends refresh themselves with copious libations. . . . Between the acts of the opera the cavern is crowded, but as soon as the music commences, the rotund German drops his lager; the Frenchman shrugs his shoulders and says "Mon Dieu"; the Italian quotes Count Luna in *Trovatore* and sings "Andiamo"; the yellow Cubans and Spaniards give a twirl to their moustaches; the English or New York swell struts towards the stairs, and in a few moments the motley crowd are in the seats or lobbies.

Before 1900, opera in America was riotous or reverent, vernacular or exotic, intimate or grandiose. It had not yet been reduced to a single governing template: elitist "grand opera." That happened at the Metropolitan Opera decades later. The *early* history of the Met, moreover, can no more be summarized by Caroline Astor's diamond stomacher than the Academy was a WASP preserve favoring Newland Archer and the etiquette of arriving late. Rather—as glimpsed in an earlier chapter of this book—the pre-1900 Met was a battlefield of class and ethnic warfare, as often as not more German than WASP even to the inclusion of German-American singing societies onstage. On Wagner nights the house was rocked by "unruly feeling," thronged by lady acolytes whose answer to Isolde's love-death was to stand on their chairs and scream. The larger picture of classical music in New York was one of rivalry and rancorous conflict: the Metropolitan versus the renegade Manhattan Opera of Oscar Hammerstein (who was hostile to all great wealth except his own); the New York Philharmonic (a self-made musicians' cooperative) versus Andrew Carnegie's New York Symphony; Anton Seidl's world-class New York Wagner ensemble versus Walter Damrosch's itinerant Wagner troupe—institutions that, generally considered, more sidelined than empowered any "WASP elite." Meanwhile, Dvořák, Henry Krehbiel, and Jeannette Thurber influentially espoused "negro melodies." Even a sophistry inferring hidden capitalist dynamics of class and wealth could not possibly discover "social control" in this actual picture of late Gilded Age culture.

If Trachtenberg's purview of "older Anglo-Saxon America" knows nothing of German-American *Kultur,* what about Boston Brahmins to the north? Here Levine furnishes a "social control" snapshot of Henry Higginson, the Boston Symphony being his fiefdom and its musicians his slaves. Higginson "spent four years in Europe studying music" as a young man. He subsequently was a failed "cotton planter." Bowing to the inevitable, he joined the family firm as a stockbroker. In 1881, by fiat, he established a Boston Symphony Orchestra, owned and operated solely by himself. His musicians were compelled to rehearse and perform for four consecutive days per concert. When not doing so, they were forbidden to play "for dances." They could not unionize. An elitist, Higginson charged high ticket prices and insisted on conservative programs. A monopolist, he drove Boston's other orchestras out of business. A paternalist, he disciplined audiences and performers.

This Gilded Age cartoon—the tyrannical captain of culture—is as distant from the actual Henry Higginson as are Alan Trachtenburg's culture palaces from the Symphony Hall that Higginson built: an auditorium, sans boxes, remarkable for its democratic plainness. Higginson was not born to wealth. He was not even born in Boston. The "Europe" in which he studied music was Vienna, with distinguished teachers: he was a trained musician who composed art songs. During those student days abroad, he usually lacked money enough for supper. A passionate abolitionist, he fought in the Civil War, encountering men from all walks of life (he inherited a regiment from a barkeeper). His tenure as "a cotton planter" was a failed but idealistic attempt to revive a dormant Georgia plantation by employing freed slaves. Capitulating to joining a middling family business, he amassed a fortune sufficient to realize his dream of creating a world-class concert orchestra for Boston. To counteract the instability of the city's existing symphonic organizations, he insisted on strict attendance (but did not forbid his musicians to otherwise play lighter fare—one of several errors of fact in Levine's account). He would not tolerate a union because he needed to hire expert players from abroad (his Vienna scout being the distinguished pianist Julius Epstein; Higginson defied Brahmin prejudice against Jews). The miraculous result was an orchestra of international standing.

Not the least remarkable feature of this story was Higginson's insistence on public rehearsals—concerts in everything but name—for which all tickets would cost twenty-five cents. He also reserved twenty-five-cent nonsubscription tickets for all concerts on subscription. This is one reason John Sullivan Dwight complained that Higginson would drive Boston's other orchestras out of business—which he did. The Harvard Musical Association—Dwight's orchestra—had played for an invited audience. Its repertoire was archaic. Dwight himself—Boston's leading music critic until Higginson's new order swiftly dethroned him—was the Boston embodiment of "social control." He feared the immigrant rabble and disparaged the "reason and intellect" of Black Bostonians. Higginson was cosmopolitan. He delighted in the diversity of a Symphony Hall crowd "not from the Back Bay or from any particular set of people." That "to his true comrades he was like a lover" is not the only encomium testifying to a "feminine" predisposition toward cherished friendships. No less than Mark Twain and Charles Ives, he married art and business, with art coming first; no less than Twain and Ives, he led

multiple lives and inhabited multiple communities. The very embodiment of musical Boston at the turn of the twentieth century, Henry Higginson was a colossus, an American musical hero with no successors.

The larger topic of Lawrence Levine's book—a necessary topic—is the
sacralization of American culture: the bifurcation of "high" and "low"
that we have already observed penalizing jazz during the post–World
War I era. But Levine deals with an earlier era—during which sacralization had a different aspect that eludes him. The driving agents of sacralization during the late Gilded Age were less elitist snobs than the music
dramas of Richard Wagner. Wagner's "Music of the Future" demanded
disciplined, even reverent audiences, audiences that themselves disciplined the snobs who came to chat. The Wagnerites were both religiously
attentive and wildly demonstrative. They understood that late Romantic
art itself embraced an aesthetic—a *Weltanschaung*—of sacralization.

In New York, the erotic maelstrom of *Tristan und Isolde* more provoked than suppressed "rebellious impulses." Equally pertinent: when
not conducting *Tristan* at the Met, Anton Seidl led twice-daily summer
concerts on Coney Island for audiences paying as little as fifteen cents.
An outspoken populist democrat, Seidl alternated Wagner Nights with
lighter fare, including concerts for children. In Boston, Artur Nikisch's
incendiary Wagnerian interpretation of Beethoven's Fifth ignited a five-
week dispute in the local press: a torrid debate over Boston's destabi-
lized cultural pedigree. The fashion-enslaved, overdisciplined audiences
Levine deplores, sacralizing dead European masterpieces and living
European maestros, are a post–World War I phenomenon. He unwittingly invents the past in imagining that Seidl's Germanic Metropolitan Opera was "deeply influenced if not controlled by wealthy patrons
whose impresarios and conductors strove to keep the opera they presented free from the influence of other genres and other groups."

If anything like the social-control model existed in turn-of-the-
century American music, it would likely be in Chicago, where the deadly
1886 Haymarket Riot impelled Ferdinand Peck to create his 4,200-seat
Auditorium Building as a socially engineered temple for class harmo-

nization. And yet Peck was a utopian pragmatist, a social reformer for whom the auditorium would bridge the gap between rich and poor. The truest agents of the sacralization Levine deplores, sucking the life out of contemporary culture, are to be found among the "popularizers" of the interwar decades, including NBC's David Sarnoff and the musical power-broker Arthur Judson. The music appreciation movement, instilling reverence for foreign masterworks, extolling Arturo Toscanini as "high priest," "consecrated celebrant," and "custodian of holy things," excluding from heavenly climes unsavory popular and contemporary music, is the kind of sacralization that most bothers Lawrence Levine. He looks for culprits and misplaces the blame.

Trigger Warnings

For Virgil Thomson, Aaron Copland, and Leonard Bernstein, the past was a blank to which little attention need be paid; none of them posed as a professional historian. For Van Wyck Brooks and Lewis Mumford, early on, the past was a polemic: a caricature explicitly concocted to goad present-day achievement; neither posed as a disinterested chronicler. Oblivious of the humane New York of Antonín Dvořák and Anton Seidl, of the dynamic Boston of Henry Higginson, Trachtenberg and Levine, by comparison, write of the past with outright hostility; "a weird and ghastly story" is for Trachtenberg a fair summary of "the last quarter of the nineteenth century."

Inspired by the New Left populism of my own 1960s coming-of-age, aroused by acute awareness of racial and social injustice (and also, in Levine's case, by a passion for jazz), the social-control model remains perilously speculative, at least insofar as American classical music is concerned. It distorts the past to conjure hegemonic cultural configurations penalizing the underdog.

The irrelevance of social control to Mark Twain and Charles Ives need not be belabored. They reviled snobs. They inhabited both "high" and "low." So far as I am aware, neither has yet been depicted as an instrument of class hegemony. But both have suffered from fresh currents of historical—or, rather, ahistorical—interpretation.

My first experience of trigger warnings was a rereading of Willa Cather's *The Song of the Lark*. This tale of a New World opera diva is partly based on the life story of the galvanizing Wagnerian soprano Olive Fremstad, whom Cather knew rather well. Cather was herself a fervent Wagnerite many of whose predilections, personal and creative, correlate with the Wagner movement and its protofeminist message for American women of her generation. Sharing all of that with present-day readers would seem a pertinent use of history—but my 1991 Signet edition offered a very different 13-page preface by the Cather scholar Sharon O'Brien. It seems that Cather had in 1915 unwittingly committed transgressions requiring scrutiny and censure. And so I discovered myself reading with bewilderment that

> some readers may find Thea's theft of the pot fragments and her imaginative connection to Indian women ancestors acts of cultural appropriation in which Cather, despite her sympathy for native cultures, is still using them for her own purposes. . . . I find Cather's and Thea's treatment of the Indian women and their pottery problematic. Not only do Cather and her heroine take something that does not belong to them, but both are using the art of a communal (and eventually colonized) culture—which is anonymous, domestic, ritualistic—to empower an individualistic notion of the artist that is anything but anonymous. . . . We never know what the Indian women might have thought of such desires, since they are not given voices in the novel.

The back story here is that Willa Cather experienced the American Southwest as a spiritual respite. She admires Native American women decorating pots; she leaves with some pot fragments. Thea does the same. Neither asks permission. Both violate twenty-first century behavioral codes.

To understand Cather and Thea, a useful starting point would be the contemporaneous Indianists movement and practitioners like Arthur Farwell—who admired Native Americans to a point of reverence. In fact, the collection and application of Indian tunes was mainly undertaken by women who shared the epiphanies of Cather and Thea. One of the most prominent, Natalie Curtis, was, like Cather, a protofeminist Wagnerite. Opinions about Farwell and Curtis may differ—but referencing their activities is at the very least a pertinent way of using the past. Invoking "cultural appropriation" is serenely ahistorical.

I suppose the mother of all trigger warnings must be "nigger Jim," a phrase attributed to Huck though he never says it. That he says "nigger" is indisputable—it is a word Huck would surely have used. From the start, his foul language provoked suppression. I learn from Shelley Fisher Fishkin's *Lighting Out for the Territory* that this activity continues, lest a classic American novel give offense. And Mark Twain is surely a practitioner of cultural appropriation—it is the very engine of his genius that he borrows the inspired idiom of an oppressed minority.

What are we to make of Mark Twain and race today? Fishkin makes a case for contextual understanding. She acknowledges that Jim (not unlike Gershwin's Porgy) partakes of the gullible and superstitious minstrel-show darky of Twain's America, and that in a twenty-first-century classroom some Black students will sensibly be repulsed. She knows that Twain was blatantly racist until his thirty-second year, and that a subcurrent of paternalism toward Blacks was part of his Missouri inheritance. But she adds:

> We can accept the idea that Twain shared, with peers of his race and class, simple assumptions about "the existence of a natural racial hierarchy" only if we blind ourselves to those instances in which Twain subverted and radically deconstructed the racial categories of his day.... Of interest here is not so much the question "Was Twain a racist?," which may be answered "yes" or "no" depending on how the term is defined, but rather how

Twain intermittently played havoc with his culture's categories of "blackness" and "whiteness" in fresh and surprising ways.[*]

And what of Charles Ives's appropriation in his Second Symphony of "Camptown Races," itself a Stephen Foster theft—we are now told—of a song sung by Yoruba mothers to their children? I am not aware that the Ives literature has gotten around to that; the chief trigger warnings to date have to do with gender and sexuality. In his notorious tirades against philistines, Ives's typical terms of opprobrium include "pansies" and "lillypads" and "ladies." And when he discovered that his friend Henry Cowell was an alleged homosexual, he cut Cowell off. To investigate Ives the alleged homophobe and misogynist is, I suppose, necessary enough—if only to insist that Ives's gendered invective signified not hostility to women, but to a cultural environment he both loathed and feared. Instead, Ives has been thrust on a couch as a freakish object of analysis, with his diatribes interpreted as evidence of psychological derangement. These commentaries—I am mainly thinking of Frank Rossiter, Maynard Solomon, Lawrence Kramer, and Stuart Feder—fail to absorb what it meant to grow up in the late nineteenth century rather than fifty years later. An exemplary antidote is Judith Tick's 1993 essay "Charles Ives and Gender Ideology," which elegantly discerns—with much historical evidence—a metaphoric discourse of dissidence. As twentieth-century composers of stature go, Ives was no less eccentric than Schoenberg, Bartók, or Shostakovich. Unlike Stravinsky, he was an invariably loving husband and father. His friends and business associates adored him. His daughter plausibly judged him a "great man."

And yet tangential perspectives continue disproportionately to infiltrate depictions of Ives the man and artist. What we need—still—are considered treatments of Charles Ives as a historical actor grounded in his own elusive time and place. Jan Swafford's 1996 biography should

---

[*] I leave to others the endless controversy over the novel's odd and ill-formed ending, and its bearing on Twain's treatment of slavery and race.

have been a strong starting point; he pointedly resists modernist readings of Ives the anomaly. My own *Moral Fire: Musical Portraits from America's Fin-de-Siècle* (2012) includes a 50-page chapter linking Ives not to twentieth-century musical progressives, but to Henry Higginson, Henry Krehbiel, and the protofeminist Brooklyn impresario Laura Langford. I here extrapolate a five-point template, ca. 1900, Ives being the wild card—the surprise portrait—with which I load my deck.

However much a renegade, I argue, Ives possessed in common with these archetypal American culture-bearers five signature traits. All four were agents of uplift for whom great art seemed inherently ennobling; for Ives, art was about divinity and God was "nothing but love." All four espoused a democratic ethos: Ives, in Redding, identified with the barber and the farmer; no previous American composer had so wedded the quotidian with high art. A corollary: for all four, empathy for the common man dictated empathy for the Black man; Ives composed his dead march in honor of the Black Civil War regiment led by Robert Shaw—whom Higginson had memorialized as a fallen comrade. Thirdly, all four were combative: fighters. Estrangement from the new century is a fourth linked trait; Ives railed against airplanes, disdained the telephone, radio, and phonograph. Finally, all my subjects were *fin-de-siècle* fulcrum figures. Ives, I here write, shares with Mark Twain a series of dualities: gentility and rebellion; business and art; philosophic gravitas and vernacular exuberance. "But their most telling affinity, the one they most shared with other fin-de-siècle activists, was the restlessness of Americans jostled and challenged by changing times. Their multiple worlds, and unruly energies were equally self-generated and outwardly inflicted."

Such was my effort to recontextualize Charles Ives within a capacious historical framework transcending music and merged with the work of intellectual and social historians for whom Ives is barely a name. Whether this attempt to connect silos will ever gain traction I have no idea—even in the *Journal of the Gilded Age and Progressive Era, Moral Fire* was reviewed by a music historian; Alan Lessoff, the journal's editor, tried fruitlessly to find a cultural historian to consider my argument.

Incredibly, Frank Rossiter's *Charles Ives and His America* (1975) remains the only book-length treatment of that topic—and it's a wrong turn, an earnest rewrite of Van Wyck Brooks's *The Ordeal of Mark Twain* heedless of the passage of historiographic time. Ives is here portrayed as a tragic victim of late Gilded Age mores both sclerotic and philistine. He "succumbed to a series of pressures that his society and culture brought to bear upon him," pressing him toward Yale, business, and family—pressures "so powerful and baleful as to bear comparison with the more obvious pressures" exerted upon Shostakovich in Soviet Russia. "He never reached that degree of independence which would have allowed him to define himself primarily as an artist." "As an artist, he became literally his own worst enemy. He willingly—even eagerly—subordinated both his art and his life as an artist to a rigid ideology that was based upon non-artistic considerations." "The thought of making art his life's work was too much for him for it seemed to imply that he must cut himself off from the common life of America." Rather than an artist, he "chose to be a good American" and wound up "utterly isolated." "Tremendous pressures" had "narrowed his creativity, stifled his autonomy, and driven him into artistic isolation."

It does not occur to Rossiter that he himself exerts the pressures that drive "Ives" into isolation and stifle his autonomy: Rossiter's Ives abjectly lacks agency or self-knowledge. Would the real Charles Ives—so formidable both in aspiration and accomplishment—have been a more fulfilled, less "narrowed" composer in the modernist America he detested? *

Reencountering Harry Burleigh

During the writing of *Dvořák's Prophecy*, the uses of history have grown steadily more problematic.

---

* A backstory, related by David C. Paul in *Charles Ives in the Mirror* (2013), suggests to Paul "compelling evidence that Rossiter sometimes conflated his own America with that of Charles Ives." Rossiter was an embattled gay scholar denied tenure by the University of Michigan.

An ongoing debate over the proper fate of public statues has illustrated the seeming futility of referencing the past. When the mayor of New Orleans, in a speech so eloquent as to seem anachronistic, distinguished between "remembrance of history and reverence for it," between chronicling history and "rebranding" it to "celebrate a fictional, sanitized Confederacy," the response was a chorus of political catcalls.

As of this writing, a viral pandemic threatens American institutions of culture and newly discloses our confusion over what our cultural inheritance may be and how much it may matter. I do not pretend to know the answers. But I am certain that, absent the ballast of history, a psychological condition of weightlessness is a likely national malady.

My own work exploring America's musical past with concert audiences continues apace. But the obstacles feel new. The case of Harry Burleigh will explain the reasons. Burleigh's story is of course integral to the Dvořák story. I have had occasion to tell it many times. The first came during my tenure as executive director of the Brooklyn Philharmonic Orchestra at the Brooklyn Academy of Music, where I produced a 1994 Dvořák festival to celebrate the centenary of the *New World* Symphony. A distinguished Black tenor, Thomas Young, sang a set of Burleigh spiritual arrangements and art songs. He was followed by a distinguished Black scholar: the late Samuel Floyd, then director of the Center for Black Music Research, who gave a talk about Will Marion Cook. Floyd used Cook to punish Burleigh for sanitizing Black music: he turned it white, Floyd said. In response, Young improvised one of the most stirring speeches I have ever heard. He said that no one in that room had the right to judge Harry Burleigh. These remarks constituted an impassioned act of historic contextualization. Sam Floyd offered no rejoinder.

For more than a decade I have produced a "Harry Burleigh Show" at elementary, middle, and high schools, at colleges and universities, conservatories and festivals. I subsequently created a more elaborate Burleigh tribute: "Deep River: The Art of the Spiritual." My intention was to explore Burleigh's inspiration, his method, and his legacy. The final half-hour documents in detail the evolution of "Deep River" via the Fisk Jubilee Singers, who sang it early on; Samuel Coleridge-Taylor, who created a 1905 solo piano version; Maud Powell, who played and recorded Coleridge-Taylor's version on the violin; and finally Burleigh, whose 1917 transcription for solo voice was an overnight sensation. At the show's 2015 premiere, I discovered myself dealing with sensitivities I had not anticipated. All mention of blackface minstrelsy was expunged from my script so as not to give offense. So was Burleigh's page of admonition to performers, with its dated notions of racial traits. Dvořák had said: "In the negro melodies of America I discover all that is needed for a great and noble school of music. They are pathetic, tender, passionate, melancholy, solemn, religious, bold, merry, gay, or what you will. It is music that suits itself to any mood or purpose." From this list of adjectives, "pathetic" and "gay" were deleted.

My Burleigh partner has long been the African-American bass-baritone Kevin Deas, a supreme exponent of spirituals in concert. When Kevin studied at Julliard, his ambition was to sing Bach and Handel—which he does to this day. He came late to Burleigh—so much so that he and I have discovered this music together. Kevin also participates in most of the "Dvořák and America" festivals I produce. The core component is a concert with the *New World* Symphony on the second half. The first half is a multimedia exegesis during which Kevin sings "Swing Low, Sweet Chariot" (virtually quoted by Dvořák). He also sings "Goin' Home" (adapting Dvořák). Finally, he portrays both Dvořák espousing "negro melodies" and (hilariously) Dvořák's Boston nemesis Philp Hale declaiming that "the Negro is not inherently musical." It was Kevin's "Deep River" script that was abridged so as not to give offense. I asked him what he thought. "Ridiculous," he replied.

On another occasion, an unhappy local reviewer reinvented Burleigh as a heroic victim who "overcame racial discrimination to . . . become the personal assistant" of Dvořák in New York. He "used to sing Negro Spirituals while cleaning the halls as a janitor during his musical education." His "arrangements prompted Dvořák to explore this musical genre." Dvořák's *New World* Symphony "included strong elements of

Harry Burleigh's astute musical creativity." The critic also complained that our choral forces were mainly white. But Burleigh, take him or leave him, mainly sang in white choruses. His arrangements were initially mainly sung by white recitalists. Erie's citizens, white and Black, enthusiastically supported his trek to New York. Dvořák and Jeannette Thurber would no more have put a mop and bucket in his hands than they would have manacled his legs (it is Harry's mother who was the janitor). His transcriptions did not prompt Dvořák's explorations of "negro melodies"; it was the other way around.

For some who question the wisdom of transforming the sorrow songs into concert songs, Burleigh did so conditioned by social and economic forces impinging on Black Americans of his generation: it was an accommodation with the white elite, a way of attaining mainstream influence and success. I would differently account for Burleigh's initiative. It is true that he brought the spirituals into white concert halls in a new format predicated on European art song; that his circle included J. P. Morgan; that he was the soloist at a church and a synagogue both of which were citadels of white affluence and power.

Burleigh himself repeatedly testified that one reason he turned spirituals into concert songs was to preserve them. Just as it was once widely believed that the Native American would grow extinct, many admirers of the sorrow songs feared that they would be forgotten. But very likely Burleigh mainly did what he did because he spent three years at the side of a white composer of genius whom he revered. He intimately knew the Dvořák home, the Dvořák family. And he perceived Dvořák not only as a musician of genius, but a great humanitarian. When Dvořák espoused taking "negro melodies" into the concert hall, Burleigh subscribed wholly to this artistic aspiration. It fit the European template Dvořák embodied. It fired Burleigh's creative imagination. Burleigh initially imagined that Samuel Coleridge-Taylor might do the job—and Burleigh urged it upon Coleridge-Taylor. But at some point Burleigh began to think: I can do it better. And he did.

Of course, one can infer a sociocultural framework, based in history and ideology, that second-guesses Burleigh and infers "real reasons." But that risks an act of sophistry. While it is not necessary to agree with what Burleigh did, the Uncle Tom view patronizes him as a victim; it denies him agency. I read Harry Burleigh as an individual of formidable personal integrity and moral stature—you can observe that in his dealings with others all his life. It is pertinent to recall that Burleigh and Will Marion Cook—embodying antithetical approaches to the proper use of "negro melodies"—were longtime friends. They respected one another. Very likely they were able to discuss issues of race and culture that no longer invite constructive disagreement. Perhaps the legacy of slavery is so onerous that it would be as naïve to expect a common understanding of Burleigh as it would be to expect an experience of America common to both whites and Blacks. Perhaps we are today enacting a fated and poisoned scenario.

In fact, all aspects of the Dvořák/America story ignite a racial minefield. Like so many Europeans of his time, Dvořák was fascinated by American Indians. When he landed in New York, he wanted to meet them, question them, see and hear them making music. And he did. He also arrived in New York having already read *The Song of Hiawatha* in Czech. He reread it in English (a language he could speak imperfectly). He became consumed by an ambition to compose a Hiawatha opera or cantata. Dvořák's American style in such works as the *New World* Symphony, the *American* Suite, and the Violin Sonatina is saturated with African-American and Native American influences. The former are musical. The latter are not. Black music was tonal, harmonic, Christian—adaptable. Indian music had scales of its own and unharmonized tunes. Dvořák took a pass and opted for an Indian musical impression little related to Indian chant. It is primal and exotic—gapped scales, drone accompaniments, simple textures, odd accents. (The G minor second theme of the *New World* Symphony's first movement, sung by oboe and flute, is an example.) Dvořák's Indian music is often elegiac; it conveys intimations of tragedy.

Longfellow's Indians are obviously pertinent. What is their provenance? Mainly tales and legends collected by Henry R. Schoolcraft (1793–1864). Schoolcraft garbled some of this information, and Longfellow garbled it some more. Hiawatha emerges as a premodern superman at one with nature (like Porgy, he is endowed with "plenty o' nuttin'"). Longfellow himself was a passionate abolitionist who also espoused Indian rights. His poem "The Revenge of Rain-in-the-Face" blames the massacre of Custer's troops on the "broken faith" of the U.S. government.

As with George Gershwin and *Porgy*, issues of authenticity are beside the point. Dvořák was no Bartók, for whom specific folk sources were paramount. He was not even a Brahms, whose Hungarian Dances use actual Hungarian dances. Like his "Bohemian" music, Dvořák's "American" music is happily synthetic. As for Longfellow, he said his Hiawatha lived "purely in the realm of fancy." Far from marginalizing the Native American, *The Song of Hiawatha* binds indigenous and European traditions. It bears mentioning, as well, that the noble savage was not wholly mythic. Many are the reports describing Indians of rare self-possession and authority.

But the most intractable obstacles arise once *Porgy and Bess* is broached. At one Coleridge-Taylor tribute at a major American university, I was advised by a member of the music faculty that my program note should not so much as mention George Gershwin, let alone state that, while Nathaniel Dett, Florence Price, William Dawson, and William Grant Still "notably culled the sorrow songs in ambitious works with orchestra, . . . this 'Black' symphonic music did not find an enduring place on concert and operatic programs with a solitary exception: . . . *Porgy and Bess* extrapolated the sorrow songs to produce what is arguably America's highest achievement in the realm of classical music." And yet this statement is as pertinent as it is irrefutable. It asks: Why did African-American musical genius find a home in the Cotton Club, not Broadway, Carnegie Hall, or the Metropolitan Opera? Gershwin's appropriation of Black sources remains properly controversial. But the controversy requires context.

Reencountering John Singer Sargent

I next offer a personal experience bearing on readings of Gilded Age culture and how silos obtrude on understanding history.

In 2016 the Metropolitan Museum mounted a John Singer Sargent retrospective. Standing in contradistinction to American nostalgia, to the originalities of Mark Twain and Charles Ives, was the most gifted American painter of the day, born in Tuscany and schooled in Paris. If Sargent therefore limns a different *fin-de-siècle* portrait, it is one that equally contradicts the Oedipal conventional wisdom long ago spawned by Van Wyck Brooks.

Though he principally resided in France, then England, Sargent was nomadic. From an early age he was fluent in English, French, and Italian. An American citizen, he often visited the United States, was patriotic, but was never tempted to settle in Boston or New York. In 1882, when Sargent was all of twenty-six, Henry James observed in him "the slightly 'uncanny' spectacle of a talent which on the very threshold of its career has nothing more to learn. It is not simply precocity in the guise of maturity—a phenomenon we very often meet, which deceives us only for an hour; it is the freshness of youth combined with the artistic experience, really felt and assimilated, of generations." Sargent found inspiration in masters as diverse as Velázquez, Goya, and Monet. He excelled in oil and watercolor, in portraits and landscapes and exotic tableaux. His mastery was cosmopolitan, frictionless, effortless. A dash of spontaneity was a Sargent hallmark. Sensuality and painterly bravura were constant features of his work.

From the start, Sargent was a victim or beneficiary of his supreme facility and irrepressible elegance. The finish of his canvases can seem deflective. His self-portraits are among his least revealing. Sargent the man was reserved, gracious, liked and admired—and not all there. His paintings of male nudes are suggestive. He was a lifelong bachelor whose sexual proclivities are unknowable.

Gilded Age stereotypes classify Sargent as a "society portraitist"—a risible simplification. His obliviousness to the criterion of newness was viewed by modernists as a fatal weakness. He disdained the avant-garde and never quite succumbed to Impressionism. Unlike Monet or Matisse, Kandinsky or Picasso, he refused to regard art history as a teleological narrative: he belongs to no trajectory. He has been variously admired for fabricating a "cool glass of mastery," for creating an art "one with itself" conjoining past and present, for showing "the exhalation of breath that an American can feel in Europe" and the disillusion that comes after.

Sargent is an artist whose work cannot be reproduced in books. If *The Daughters of Edward Darley Boit* (1882) is obviously an homage to Velázquez's *Las Meninas*, it is partly because its palpitating painterly textures, eschewing sharp outlines, are only appreciable if one visits the Boston Museum of Fine Art. In this canvas, James appreciated "the sense it gives us of assimilated secrets and of instinct and knowledge playing together"—that is, a gift for Jamesian insinuation. The copious Sargent retrospective mounted in 2016 by the Metropolitan Museum was a visual feast testifying to the variety and resilience of Sargent's genius. I happened some months afterward to visit the Phillips Collection in Washington, D.C., with its superb cross section of twentieth-century American painting, a collection espousing a new day. There is no Sargent, no Homer, no Frederic Church or Thomas Eakins. Their absence is gaping.

Sargent clarifies what the "unfinished" nostalgic subversives Twain and Ives were not. He also happens to present a ripe opportunity for cross-disciplinary inquiry. That Sargent was a skilled musician is well known. He played the piano with professional skill (and even considered giving up art for music). He liked to play keyboard duets with his friend Gabriel Fauré. He was also a Wagnerite. Fauré and Wagner speak to Sargent's sensuality—albeit from contradictory aesthetic postures counterposing Gallic objectivity with Germanic *Innerlichkeit*.

It is insufficiently remembered that there is an American milieu into which Sargent fits: the *fin-de-siècle* Boston aesthetes, a cocoon within which America's prevailing moral criterion of art was disdained. Boston's "visualists" encircled the bibliophile/philosopher Fred Holland Day, who with his Turkish robes and Chinese silk shirts might have stepped out of a Sargent painting. The aesthetes' queen bee, Isabella Stewart Gardner, was in fact famously painted by Sargent—in décolleté. She was also known to appear at parties swathed in gauze as an Egyptian "nautch girl" or wearing diamonds attached to bobbing gold antennae. Gardner's palazzo, Fenway Court, housed paintings by Titian, Vermeer, and—its largest canvas—Sargent's eight-by-eleven-foot *El Jaleo*.

Gardner's refined male coterie included Sargent alongside a swarm of handsome musicians, her court violinist being Charles Martin Loeffler (1861–1935). Ignored today, Loeffler was briefly the most eminent American concert composer. He was also a deracinated aesthete as placeless as his friend John Singer Sargent. Loeffler's compositional style was changeable, sensual, and polished, as ultimately inscrutable as his persona. Though he claimed to have been born in Alsace, recent scholarship establishes Berlin as his birthplace. As a child, he also lived in Hungary and Russia. In the United States—his home beginning in 1881—he was presumed to be French. He married after an engagement lasting more than two decades; a not atypical letter to his wife read: "We love each other without loving and yet we love each other."

Among Sargent's too many portraits, the one of Loeffler (1903) is among the most compelling. Loeffler's erect bearing, slender carriage, fine features, blond hair, and clear blue eyes impressed as regal or aristocratic. And so he seems in Sargent's picture. But there is more. The glistening wetness of his lips—a detail barely appreciable in reproductions—is startlingly suggestive. His worried eyes contradict his refinement of posture. An undercurrent of unease—of homoerotic ambivalence?—is the picture's crowning affect.

Inscribed "to Mrs. Gardner con buone feste," Sargent's *Charles Martin Loeffler* is a Jamesian feat of observational acuity. Is its object equally the observer? Could this polyvalent canvas possibly be regarded as a tacit self-portrait the painter did not permit himself in life, or explicit self-depiction? Anchored abroad, did John Singer Sargent transcend the disillusion and ambiguity of Gardner's decadent Boston sideshow, snubbing the America of Ives and Mark Twain? Or is his understanding of Boston also self-understanding? We will never know.

The catalogue for the exhibit, *Sargent: Portraits of Artists and Friends* by Richard Ormond (2015), gets Loeffler's birthplace wrong. But that is the least of its misrepresentations. The thesis of this volume turns out to be revisionist. Ormond writes:

> This exhibition challenges the conventional view of John Singer Sargent as a bravura painter of the old school, of limited imagination and originality. What materializes here is a painter in the vanguard of contemporary movements in the arts, in music, in literature and the theatre. His enthusiasms were for all things new and exciting, . . . and in music his influence on behalf of modern composers and musicians ranged far and wide. . . . Sargent the painter is well known; but Sargent the intellectual, the connoisseur of music, the literary polymath is something new. . . . He was by instinct an aesthete and a modernist.

The point of it all is to rescue Sargent from the incriminating Victorianism of pre–World War I culture—from Mark Twain's ordeal as depicted by Van Wyck Brooks, or that of Charles Ives as invented by Frank Rossiter. Rather, Sargent is a knowing aesthetician, a sophisticate standing outside the rigid confines of his apparent milieu. But Sargent's admiration for Manet and friendship with Monet do not make him an Impressionist. And his passions for Wagner and Fauré do not transport him into "the vanguard of contemporary movements in music"; by the time he died in 1925, still vigorously productive at the age of 69, Schoenberg and Stravinsky were the established musical modernists. Sargent inhabited an older world of feeling and sensibility.

If the modernist criterion of originality is to be applied to Sargent, he is diminished, not enhanced. Removing him from the *fin-de-siècle* is prejudicial; Ormond misuses the past.

Reencountering Arthur Farwell

I close this litany with an account of futile advocacy.

In 2014, I produced a Naxos CD entitled *Dvořák and America*. It included three top-drawer Arthur Farwell cameos in terrific performances: the piano pieces *Pawnee Horses* and *Navajo War Dance* No. 2 played by Benjamin Pasternack, and the a cappella version of *Pawnee Horses* sung (in Navajo) by the University of Texas Chamber Singers under James Morrow—one of half a dozen distinguished choral conductors whom I have observed discovering Farwell with incredulity. Then came a weeklong festival produced in Washington D.C., by PostClassical Ensemble—the "experimental" chamber orchestra I cofounded in 2003. This was "Native American Inspirations," surveying 125 years of music inspired by Native America. That is—we linked Dvořák, Farwell, and the Indianists to contemporary composers, Native and non-Native, who mine Native American songs and ceremony. In Fall 2021 will come a PCE-produced Farwell release, again on Naxos, with multiple world premiere recordings.

Presented at the Washington National Cathedral, the D.C. festival provoked divergent reviews from Anne Midgette in the *Washington Post* and Sudip Bose in the *American Scholar*. Midgette gave short shrift to Farwell; she wanted to hear more music composed by Native Americans. Her review was buttressed by a flood of supportive tweets condemning Farwell as an appropriator. Bose mounted a considered rebuttal, contending in part:

> To be sure, we can look back at Farwell's interactions with Native
> American cultures, and find him lacking in certain areas. . . . Yet
> it cannot be denied that Farwell's reverence for Native American
> music was genuine. . . . It's a tricky thing—trying to come to terms
> with Farwell in our time. His perceived flaws provide detractors
> with enough justification to reject him out of hand. To them, it
> doesn't matter what his music sounds like, or what part it played

in the evolution of classical music in the United States. To them, Farwell is simply a white man who made a living at the expense of marginalized peoples. This, I believe, not only misrepresents the composer and his intentions, but it also uses the politics of our current moment to form loose judgments about a very distant time. . . . I would also like to assert that Farwell, despite his keenest ethnographic instincts, was *not* an ethnographer. His principal aim was not to document Native music, and certainly not to compose it. Rather, he was writing classical music—an anti-modernist classical music, rooted in diatonic harmony and sonata form, that he felt best represented America.

It is indeed "a tricky thing" to advocate for Farwell today. One of the challenges is enlisting Native American participants. For our D.C. festival, I unsuccessfully attempted to engage Native American scholars and musicians from as far away as Texas, New Mexico, and California. My greatest disappointment was the Smithsonian Museum of the American Indian, which declined to partner the festival even though it presented in concert the South Dakota Symphony's Lakota Music Project, brought to Washington at the invitation of PostClassical Ensemble. The visitors included nine orchestral musicians and two distinguished Native performers: a Lakota singer—Emmanuel Black Bear, from the Pine Ridge reservation—and a Dakota flutist—Bryan Akipa of the Sisseton Wahpeton Sioux Tribe, who is also a vibrant dancer. We opened the first concert with a stomping dance, in headdress and moccasins, down the length of the nave, partnered by a solo song, immense in volume, that set the huge space throbbing. The week's concerts included compositions, by composers Native and non-Native, in which our two Native performers partnered Western strings and winds. These works were born in patient collaboration between the composers and performers. A distinguished concert baritone, William Sharp, sang music by Farwell and by the contemporary Chickasaw composer Jerod Impichchaachaaha' Tate. Sharp was overwhelmed by the expressive power of Black Bear's songs.

And yet the paucity of Native participants caused discomfort on all sides. Inescapably, Black Bear and Akipa seemed a token presence, out of place alongside our orchestra and chorus. And so it is, still, for Native America generally. Tracking a musical narrative beginning with Dvořák, the festival exposed a self-critical, self-confrontational United States that feels newly inchoate. In Dvořák's day, America rhymed with Thomas Jefferson's Enlightenment philosophy of brotherhood and equality; with a buoyant and sanitized national epic, Longfellow's *The Song of Hiawatha*, still resilient in 1900; with the religious message of Manifest Destiny imparted by Frederic Church's megalandscapes; with Walt Whitman's democratic paeans. Today Jefferson and even Whitman are impugned for racial insensitivity, and Longfellow and Church are irrelevant. New candidates for the American cultural pantheon await in the wings: that Frederick Douglass and W. E. B. Du Bois are iconic Americans is unarguable. Both, of course, are militant, confrontational personalities who probe American fissures. It bears mentioning, as well, that both happened to be devotees of Old World culture—Shakespeare and Wagner, for them, did not occupy alien terrain.

But what of the formidable, formidably wronged Crazy Horse? With Black America, the question "Whose America?" is at least on the table.

Porgy and Dvořák's Prophecy

Dvořák's prophecy lists no fewer than nine adjectives for the sorrow songs; he foresaw a musical idiom, inspired by Black America, ranging "great and noble" from tragedy to exaltation. By this criterion, Gershwin fully melded symphony and opera with the legacy of the cotton fields. When Shostakovich called *Porgy and Bess* "as great as *Boris Godunov*," he was probably thinking of native roots and usable pasts. It is Gershwin who amasses a full gamut of "negro melodies": from Charleston and Folly Island, from Harlem and Broadway. The street cries of his vendors, the superimposed spirituals in the hurricane scene, Serena's wailing "Dr. Jesus" prayer, her great lament for Robbins, Porgy's yearning for the absent Bess—all this and more derives from the songs Dvořák heard and Du Bois extolled as "the most beautiful expression of human experience born this side the seas." In fact, the entire opera adapts a template of sorrow and redemption, culminating with a great Gershwin spiritual: "Oh Lawd, I'm on My Way."

Assuredly, *Porgy and Bess* is not as "finished" as *The Marriage of Figaro*. If its instances of crude transition or stylistic inconsistency are obvious enough, it far surpasses the first operas of just about anyone else. What is more, unfinished—as I have stressed throughout this narrative—can mean self-directed, even self-invented. In Gershwin's case, his opera is a product of unsystematic but assiduous self-guided instruction. Its eclectic amalgam of originality and emulation is egalitarian. It equally absorbs the unschooled oral counterpoint of Gullah shouts (in the hurricane scene, with its simultaneous songs) and the specific fugal techniques of Berg's *Wozzeck* (in the crap game, with its melodic palindrome). Its particular recourse to a lullaby, a mock sermon, and an out-of-tune upright piano also evidences close study of Berg's score. The ingenious application of leitmotifs to "O Lawd, I'm on My Way"—the way Gershwin's orchestra summarizes the heartbreak and courage of Porgy's journey to manhood—is Wagnerian, as are the subtle relationships binding variants of Porgy's theme, manipulated to convey both suffering (a blue minor third crippled by a mashed grace note) and the underlying wholeness of his nature (a primal fifth, used down or up). Gershwin truly said of *Porgy and Bess* that "it brings to the operatic form elements that have never appeared in opera. . . . If, in doing this, I have created a new form . . . , this new form has come quite naturally out of the material."

The same American trope of the "unfinished," I have argued, links to a largesse of personal and creative experience. Gershwin's 1918 contract with T. P. Harms, the starting point of his composer's career, plunged him toward a wide variety of popular styles—as well as fame and fortune in his mid-twenties. Previously, aiming elsewhere, he chose a classical piano teacher, Charles Hambitzer, whom he knew would not object to "ragging the classics." This self-made odyssey aligns with Melville and the South Seas, with Whitman and Washington's Civil War hospitals, with Dvořák and Iowa pastures and porches. Ives said of his insurance job, once cited as certain evidence of confusion or indecision, that it sealed his relationship to the "average man." *

No less than Ives was Gershwin demeaned as an interloping dilettante. And of course there are voices who argued that any such appropriation of Black music into the white milieu of the concert hall inherently sanitized and delimited it. Was Dvořák's prophecy therefore bad advice? A wrong turn?

---

* See page 93.

Summing Up

A New Paradigm—The Paradigm Summarized—
Dvořák's Prophecy

A New Paradigm

I t is now more than four decades since I quit my music critic's job at the *New York Times* determined to figure out why classical music in America remained a Eurocentric subsidiary. The central fact, I knew, was that American composers had failed to supply an American repertoire of sufficient size and variety to secure the "native school" Dvořák had foreseen in the decades before World War I. Seeking to account for a "mutant musical high culture," I scrutinized the past and found in the late Gilded Age a robust phase of dramatic growth I had not realized existed—followed by a more quiescent twentieth-century "culture of performance" in which composers played a secondary role. I also documented a bifurcation of musical experience—high and low—more pronounced than in the European parent culture.

My various historical accounts—chiefly *Understanding Toscanini: How He Became an American Culture-God and Helped Create a New Audience for Old Music*; *Wagner Nights: An American History*; and *Classical Music in America: A History of Its Rise and Fall*—were not without culprits of a sort. One was Arthur Judson, the managerial powerbroker who decided that audiences, not cultural leaders, should shape taste. Another was David Sarnoff, whose "music appreciation" empire prioritized European masterpieces and their proponents—in particular, the conductor Arturo Toscanini, who was both an agent and a tool. But the currents of change at the same time seemed ineluctable. The new middle classes, with their vague cultural aspirations, comprised a sociological factor. New technologies facilitating the manipulation of taste comprised another. And the United States was and is a young, polyglot nation; it was incompletely prepared to capitalize on nineteenth-century cultural nationalism.

America's interwar composers figured in my accounts more as victims than as conspirators. That at heart they were primarily modernists, aloof from the new, democratized audience, seemed to me an inescapable aesthetic current contributing to their relative insignificance. In *Classical Music in America*, I appointed Ives and Gershwin the twin creative geniuses of American classical music—both ineffectually situated outside the mainstream. The most prominent and influential American concert composer—Aaron Copland—seemed to me a lesser talent who in his understandable eagerness to redirect new listeners toward American works compromised his modernist prowess, producing instead an American style at times verging on kitsch.

The present meditation began with a review for the *Wall Street Journal* of certain writings by Virgil Thomson in which a false history of American music decreed a useless condition of pastlessness. I concurrently encountered an environment of political rectitude that can interfere with the proper pursuit and appreciation of history, rendering the past increasingly irrelevant. I proceeded to extol the uses of nostalgia and explored how Mark Twain and Charles Ives comparably used the past. This strategy intertwined musical and literary narratives. It also stressed the potency not of shifting aesthetic currents, but of permanent vernacular resources.

The resulting book has taken me to some places I anticipated and others I did not. I had not initially envisioned proposing a second American music narrative to supplement the institutional history I have long pursued: an unfulfilled composers' narrative keying on the American Dvořák and his espousal of the sorrow songs of Black slaves. And I did

not at first realize that an inquiry into the pastlessness of American classical music—showing how Copland, Thomson, and Leonard Bernstein
had failed to identify pertinent forebears—would invite comparison
with the quest for a "usable" literary past famously undertaken by Van
Wyck Brooks and other gifted literary historians conspicuously unpart-
nered by scholarly historians of American music.

Once I absorbed that Brooks's quest had been both serious and productive, many things snapped into place. If American writers, artists,
and architects can today cite a long and continuous lineage of relevant
precursors, it is (I have argued) not solely because they enjoyed an earlier start than did American composers. In the decades of Ernest Hemingway, William Faulkner, and Frank Lloyd Wright, American music
split in two—with classical music coming up short. Jazz drew on a profound inheritance of "negro melodies." Concert composers decided to
start anew. Copland and Harris were not to be compared with Faulkner,
Hemingway, or Wright as world creative figures. Gershwin, who mattered greatly abroad, was a limbo figure—and yet rooted in the same
past as Duke Ellington and Louis Armstrong.

In retrospect, the standard narrative proved self-evidently defec-
tive. Copland, Thomson, and Bernstein anticipated that the newfound
"maturity" of the come-of-age composers would anchor a native repertoire to come—a consolidated American school generating symphonies and operas for American orchestras and opera companies. With its
emphasis on craftsmanship and pedigree, the come-of-age precedent,
pursued by such skilled practitioners as Copland and Bernstein, Samuel Barber and William Schuman, catalyzed a subsequent generation of
high modernists, of whom Elliott Carter was the most performed and
admired. Then, quite suddenly, the entire exercise was effaced by a coun-
terrevolution of minimalists and globalists: a succession of younger, ever
more promiscuous composers transgressing boundaries once erected
to ensure premium quality. The nascent American school glimpsed by
Copland quietly shrank and expired.

My *Classical Music in America* challenged the standard narrative, but without attempting a replacement. Rather, I discerned by 1950 "at least four distinct streams of music, all of which achieved substantial results and none of which reached fruition." First there was "a variegated pre-1920 bunch." Then came Aaron Copland's come-of-age composers and, alongside, Henry Cowell and the "ultramoderns." George Gershwin was the first and best of a series of interlopers who moved in and out of popular realms. That these four streams, I wrote, did not intersect "points to a pervasive fragmentation, to an absence of lineage and continuity complicated by a late start and heterogeneous population, by two world wars and the confusing influx of powerful refugees" —and, I would now add, by a failure of historical memory. The new paradigm here proposed would connect some dots, however far apart, with Dvořák's prophecy furnishing a central impetus. Proximity to the vernacular is one dominant feature. An American trope of the "unfinished," self-created artist is another, mirroring a larger cultural-political New World reality.

And so I have extrapolated a crippled spine of American classical music, one less continuous than what Copland and Thomson began, *tabula rasa*, in the 1920s. It favors Dvořák and the notion that American composers would prioritize a vernacular legacy. It continues with Ives and his absorption of American tunes of every stripe. And it connects, in a later period, to *Porgy and Bess*. Filling in the blanks, it ranges to William Billings and hymn tunes, to sorrow songs and minstrelsy, to Louis Moreau Gottschalk and William Henry Fry. It incorporates such prejazz limbo composers as Scott Joplin and Harry Burleigh, and also Black symphonic composers such as Samuel Coleridge-Taylor, William Dawson, and Florence Price. Hugging the high/low schism, it does not shun the amalgamation of a "Black Virtuoso Tradition" ranging from Dvořák's G-flat Humoresque to Art Tatum's "Humoresque." It treats Aaron Copland, his colleagues, and his high-modernist progeny, as a formidable side trip—an ascent to ever higher climes not without conquests, but more circumscribed and short-lived than its proponents could possibly have imagined. Gershwin's opera and William Dawson's symphony are but two of the high achievements falling outside Copland's circle of influence and rapport. Hollywood's supreme composer, Bernard Herrmann, also left a concert catalogue—including a string quartet, a clarinet quintet, a *Psycho* "narrative," a symphony, and a cantata—that bears comparison with the output of East Coast composers (not excluding Copland) whose self-esteem he seethingly resented.*

Expanding the parameters of the standard narrative, the new paradigm proposes a more porous line between highbrow and popular expression. "Classical music" was influentially defined by the Boston critic John Sullivan Dwight as the highest stratum of musical expression. That was during the mid nineteenth century, when American music was a melee seeking stratification and organization. After World War I, the classical stratum consolidated, then calcified: a cul-de-sac. Today, "classical music" refers to a bygone moment. What has taken its place? For some time, I have used the term "postclassical" to frame a wide terrain within which many types of music comingle. Its landmarks include Steve Reich's *Music for 18 Musicians* and *Einstein on the Beach* by Philip Glass, both premiered in 1976. Its supreme harbinger was Lou Harrison, a self-created synergist of East and West whose time will come. Neither the standard narrative nor the new paradigm connects to all of that. But the paradigm cuts a broader swath. It more productively uses the past. It properly credits Ives and Gershwin. It segues to today's transgressional strategies of renewal. And it suggests a narrative, however interrupted and truncated, that aligns with the most protean, most capacious currents of American culture and experience.

* I would call Herrmann the most underrated twentieth-century American composer. Listeners new to his concert output should start with the intoxicating 1967 clarinet quintet, *Souvenirs de Voyage*. When the long first movement's hypnotic *molto tranquillo* beginning returns at the close, we feel we have journeyed somewhere, even if that makes no ultimate difference in a world of sadness and remembrance. Herrmann once confessed, "My feelings and yearnings are those of a composer of the nineteenth century. I am completely out of step with the present." His favorite composers, an unfashionable twentieth-century list, included Debussy, Ravel, Elgar, Delius, Holst, and Ives.

THE WESTERN CLASSICAL music tradition is formidably Germanic—and German classical music is formidably consumed by an awareness of lineage. In the twentieth century, Gustav Mahler's reverence for Richard Wagner, and the humility with which Arnold Schoenberg regarded Mahler, were necessary resources of empowerment. "I am now really truly yours," Schoenberg wrote to Mahler upon hearing the latter's Seventh Symphony. "To express very clearly one thing that I principally felt: I reacted to you as a classic. But one who is still a *model* to me." He also wrote: "It is my ambition to become as pure as yourself, since it is not permitted to me to be so great." The letters are signed "With very cordial regards and deep veneration" and "With affectionate veneration and devotion." Mahler the father figure enabled Schoenberg to position himself in the German pantheon. Exiled in the United States, Schoenberg never acquired an American disciple remotely as significant as his Old World pupils Alban Berg and Anton Webern.

The first stirrings of the Germanic lineage Schoenberg revered began in the Renaissance. More pertinent to the American musical experience is Russia—like the United States, musically colonized by Europeans during the eighteenth and nineteenth centuries. Russia's own composers, like America's, naturally began by emulating European models (but these works, of which Glinka's *Trio pathétique* is an excellent example, were not therefore discarded). Russian-sounding composers followed in profusion: a lineage was born. Concomitantly, Russian traditions of performance materialized, based in Russian repertoire and language. Not least significant were musical settings of classic Russian texts. The composers were also teachers, bulwarks of important pedagogical institutions linked in turn to important institutions of performance.

The institutional memory of today's Mariinsky Theatre is curated by its presiding artistic leader, Valery Gergiev. Gergiev has prioritized reviving operas by Glinka, Mussorgsky, and Rimski-Korsakov that helped to shape the Mariinsky's 150-year history. That Verdi's *La forza del destino* was first given in St. Petersburg, that Berlioz twice visited St. Petersburg and left a profound impression are events that matter to Gergiev's way of using the past. He has also mounted and remounted major retrospectives of Stravinsky, Prokofiev, and Shostakovich, filling in the blanks for compositions that were ignored, proscribed, or forgotten.

No comparable exercise has ever been undertaken by the Metropolitan Opera. The New York Philharmonic has not honored its great formative conductors Theodore Thomas and Anton Seidl. That the Boston Symphony and Philadelphia Orchestra once regularly premiered the new works of George Chadwick and Edgard Varèse, that Boston enjoyed a historic relationship with Igor Stravinsky via Serge Koussevitzky and Harvard University are chapters in the American musical past mainly unknown to the very institutions that once wrote them. That cultural institutions exert enormous influence on how the past is perceived was last a pervasive priority for American orchestras in their early heyday, promulgated by the likes of Thomas and Seidl; both tirelessly and inquisitively espoused new music of consequence. In recent decades, Michael Tilson Thomas, in San Francisco, has systematically celebrated a "maverick" strain in American musical life. Esa-Pekka Salonen, in Los Angeles, tenaciously sought a usable local past and came up big with Bernard Herrmann and Silvestre Revueltas, and the underexplored L.A. sojourns of Schoenberg and Stravinsky. But nothing of the kind has occurred in Chicago, Cleveland, Philadelphia, Pittsburgh, New York,* Boston—cities whose art museums, I am sure, regularly scrutinize the American cultural narrative. †

---

* I here of course refer to the New York Philharmonic. Leon Botstein's New York–based American Symphony Orchestra, like my own PostClassical Ensemble in Washington, D.C., exercises a fundamentally curatorial mission, albeit on the margins of American symphonic culture. The same was true of the Brooklyn Philharmonic in the 1990s.

† In early 2018, the Metropolitan Museum of Art produced and presented an exhibit entitled "Thomas Cole's Journey: Atlantic Crossings." Cole was the teacher of the most prominent, most influential postbellum American painter: Frederic Church. You cannot grasp Gilded Age America without referencing Church. The same is true for *The Song of Hiawatha* and Dvořák's *New World* Symphony: they are essential reference points for understanding how Americans viewed themselves before the turn of the twentieth century. In a splendid video presentation that introduced the Met exhibit, Cole was called "a torchbearer who created a defining aesthetic" for the New World. Thanks to Cole and

Even with the strictures and interruptions imposed by Soviet aesthetics, Russian music retained contact with folk roots and forebears. The United States, by comparison, was not even able to consolidate a tradition of opera in the vernacular—a fundamental precondition to a native operatic canon. Russian composers fed on Pushkin, Tolstoy, Dostoyevsky, Gogol; they turned *Boris Godunov, Queen of Spades, Eugene Onegin, War and Peace, The Gambler,* and *The Nose* into notable operas. The most eloquent musical settings of Melville and Whitman are British: Benjamin Britten's *Billy Budd*, Frederick Delius's *Sea Drift*.

CHARLES IVES AND George Gershwin, I have proposed, are composers steeped in an American past both varied and sustained. One way or another, they connect to the sorrow songs and to minstrelsy, to slavery and ragtime, to Huck Finn, *Moby-Dick*, and *Leaves of Grass*.

If at first glance Ives and Gershwin make strange bedfellows, look again. To begin with: as one learns from a 1934 Gershwin letter, he was powerfully drawn to the music of Ives long before others discovered

---

Church, landscape became the defining American genre for visual art. Including major works by Turner and Constable, the exhibit dramatized how the European landscape masters that Cole revered inspired epic canvases of mountains and plains inhabited not by peasants and farmers, but—a transformational ingredient—by ceremonial Native Americans. This achievement, clinched by Church, parallels the achievements of Mark Twain and Charles Ives, who likewise transformed hallowed Old World genres into something New. Created by Elizabeth Kornhauser, the museum's curator of American paintings and sculpture, the exhibit linked to nine exhibition tours, two concerts, and various other presentations—in addition to a major publication: *Thomas Cole's Journey: Atlantic Crossings,* which "breaks new ground by presenting British-born American painter Thomas Cole as an international figure in direct dialogue with the major landscape painters of the age." Personally, I would never call Cole a "great painter" (Church is another matter). But he is a great and necessary figure in the history of American painting.

Were an orchestra to do something similar, it might be a contextualized presentation of the symphonies of John Knowles Paine (1875, 1879)—crucial progenitors of the American-sounding Second and Third Symphonies of George Chadwick en route to Ives. I would not call Paine a "great composer." But he is a great and necessary figure in the history of American classical music. American orchestras do not even know him.

it. He tried without success to meet Ives. A related note in Ives's hand, responding to news from an acquaintance, reads: "G said my music has been a help to him—had known it from several years back. . . . Gershwin said he had gotten more out of my music than of any other[,] especially new chords and new rhythms and that he wants to ask about more copies etc." And Gershwin's access to the vernacular could not have been irrelevant. The ramifications are manifold.

The second chapter of this book extolled the uses of nostalgia: James Gibbons Huneker, William J. Henderson, and Henry Edward Krehbiel as exemplars of a species of retrospection compatible with progressive thought. Chapter 3 proposed Ives and Mark Twain as agents of "subversive nostalgia." Using nostalgia is one way of using the past.

After World War I, nostalgia fell into sharp disfavor. Even when looking back—upon cowboys or farmers or Shakers—Aaron Copland and Virgil Thomson do not wax nostalgic. The most telling contemporaneous counterexample I can think of occurs in *Porgy and Bess*:

> Summertime an' the livin' is easy
> Fish are jumpin' an the cotton is high
> Oh yo' daddy's rich, an' yo' ma is good-lookin',
> So hush, little baby, don' yo' cry.

Gershwin's immortal lullaby, to words by DuBose Heyward, was inspired by the Edenic opening sentence of Heyward's novella *Porgy*: "Porgy lived in the Golden Age." Musically, it affectionately absorbs the sorrow songs and jazz. It cadences on an operatic high B.* The influence of Marie's lullaby from Alban Berg's *Wozzeck* is tangible. Gershwin himself called "Summertime" cantorial. Perhaps cantors have actually sung it—in any case, Billie Holiday, Ella Fitzgerald, and Leontyne Price all did.

---

* An interpolation—the original score has Clara descend to B an octave lower. But no one sings "Summertime" that way anymore.

Like Mark Twain's Mississippi wharf and Charles Ives's Connecticut porch, Gershwin's Catfish Row is here a site of remembered premodern innocence. As with Twain and Ives, it invites seasoned vernacular speech and song. As with Twain and Ives, it contributes to a range and depth of feeling and experience. The paradisal nostalgia of "Summertime" is a necessary preamble to the fall-and-resurrection parable to come.

I have suggested that the core attribute of American classical music is a confluence of Old World and New incorporating American vernacular voices. That "Summertime" is steeped in a multifarious past is an American trait, an Ivesian trait. "Summertime" is also—as in Ives—a high/low synthesis: an aria and a nightclub song. *Wozzeck* infiltrates the whole of *Porgy and Bess*. So do *Carmen* and *Die Meistersinger*—and Broadway and Hollywood, Tin Pan Alley and Folly Island. No less than Ives—no less than Mark Twain or Walt Whitman or Herman Melville— Gershwin resolves the schism of "highbrow" and "lowbrow" that Van Wyck Brooks in 1915 claimed was a fundamental barrier to American artistic distinction. Mark Twain's Jim uses Mississippi River metaphors to philosophize about the human condition. Melville's sailors combine Shakespearean rhetoric with South Seas praxis. Whitman's democratic "I" is in equal parts worldly and mundane. Ives's symphonies merge Beethoven with "Old Back Joe." And *Porgy and Bess* applies Old World models to a gamut of New World styles and experiences. No less than Huck, Porgy speaks through, not of, the popular.

I have applied the trope of the "unfinished" to Twain, Whitman, and Melville, to Ives and Gershwin. The ragged edges of *Huckleberry Finn* or *Moby-Dick* or *Leaves of Grass* or the *Concord* Sonata—the inconsistencies of tone, the vagaries of structure—are "American": unbridled. Whitman swims between poetry and narrative prose. Melville intermingles fiction, reportage, and the stage (*Moby-Dick* even incorporates stage directions). Huck's vernacular voice broaches the national battleground of morality and race. Ives's symphonies and sonatas likewise find a new sphere. So does Gershwin's unclassifiable opera. Without brandishing the twentieth-century criterion of originality, Ives and

Gershwin achieve an originality as valid as that of any American modernist composer.

The trope of the uncategorizable and "unfinished" provokes the same cross-disciplinary critique. When R. P. Blackmur complains that *Moby-Dick* fails to "establish direction," when Newton Arvin contends that Melville cannot sustain "the mentality of the professional," they could equally be complaining about Twain, Whitman, Ives, or Gershwin. And these complaints, however disproportionate or obtuse, are not without merit. Ultimately, what most matters about America's iconic unfinished masterpieces—what most justifies their "immaturity"—is that America is itself unfinished. Ralph Ellison put it this way:

> The major ideas of our society [are] grounded [in] a body of assumptions about human possibility which is shared by all Americans—even those who resist most violently any attempt to embody them in social action. Indeed, these assumptions have been questioned and resisted from the very beginning, for man cannot simply say, "Let us have liberty and justice and equality for all," and have it; and a democracy more than any other system is always pregnant with its contradiction.

Ellison also wrote:

> American culture is ... the product of a process which was in motion even before the founding of this nation, and it began with the interaction between Englishmen, Europeans, and Africans and American geography. When our society was established this "natural" process of Americanization continued in its own unobserved fashion, defying the social, aesthetic, and political assumptions of our political leaders and tastemakers alike.

For Ellison, the contradictions between American ideals and realities, articulated in "critical and morally affirmative novels" before World War

I, were ignored by a later generation of morally diffident, stylistically experimental writers. As I have earlier noted, he endorsed the vernacular as "our most characteristic American style," by which "the high styles of the past are democratized." The vernacular is wholesome, subversive:

> Ironically it was the vernacular which gave expression to that new-
> ness of spirit and outlook of which the leaders of the nation liked to
> boast. Such Founding Fathers as Franklin and Webster feared the
> linguistic vernacular as a disruptive influence and sought to dis-
> courage it, but fortunately they failed. For otherwise there would
> have been no Mark Twain.

An American "morality of craftsmanship" in pursuit of perfection of style and form, for Ellison, not only sidesteps the conundrum of America; it sacrifices truth and integrity. He rather espouses a methodology of "play-it-by-eye-and-ear improvisations" to "merge" the vernacular with "the most refined styles from the past." This is the very methodology of the "unfinished" in the *Concord* Sonata and *Porgy and Bess*.

Ellison names Mark Twain, Walt Whitman, and Herman Melville as writers who anoint "the Negro as a symbol of man." So it is, as well, when Ives evokes the stoic endurance of Colonel Shaw's Black Civil War regiment, or when Gershwin's Porgy surmounts hardship and betrayal to attain an ecumenical pulpit. *Porgy and Bess* verily embodies the "vernacular as a disruptive influence," shunned alike by the Founding Fathers and by the self-appointed founders of American classical music.

If the forebears of the late-nineteenth-century writers admired by Ellison prominently include the Transcendentalists, Antonín Dvořák was assuredly a precursor of the fractured American musical lineage of which Ives and Gershwin are part. Porgy at length discovers the "long, long road" to "a Heavn'ly Land." But Gershwin notwithstanding, Dvořák's was mainly a long road not taken. A shorter road—a road without a past—was pursued. The modernists were Oedipal. They mistrusted the vernacular. They hastily invented a pastless musical history. Inconveniently, the interwar American composer of genius was an outsider. A fixation on European pedigree penalized him for an alleged insufficiency of professional training. The sorrow songs he beautifully and ingeniously appropriated were meanwhile undervalued by American concert composers in favor of white spirituals. Concurrently, institutions of performance—opera companies—shunned potential Black participants, even those who enjoyed major international careers. Henry Krehbiel's admonitions of 1914, rebuking Boston's music journalists, long retained pertinence—that Dvořák's "aims . . . called out a clamor from one class of critics which disclosed nothing so much as their . . . ungenerous and illiberal attitude toward a body of American citizens to whom at the least must be credited the creation of a species of song in which an undeniably great composer had recognized artistic potentialities thitherto neglected, if not unsuspected, in the land of its origin."

Did Dvořák really inhabit the "kindergarten" period of American classical music? Was Gershwin the equivalent of "high school"? Was the post–World War I generation of American composers pivotal? Today's American classical music of most consequence has nothing to do with the interwar pursuit of the Great American Symphony. Composers like Lou Harrison, Philip Glass, Steve Reich, and John Adams have no precise American musical precursors. Rather they embody American confluence, drawing on vernacular and popular sources as far afield as Javanese gamelan, West African drumming, Indian ragas, and the Benny Goodman Band.

What if Gershwin had lived as long as Aaron Copland? Would he have composed the violin concerto Jascha Heifetz sought from him? The string quartet he was mulling when he died? A body of musical theater building on his historic first opera? What if William Dawson had been permitted to pursue his evident vocation as a consequential Black symphonist? To explore his aspirations to conduct? We will never know.

The Paradigm Summarized

In sum: the new paradigm for American classical music that I have proposed may be extrapolated as a series of musical threads. Due in part to a failure of historical memory, the threads remained separate rather than knit.

The first American composer of world consequence was Louis Moreau Gottschalk, whose roots included Black Creole music. The thread he begins may be called "Black." It includes enduring piano works and an important "symphony": *Night in the Tropics* (1858).

Gottschalk notwithstanding, American music of the second half of the nineteenth century was predominantly "German" in style. Here, the first symphonist of high polish and individuality was John Knowles Paine. Paine inspired a second such symphonist whose music (like Gottschalk's, unlike Paine's) sounds "American": George Chadwick. Chadwick's peak achievement may be *Jubilee* (1895). The scherzos of his Second and Third Symphonies (1885, 1894) are notable creations in the same American vein. Edward MacDowell and George Templeton Strong are "German" high Romantics, Strong's *Sintram* Symphony (1888) being an American symphony in something like the heroic Liszt/Wagner/Bruckner mold.

Antonin Dvořák, a pivotal figure in this narrative, singularly consolidates the Black and German threads and adds a third: "Indian." Dvořák's American style embraces a multiplicity of compositions, some of which remain remarkably little known. His once-influential engagement with African-American and Native American sources deserves to be remembered as an act of empathy.

Post-Dvořák, the German thread produced its highest embodiment in Charles Ives. An important German sequel to Ives is Carl Ruggles. The Indian thread led to Arthur Farwell, a still-forgotten American original, and Ferruccio Busoni, whose *Indian* Fantasy (1914) is an American piano concerto we should know. A composer who doesn't fit is Charles Griffes, who died young on the cusp of maturity. His Piano Sonata (1918) is ignited by a passion for Scriabin; his *Two Sketches on Indian Themes* belongs to the Indianist movement spearheaded by Farwell.

After World War I comes a French/modernist thread: the Boulangerie and its progeny. The main names include Aaron Copland, Virgil Thomson, and Roy Harris. This come-of-age generation, also including Samuel Barber, denied the pertinence of prior American music. Leonard Bernstein is and is not part of this picture.

The Black thread, meanwhile, was embroidered by Scott Joplin and by Dvořák's onetime assistant Harry Burleigh. A "Dvořák school," fostered by Dvořák's prophecy, included the Black British composer Samuel Coleridge-Taylor and the African Americans Nathaniel Dett, William Dawson, William Grant Still, Florence Price, and Margaret Bonds. Their peak achievement may be Dawson's *Negro Folk Symphony* (1934). George Gershwin was a master practitioner of the Black thread. The many other pertinent white composers include Bernstein and such eager Europeans as Ravel and Milhaud.

A keyboard outgrowth of the Black thread is what I call a Black Virtuoso Tradition in which American popular and classical music, Black and white, for once found common ground. Its many inspired exponents included Gottschalk, Dvořák, Joplin, Gershwin, Bernstein, and William Bolcom; also James P. Johnson, Jelly Roll Morton, Fats Waller— and Art Tatum, whose "Humoresque" circles back to Dvořák's classic G-flat major Humoresque (1894).

More broadly considered, Gershwin is an Interloper—had he not died in 1937, he would have been the most likely candidate to ameliorate the bifurcation of American music. In the realm of musical theater, other Interlopers of note include Kurt Weill, Marc Blitzstein, and Bernstein again—composers whose *Street Scene* (1946), *Regina* (1949), and *West Side Story* (1957) do not, however, rise to the level of *Porgy and Bess* (1935). In the realm of American cinema, the most notable Interloper is Bernard Herrmann.

After 1950, classical music in America acquired a gathering global thread. A pioneer figure was Lou Harrison, whose Concerto for Violin and Percussion (1959) and Piano Concerto (1985) are high American achievements as yet little heard. His notable precursors, lesser composers, included Henry Cowell and Colin McPhee. After Harrison come Steve Reich and Philip Glass, both of whom like Harrison turn East for inspiration. Their contemporary John Adams is a composer of exceptional promiscuous range. Concurrently, evolving musical synergies have produced what I call "postclassical music," finally superseding the high/low and Western/Eastern schisms of the past.

Though the French/Modernist thread was once widely perceived as a crowning achievement, in retrospect its priority cannot be substantiated. Its advocates, who undervalued the vernacular, misread Ives and Gershwin. Such early Ives as "Feldeinsamkeit" and the Symphony No. 2 disclose a foundation of craftsmanship. Similarly, *An American in Paris* (1928)—in which a big tune, variously deployed, directs an organic trajectory—defies the onetime marginalization of Gershwin as a mass producer of "pops" confections. A comparable next-door composer, likewise a born populist once marginalized, was the Mexican Silvestre Revueltas.

The multifarious New World classical-music tapestry thus adduced richly intersects with American literature and visual art. It peaks, I have argued, where the act of memory peaks. It is the weighty presence of the past, artfully conveyed, that seals the dimensionality of Huck Finn's bardic adventures, of Faulkner's cursed and haunted Yoknapatawpha County, of Gershwin's biblical Catfish Row, of Toni Morrison's mythic *Beloved*—and also of Dvořák's yearning Largo, or the Lento of his *American* Quartet in which Nathaniel Dett heard the long-ago voice of his grandmother. In Ives, the regional past is, again, protean, even cosmic. In *Moby-Dick*, the past is ultimately primordial.

Toni Morrison, in *Playing in the Dark: Whiteness and the Literary Imagination* (1990), embraces writers willing "to project consciously into the danger zones [that] others may represent." She mentions Dostoyevsky's "compelling intimacy" with the tormented, tormenting Svidrigailov in *Crime and Punishment*. She is "in awe of the authority of Faulkner's Benjy," whose deranged narration so tellingly begins *The Sound and the Fury*. She endorses "entering what one is estranged from . . . into corners of the consciousness held off and away from the reach of the writer's imagination"—as when, knowingly or unwittingly, a white writer broaches the African American experience. It is "one of the most furtively radical impinging forces on the country's literature. The contemplation of this black presence is central to any understanding of our national literature and should not be permitted to hover at the margins of the literary imagination."

For me, a white listener, Charles Ives's musical rumination on Colonel Shaw's Black regiment—stoic, inscrutable, dispersing particles of national and racial memory, an embattled freedom march eschewing trumpets and drums—"compels intimacy" of this kind.* So does Ives's fractured, visionary "Emerson." So, if his grave physical disability is truthfully presented, does Gershwin's Porgy.

The American artistic trope to which Faulkner, Ives, and Gershwin belong, I have suggested, is the self-created, unfinished genius for whom creative improvisation—as in the sorrow songs and the blues—is a necessary means of expression. It reveals an empowering susceptibility to the "American Africanism" Morrison extols. What was Ives thinking when he interpolated "Old Black Joe" into the finale of his Second Symphony? Why did Gershwin choose a story about African Americans for his opera? Morrison would have us believe that the reasons were not wholly conscious, that the Black experience impinged "furtively," "radically," inescapably. That sounds right to me, so pregnant and formative is our Black musical inheritance.

Aaron Copland's Piano Variations, which I am not alone in considering his highest compositional achievement, is a taut modernist credo the musical sinews of which are flexed—agitated or relaxed—by a subliminal jazz influence. Copland's warning of the "severe limitations" of jazz as grist for "serious composers," of its self-restriction to "only two

* See page 65.

expressions," records conscious awareness, not actual practice. Earlier in this account, I have written: "An aversion to jazz, less virulent abroad, became a defining feature of the interwar musical high culture of the United States." As we have seen, Roy Harris went so far as to counsel Copland: "A word of warning to you—dear brother Aaron . . . Don't disappoint us with jazz." Whence this trepidation?

"In the scholarship on the formation of an American character and the production of a national literature, a number of items have been catalogued," Morrison writes. "A major item to be added to the list must be an Africanist presence—decidedly not American, decidedly other." "Canonical American literature," she elsewhere says, "is begging for such attention."

Reframing American classical music is part of a larger, ongoing project reframing the American experience.

Dvořák's Prophecy

One hundred twenty-five years have now elapsed since Dvořák prophesied that "negro melodies" would foster a "great and noble" canon of American symphonies, concertos, art songs, and operas. What are we to make of his prophecy today?

Culling the past, I reprise a pertinent vignette from early on in this narrative—that when Dvořák conducted a Black chorus and an interracial orchestra at the Madison Square Garden concert hall on January 23, 1894, his soloists were Harry Burleigh and Sissieretta Jones, the latter being the celebrated African-American soprano known as the "Black Patti." Jones took part in Dvořák's new arrangement of Stephen Foster's "Old Folks at Home." She also sang the "Inflammatus" from Rossini's *Stabat Mater* and an aria from Meyerbeer's *Les Huguenots*. Her repertoire, while mainly American, also included some Verdi and Gounod. She sang for four presidents. The highest-paid African-American performer of her day, she achieved international acclaim before retiring in 1915. But the Black Patti could not sing on white American opera stages.* Dvořák's prophecy was aborted.

Decades later, Gershwin's 1935 *Porgy and Bess* cast included Ruby Elzy, who succumbed to a botched operation for a benign tumor in 1943 at the age of thirty-five. Elzy's broadcast performance of "My Man's Gone Now" at the Hollywood Bowl Gershwin Memorial Concert documents a silvery soprano combining the bluesy pathos of a Billie Holiday with the stratospheric high B's of a Leontyne Price. When she died, Elzy was preparing to sing Aida with the National Negro Opera Company—which in the 1940s successfully mounted *Aida*, *La traviata*, and *Carmen*. Lillian Evanti, the company's Violetta, also sang opera in Paris, Genoa, Naples, and Milan. Giulio Gatti-Casazza had hoped to engage her at the Metropolitan, but not even an audition proved feasible.

Dvořák, in America, was widely perceived as a *naïf*. The justice of that claim, it turns out, had nothing to do with musical aptitude; rather, he was naïve about human nature and the American experience. He appreciated that Washington's refusal to subsidize gifted composers, or institutions of musical instruction, would make it harder to implement an American classical music. But his sanguine temperament failed to reckon with insuperable barriers of race. Black music would make its own way.

That the "negro melodies" Dvořák endorsed for their beauty and

---

* At the same moment that Dvořák was teaching and conducting African-American composers, singers, and instrumentalists, Laura Langford, Brooklyn's most notable impresario, was bringing African-American orphans to the superb Brighton Beach childrens' matinee concerts presented by her Seidl Society with Anton Seidl conducting. These Seidl Society excursions also included the train ride, beach time, and lunch. An "inflexible" rule required Seidl Society members to accompany young "protégés." Tents with cots were furnished for tired bodies—as were milk, ice cream, chewing gum, and candy. The children also got to sing with the orchestra. A typical program (August 3, 1896) included music by Nicolai, Delibes, Humperdinck, Bizet, Auber, Wagner, and "America the Beautiful." A fearless and intrepid cultural philanthropist, Langford was impervious to pockets of resistance. (See Joseph Horowitz, *Moral Fire: Musical Portraits from America's Fin-de-Siècle* [2012], pp. 146–47.) This Brighton Beach vignette deserves to be juxtaposed with Arthur Judson's failure to promote Marian Anderson and the Metropolitan Opera's failure to engage African-American singers.

range of feeling might have generated a distinctive American classical music, deep in sentiment, varied in mood, broad in appeal, was demonstrated by George Gershwin. Logically, the same native music might have equally served Black concert composers, just as folk roots fostered national expression in the concert halls of countless other nations—except that America, finally, is not about equality.

Ultimately, American classical music suits America after all—its aspirant energies and chronic disappointments, its fundamental racial divides. Twentieth-century American classical music was an anomaly—a culture of performance that sidelined composers, that alienated audiences from the contemporary creative act. Something similar happened in Europe, where a couple of world calamities ruptured a lineage of high achievement. But, with deeper roots in place, the impact was less drastic. And racial bias was not a factor.

The new American classical-music paradigm I have here proposed, reaching into the past, treats the twentieth century as an aberration in an Ur-narrative. The modernist juggernaut, whatever its triumphs, elevated art to lonely heights. It cherished highbrow pedigrees. It also punished the past. The triumphs remain. But the punishments, whether inflicted by Van Wyck Brooks and Lewis Mumford, or by Alfred Barr's Museum of Modern Art, proved transient. It is time that the American musical pastlessness proclaimed by Virgil Thomson, Aaron Copland, and Leonard Bernstein also be put to rest.

If American classical music can process this tale—if our performers and institutions of performance, our conservatories, our agencies of philanthropy, can awaken to the moment at hand—classical music in America may yet acquire a vital future, at last buoyed and directed by a proper past.

Acknowledgments

I pursued an unusual route toward musical scholarship—via reviewing concerts for the *New York Times*, then running an orchestra at the Brooklyn Academy of Music. I remain deeply appreciative of the warm interest in my work (and tolerance of its idiosyncrasies) expressed early on by Dale Cockrell, Richard Crawford, Bob Freeman, Wayne Shirley, and the late Wiley Hitchcock. They fostered a climate of "inclusivity" before there was a name for it—and habits of tolerance and open discussion that have since eroded. In subsequent decades, Frank Candelaria and Mark Clague have been especially supportive—they are part of a brain trust of scholars who know more than I do about many things. Their assistance has been invaluable in writing *Dvořák's Prophecy*.

In the six films I have produced for Naxos in tandem with this book, a portion of my brain trust is on camera. I would especially like to express my gratitude to Kevin Deas and George Shirley. With Kevin, it has been my privilege to perform the spirituals of Harry Burleigh for more than a dozen years; in effect, we have discovered together a wondrous repertoire which Kevin sings with exceptional authority. George has been an indispensable source of wisdom. Having lived through decades during which the place of African American vocalists in opera and recital has evolved dramatically, both are intimate witnesses to history.

The *Dvořák's Prophecy* films are ingeniously "visualized" by my long-time colleague, the media artist Peter Bogdanoff. Peter's unusual gift for marrying music with the moving image has embellished countless projects I've undertaken, going all the way back to the Brooklyn Philharmonic's 1994 centenary celebration of the *New World* Symphony.

In 2003, I cofounded PostClassical Ensemble—an "experimental" chamber orchestra in Washington, DC—with the conductor Angel Gil-Ordóñez. The musical topics covered in *Dvořák's Prophecy* have generated countless cross-disciplinary PCE programs avidly embraced by Angel—new opportunities to explore new thoughts, for which I will always be grateful. Among our regular collaborators—an extraordinary list—Bill Alves, Roberto Kolb, Steve Mayer, Ben Pasternack, and Bill Sharp have immeasurably enhanced my appreciation of the music of Aaron Copland, Arthur Farwell, Charles Ives, Lou Harrison, and Silvestre Revueltas.

Klaus Heymann, the intrepid founder and mastermind of Naxos, has said *yes* to every project I have proposed, no matter how seemingly esoteric, over a period of fifteen years. In total, I've produced five CDs and nine DVDs for Naxos—including the six *Dvořák's Prophecy* films.

Pedro Carboné graciously created the *Dvořák's Prophecy* website for me. An early version of my *Dvořák's Prophecy* chapter on Ives and *Adventures of Huckleberry Finn* was published by *Raritan* in 2019. I have never worked with a more assiduous editor than Chris Freitag at W. W. Norton. My agent, Elizabeth Kaplan, and my wife and two children have all yet again managed to tolerate the self-absorption of an author writing a book.

Notes

Chapter One: Dvořák, American Music, and Race

1 **"They would sometimes"**: Frederick Douglass, *A Narrative of the Life of Frederick Douglass, an American Slave* (1845), chap. 2.

2 **"Little of beauty"**: W. E. B. Du Bois, *The Souls of Black Folk* (1903), chap. 14.

3 **"I think these gentlemen"**: Shelley Fisher Fishkin, *Was Huck Black?* (1993), p. 150.

4 **"No one was indifferent"**: Fishkin, *Was Huck Black?* pp. 4–5, 149–50.

6 **"negrophile"**: Joseph Horowitz, *Moral Fire: Musical Portraits from America's Fin-de-Siècle* (2012), p. 96.

6 **Krehbiel studied**: On Krehbiel and race, see Horowitz, *Moral Fire*, chap. 2.

7 **The New York discourse**: Horowitz, *Moral Fire*, chap. 2; Horowitz, *Classical Music in America*, pp. 8, 67–68. For an extensive sampling of critical responses to the *New World* Symphony, see Douglas Shadle, *Antonin Dvořák's New World Symphony* (2021).

7 **"I am now satisfied"**: *New York Herald*, May 21, 1893. Michael Beckerman has shown that the probable author of this article (and of Dvořák's quote, adapting his flawed English) was the yellow journalist James Creelman. See Beckerman, *New Worlds of Dvořák* (2003).

8 **"Is there a soul"**: *New York Age*, Dec. 24, 1908, p. 4 (an article authored by Jones herself).

9 **"By the time"**: Dale Cockrell, program essay for 2004 Nashville Symphony "Dvořák and America" festival (produced by Joseph Horowitz). See also Cockrell: *Demons of Disorder: Early Blackface Minstrels and Their World* (1997).

10 **As rendered by:** Wayne Shirley, "The Coming of 'Deep River,'" *American Music* 15, no. 4 (Winter 1997).

11 **"The plantation songs known":** This preface, signed "H.T.B. New York 1917," may be found in any volume of Burleigh spirituals.

12 **in concert, he sang:** Information courtesy of Burleigh biographer Jean Snyder.

13 **Decades later, in 1928:** Frederick Delius, Foreword to James Weldon Johnson, *Der weisse Neger, ein Leben zwischen den Rassen* [*The White Negro, A Life Between the Races*] (1928). See *Delius Society Journal*, no. 126 (1999).

14 **Nationally, the *Musical Courier*:** Doris Evans McGinty, "'That You Came So Far to See Us': Coleridge-Taylor in America," *Black Music Research Journal* 21, no. 2 (2001), pp. 197–234.

16 **"The question is":** *New York Times*, Feb. 11, 2018.

17 **"He came to America":** W. E. B. Du Bois, "The Immortal Child," in Du Bois, *Darkwater: Voices from Within the Veil* (1920).

19 **"Art addresses itself":** For Henderson and the reception history of *Porgy and Bess*, see Joseph Horowitz, *"On My Way": The Untold Story of Rouben Mamoulian, George Gershwin, and "Porgy and Bess"* (2013), pp. 138–51.

21 **sinks into obscurity:** Horowitz, *"On My Way,"* chap. 1.

23 **"intimate and original development":** Alain Locke, "The Negro Spirituals," in Locke, ed., *The New Negro* (1925).

24 **Pitting authenticity against assimilation:** Paul Allen Anderson, *Deep River: Music and Memory in Harlem Renaissance Thought* (2001).

24 **Toni Morrison's reservations:** Toni Morrison, "Re-Marking Twain," reprinted in *Adventures of Huckleberry Finn*, ed. Susan K. Harris (2000), p. 377.

25 **(as I had occasion):** Horowitz, *"On My Way."*

27 **Anderson's account:** Marian Anderson, *My Lord, What a Morning* (1956), p. 117.

Chapter Two: In Defense of Nostalgia

29 **"It is only natural":** James G. Huneker, *The New Cosmopolis* (1915), pp. 75–81.

30 **"a center for actors":** Huneker, *The New Cosmopolis*, p. 30; Arnold Schwab, *James Gibbons Huneker: Critic of the Seven Arts* (1963), pp. 21, 211, 77.

31 **"There gathered":** Huneker, *The New Cosmopolis*, p. 78.

32 **The prodigious Huneker rant:** Schwab, *Huneker*, p. 234.

32 **"Men [once] seemed":** Huneker, *The New Cosmopolis*, pp. 69, 81, 82.

33 **A sequel 1998 essay:** T. Jackson Lears, "Looking Backward: In Defense of Nostalgia," *Lingua Franca*, Dec. 1997.

35 "The worst [opera]": Horowitz, *Classical Music*, p. 199.

37 "for what seemed hours": Joseph Horowitz, *Wagner Nights: An American History* (1994), p. 215.

38 "To understand the story": Henry Krehbiel, *Chapters of Opera* (1908), p. 207.

42 "whoopings": Horowitz, *Classical Music*, pp. 7–10.

42 "In Europe there is room": Huneker, *The New Cosmopolis*, p. 70.

43 "It is a pity": Henry Krehbiel, *Afro-American Folksongs: A Study in Racial and National Music* (1914), p. 91.

43 "The most refined": Krehbiel, *Afro-American Folksongs*, p. 65.

44 "disprove the theory": Krehbiel, *Afro-American Folksongs*, p. ix.

44 "[They] are Americans": Krehbiel, *Afro-American Folksongs*, pp. 22–23, 26.

44 "Your country?": Krehbiel, *Afro-American Folksongs*, pp. vii, 28.

44 "foolish pride": Krehbiel, *Afro-American Folksongs*, p. vii.

45 "more racially and musically segregated": Dale Cockrell, "Everybody's Doin' It: Sex, Music, and Dance in New York, 1840-1916," paper delivered at American Musicological Society Conference, Vancouver, B.C., Nov. 4, 2016. See also Cockrell, *Everybody's Doin' It: Sex, Music, and Dance in New York, 1840–1916* (2019).

45 "A reviewer ought": I reprint the entire review in Horowitz, *Moral Fire*, pp. 107–13.

46 "I challenge any living man": Horowitz, *Classical Music*, p. 255.

47 "The Curse and Affectation": Joseph Horowitz, *Understanding Toscanini: How He Became an American Culture-God and Helped Create a New Audience for Old Music* (1987), p. 60; Horowitz, *Moral Fire*, p. 121.

48 "The glaring badge": Horowitz, *Understanding Toscanini*, pp. 247–48.

48 "German agents": Horowitz, *Understanding Toscanini*, pp. 78–79.

48 "The concert of": Horowitz, *Understanding Toscanini*, p. 100.

Chapter Three: Nostalgic Subversions

57 "When I think of": Charles Ives, *Memos*, ed. John Kirkpatrick (1972), p. 133.

59 "a stranger to me": Albert Paine, ed., *Mark Twain's Notebook* (2006), p. 377.

63 "the most artless": Shelley Fisher Fishkin, *Was Huck Black?* (1993).

63 (a dialect coach): Joseph Horowitz, *"On My Way,"* p. 35.

64 "sadness for the slaves": Tom Owens, ed., *Selected Correspondence of Charles Ives* (2007), pp. 294–95.

66 "Time will throw": For Ives and ragtime, see Judith Tick, "Ragtime and the Music of Charles Ives," *Current Musicology* 18, pp. 105–13. Copland quote in

Aaron Copland, *The New Music* (1969), p. 66. Ives quote in Henry and Sidney Cowell, *Charles Ives and His Music* (1969), p. 94.

70 **"He has chosen":** Robert Hughes, *American Visions: The Epic History of Art in America* (1997), p. 308.

72 **"But this assumes":** Ralph Ellison, *Going to the Territory* (1986), pp. 46, 84, 109, 110.

Chapter Four: Oedipal Revolt

76 **"After all these years":** Van Wyck Brooks, *The Ordeal of Mark Twain* (1920); Charles Ives, *Essays Before a Sonata* (1920), Epilogue; Mark Twain, *Life on the Mississippi* (1883), chap. 4.

77 **George Creel's Committee:** *New Republic*, Henry James, George Creel in Horowitz, *Classical Music in America*, pp. 265–66.

79 **"the saddest":** Brooks, *The Ordeal of Mark Twain*, chaps. 1, 2, 6, 7, 8, 11.

79 **"Gilded Age":** The historian Alan Lessoff has closely studied the usage "Gilded Age" (Lessoff in conversation with the author, 2018).

79 **"the whole country":** Brooks, *The Ordeal of Mark Twain*, chaps. 3, 4.

80 **Albert Niemann:** Horowitz, *Wagner Nights,* p. 119.

81 **"purged" the "negative":** Alan Lessoff, "The Gilded Age: Provenance of a Usable Past," unpublished conference paper, Organization of American Historians, Boston, March 2004; Alan Lessoff, "The Gilded Age City in American Political Discourse and Lore," in *Stadt—Macht—Korruption*, ed., Jens-Ivo Engels et al. (Stuttgart: Franz Steiner Verlag, 2017), pp. 143–54.

81 **a Germanic musical colony:** Horowitz, *Classical Music in America*, pt. 1.

84 **In Thomson's view:** Virgil Thomson, *American Music Since 1910* (1971), chaps. 1–3.

84 **The Germans, by comparison:** Virgil Thomson, "How Dead Is Arnold Schoenberg?" (1965), and "The Tradition of Sensibility" (1965) in Virgil Thomson, *"The State of Music" and Other Writings* (2016).

84 **"a certain degree of introversion":** Virgil Thomson, *Virgil Thomson* (1966), chap. 35.

85 **"By the late twenties":** Howard Pollack, *Aaron Copland: The Life and Work of an Uncommon Man* (1999), p. 112; Aaron Copland, *Music and Imagination* (1952), p. 106; Aaron Copland, *The New Music* (1968), pp. 100–101.

86 **"Some idea":** Copland, *The New Music*, pp. 103–6.

87 **Schoenefeld's *Rural* Symphony:** E. Douglas Bomberger, *"A Tidal Wave of Encouragement": American Composers' Concerts in the Gilded Age* (2002), pp. 111–13.

87 **"baneful":** Horowitz, *Classical Music in America*, pp. 67.

88 **"a name that deserves":** Copland, *Music and Imagination*, pp. 101–2.

89 **"Don't try to prove":** Humphrey Burton, *Leonard Bernstein* (1994), pp. 50–51.

90 **five personality traits:** On Bernstein's Philharmonic programs and educational concerts: Joseph Horowitz, "The Teachings of Leonard Bernstein," in Horowitz, *The Post-Classical Predicament* (1995), and Horowitz, "As Music Director: A Quest for Meaning and Identity," in Burton Bernstein and Barbara Haws, *Leonard Bernstein: An American Original* (2008).

92 **"don't always add up":** Copland, *The New Music*, pp. 114, 117; Copland, *Music and Imagination*, p. 105; Pollack, *Aaron Copland*, p. 110.

92 **changed his mind:** See Donal Henahan in the *New York Times*, April 5, 1987. Documentation in the New York Philharmonic Archives confirms this.

93 **Such was Ives's strategy:** "Health gave out" from "double life" from Bernstein's Young People's Concert "Charles Ives: American Pioneer" (Feb. 23, 1967), Leonard Bernstein Collection, folder 04, box 111, Music Division, Library of Congress (I am indebted to David Paul for this citation). Leonard Bernstein program/album note for Ives Symphony No. 2, printed in CD booklet for DG 429220-2 (1990). Ives quoted in Pollack, *Aaron Copland*, p. 110.

95 **"All his music":** Octavio Paz, "Silvestre Revueltas," *El Nacional* (Mexico City), Dec. 1, 1940.

96 **Roberto Kolb:** Extensive conversations and correspondence with the author.

97 **"I had no idea":** Letter to Carlos Chávez (May 18, 1937), in Elizabeth Crist and Wayne Shirley, eds., *The Selected Correspondence of Aaron Copland* (2006), p. 118.

98 **Levant adds:** Oscar Levant, *A Smattering of Ignorance* (1939), pp. 223–24.

98 **both of which suffer:** Copland, *Our New Music* (1941), pp. 209–10; Copland, *The New Music* (1968), p 149.

100 **nexus of influence:** Mark Carroll, *Music and Ideology in Cold War Europe* (2003), especially pp. 80–81. An appendix lists the programs for Nabokov's Paris festival.

Chapter Five: The Bifurcation of American Music

101 **"hackneyed":** *New York Herald Tribune*, March 24, 1950.

101 **"sound Chinese":** Leonard Bernstein, *The Infinite Variety of Music* (1962), pp. 159–60.

102 **"prick his ear":** Antonín Dvořák, "Music in America," *Harper's*, Feb. 1895.

104 **"primitive arts and crafts":** Copland, *Our New Music*, pp. 86 and 89; Copland, *Music and Imagination*, p. 84.

104 **"a strange sight"**: Copland letter to Israel Citkowitz, Sept. 1934, cited in Howard Pollack, *Aaron Copland: The Life and Work of an Uncommon Man* (1999), p. 277.

105 **"I don't think"**: Copland on Gershwin: "Aaron Copland and the Composers' Forum-Laboratory: A Post-Concert Discussion," Feb. 24, 1937, in Carol A. Oja and Judith Tick, eds., *Aaron Copland and His World* (2005), p. 404; Bernstein on Gershwin: Leonard Bernstein, *The Joy of Music* (1959), p. 58.

106 **"authenticity"**: Copland, *Music and Imagination*, p. 104; Arthur Berger, *Aaron Copland* (1953).

109 **pieces that most endure:** Annegret Fauser, *Sounds of War: Music in the United States During World War II* (2013), pp. 138–60. The Thomson quote (March 12, 1944) may be found in John Rockwell, ed., *A Virgil Thomson Reader* (1984), p. 47.

112 **Gunther Schuller:** In conversation with the author.

113 **truthfulness of his opera:** Robert Wyatt and John Andrew Johnson, eds., *The George Gershwin Reader* (2004), pp. 221–27.

115 **whose genesis was:** Michael Beckerman, *New Worlds of Dvořák* (2003).

116 **Farwell expanded:** These works may be heard on the 2014 Naxos CD *Dvořák and America*. It also includes the Hiawatha Melodrama created by Joseph Horowitz in collaboration with Michael Beckerman, Dvořák's *American Suite*, etc.

120 **mutant musical high culture:** This is a central theme of Horowitz, *Classical Music in America*.

121 **"all our grandfather"**: William Rossky, "*The Reivers* and *Huckleberry Finn*: Faulkner and Twain," *Huntington Library Quarterly*, August 1965.

123 **working-class culture:** David S. Reynolds, *Walt Whitman's America: A Cultural Biography* (1995), pp. 176–93.

124 **"more notable for abundance"**: Herman Melville, *Moby-Dick*, chap. 32. F. O. Matthiessen, *American Renaissance: Art and Expression in the Age of Emerson and Whitman* (1941), pp. 405, 444, 473; Herman Melville, *Billy Budd, Sailor*, chap. 18.

124 **"superimposed idiomatic"**: Charles Ives, *Memos*, ed. John Kirkpatrick (1972), p. 240.

125 **"Very often I get"**: Copland, *The New Music*, pp. 99–100.

125 **infantilization:** Horowitz, *Understanding Toscanini*, especially pp. 189–209.

126 **"My prognostication"**: Copland, *The New Music*, p. 125.

128 **Ives's borrowings:** J. Peter Burkholder, *All Made of Tunes: Charles Ives and the Uses of Musical Borrowing* (1995).

Chapter Six: Classical Music Black and "Red"

132 **Gwynne Kuhner Brown:** Gwynne Kuhner Brown, "Whatever Happened to William Dawson's *Negro Folk Symphony?" Journal of the Society for American Music* 6, no. 4 (2012).

134 **"essence of jazz":** Wilfrid Mellers, *Music in a New Found Land: Themes and Developments in the History of American Music* (1964), p. 329.

136 **the most acclaimed:** Gwynne Kuhner Brown, "Whatever Happened?"

136 **W. C. Handy:** Rae Linda Brown, *The Heart of a Woman: The Life and Music of Florence B. Price* (2020).

137 **Brown conjectures:** Brown, *The Heart of a Woman*, pp. 231–32.

137 **"Mrs. Price . . . spoke":** Brown, *The Heart of a Woman*, p. 199.

140 **"Suddenly it seemed":** Nathaniel Dett, "From Bell Stand to Throne Room," *The Black Perspective on Music*, Spring 1973.

140 **"the lack of proper":** Jon Michael Spencer, "R. Nathaniel Dett's Views on the Preservation of Black Music," *Black Perspective in Music*, Autumn 1982.

142 **"It should be stated":** Jon Michael Spencer, "R. Nathaniel Dett's Views."

143 **1967 description:** Margaret Bonds, "A Reminiscence," *International Library of Negro Life and History*, ed. Lindsay Patterson (1967), p. 192.

144 **"We have tried":** Beth Levy, *Frontier Figures: American Music and the Mythology of the American West* (2012), p. 33.

144 **"Probably the most":** Karl Krueger, *The Musical Heritage of the United States: The Unknown Portion* (1973), p. 210.

145 **"the best composition":** Levy, *Frontier Figures*, p. 46.

146 **"race spirit":** An invaluable compendium is Arthur Farwell, *"Wanderjahre of a Revolutionist" and Other Essays on American Music*, ed. Thomas Stoner (1995).

147 **"seek permission":** Levy, *Frontier Figures*, p. 24; John W. Troutman, *Indian Blues: American Indians and the Politics of Music 1870–1934* (2009), p. 157; Tara Browner, "Breathing the Indian Spirit: Thoughts on Musical Borrowing and the 'Indianist' Movement in American Music," *American Music*, Autumn 1997.

148 **"universal expression":** Levy, *Frontier Figures*, p. 65.

Chapter Seven: Using History—A Personal Quest

152 **first dissertations:** David C. Paul, *Charles Ives in the Mirror* (1989), p. 149.

154 **Journals in general circulation:** Joseph A. Mussulman, *Music in the Cultured Generation: A Social History of Music in America, 1870–1900* (1971), pp. 200–273.

156 **Russian-American son-in-law:** Carl Dolmetsch, *"Our Famous Guest": Mark Twain in Vienna, 1897–1899* (1992); Robert Hartford, ed., *Bayreuth: The Early Years* (1980).

158 **"culture was represented":** Alan Trachtenberg, *The Incorporation of America: Culture and Society in the Gilded Age* (1982), Preface, chaps. 5, 6, 7.

159 **"A long room":** Horowitz, *Wagner Nights*, p. 243.

162 **Higginson was a colossus:** Lawrence Levine, *Highbrow/Lowbrow: The Emergence of Cultural Hierarchy in America* (1988), pp. 120–32; Horowitz, *Moral Fire*, chap. 1.

162 **"deeply influenced":** Levine, *Highbrow/Lowbrow*, p. 102.

163 **And yet Peck:** The topic is little studied. The most valuable treatment of Peck to date is Mark Clague's 2002 doctoral dissertation, "Chicago Counterpoint: The Auditorium Theatre Building and the Civic Imagination" (University of Chicago). Also see Horowitz, *Classical Music*, pp. 172–75.

163 **He looks for culprits:** Horowitz, *Understanding Toscanini.*

163 **"the last quarter":** Trachtenberg, *The Incorporation of America*, p. 102.

164 **proto-feminist message:** Horowitz, *Wagner Nights*, chap. 12 ("Proto-feminism"). For a knowledgeable overview of Cather and Wagner, see Alex Ross, *Wagnerism: Art and Politics in the Shadow of Music* (2020).

165 **"We can accept":** Shelley Fisher Fishkin, *Was Huck Black?* (1993), p. 80.

166 **Judith Tick:** Judith Tick, "Charles Ives and Gender Ideology," in Ruth Solie, ed., *Musicology and Difference: Gender and Sexuality in Music Scholarship* (1993); Frank Rossiter, *Charles Ives and His America* (1975); Maynard Solomon, "Charles Ives: Some Questions of Veracity," *Journal of the American Musicological Society* 40, no. 3 (1987); Stuart Feder, *Charles Ives, "My Father's Song": A Psychoanalytic Biography* (1992); Lawrence Kramer, "Cultural Politics and Musical Form: The Case of Charles Ives" in *Classical Music and Postmodern Knowledge* (1995).

166 **"great man":** Tom C. Owens, *Selected Correspondence of Charles Ives* (2007), p. 290.

167 **"But their most telling":** Horowitz, *Moral Fire*, pp. 226–31.

168 **"narrowed his creativity":** Frank Rossiter, *Charles Ives and His America* (1975), Epilogue. Van Wyck Brooks is not mentioned by the author, but his Selected Bibliography includes both *America's Coming-of-Age* and *The Ordeal of Mark Twain.*

169 **"celebrate a fictional":** Mayor Mitch Landrieu, May 19, 2017.

170 **overnight sensation:** Wayne Shirley, "The Coming of 'Deep River,'" *American Music* 15, no. 4 (Winter 1997).

171 **His transcriptions:** Ramona Harper, "PostClassical Ensemble's 'Deep River,'" *DC Metro Theater Arts*, online, March 1, 2018.

174 **"slightly 'uncanny'":** Henry James, *The Painter's Eye: Notes and Essays on American Pictorial Art* (1989), pp. 218–19.

175 **"cool glass of mastery":** Robert Hughes, *American Visions* (1997), p. 250; Carter Radcliff, *John Singer Sargent* (1982), p. 227; Adam Gopnik, "Sargent's Pearls," *New Yorker*, Feb. 15, 1999, p. 71.

176 **"We love each other":** Ellen Knight, *Charles Martin Loeffler: A Life Apart in American Music* (1993). Also see Horowitz, *Classical Music in America*, pp. 113–17.

177 **"This exhibition":** Richard Ormond, *Sargent: Portraits of Artists and Friends* (2015), p. 9.

178 **"To be sure":** Anne Midgette, "Lakota Music Gets Short Shrift," *Washington Post*, Oct. 22, 2019; Sudip Bose, "A Composer in an Antique Land," *American Scholar*, Nov. 1, 2019.

181 **The ingenious application:** On *Porgy* and *Wozzeck*: Christopher Reynolds, "Porgy and Bess: 'An American *Wozzeck*,'" *Journal of the Society for American Music* 1, no. 1 (Feb. 2007). On *Porgy* and Wagner: Horowitz, *"On My Way,"* pp. 6–7.

181 **"it brings to the operatic form":** George Gershwin in the *New York Times*, Oct. 20, 1935 (reprinted in Merle Armitage, *George Gershwin* (1938), pp. 72–77.

182 **"ragging the classics":** The Gershwin biographer Richard Crawford, in conversation with the author (2018).

Summing Up

186 **four streams:** Horowitz, *Classical Music in America*, pp. 473–74.

187 **John Sullivan Dwight:** Horowitz, *Classical Music in America*, p. 27.

188 **"With affectionate veneration":** Erwin Stein, ed., *Arnold Schoenberg Letters* (1987), pp. 293–98.

191 **"G said my music":** Owens, *Selected Correspondence of Charles Ives*, p. 221.

193 **"establish direction":** R. P. Blackmur, *The Lion and the Honey-Comb* (1955), pp. 125–26; Newton Arvin, *Herman Melville* (1950), pp. 77–78.

194 **Ellison names Mark Twain:** Ralph Ellison, *Going to the Territory* (1986), 139–42, 251; John F. Callahan, ed., *The Collected Essays of Ralph Ellison* (2003), p. 88.

195 **"ungenerous and illiberal":** Henry Krehbiel, *Afro-American Folksongs* (1914), pp. 22–23.

198 **"to project consciously":** Toni Morrison, *Playing in the Dark: Whiteness and the Literary Imagination* (1990), pp. 3–5.

200 **"In the scholarship":** Morrison, *Playing in the Dark*, p. 48; Morrison, *The Source of Self-Regard* (2019), p. 181.

200 **"Black Patti":** John Graziano, "The Early Life and Career of the 'Black Patti': The Odyssey of an African American Singer in the Late Nineteenth Century," *Journal of the American Musicological Society* 53, no. 3 (2000).

201 **Ruby Elzy:** On Elzy: David E. Weaver, *Black Diva of the Thirties: The Life of Ruby Elzy* (2004). On National Negro Opera Company: Fauser, *Sounds of War*, pp. 174–77.

Index

ABOUT THE AUTHOR

Joseph Horowitz's ten previous books mainly deal with the history of classical music in the United States. *Understanding Toscanini: How He Became an American Culture-God and Helped Create a New Audience for Old Music* (1987) was named one of the year's best books by the New York Book Critics Circle. *Wagner Nights: An American History* (1994) was named best-of-the-year by the Society of American Music. Both *Classical Music in America: A History of Its Rise and Fall (2005)* and *Artists in Exile: How Refugees from Twentieth Century War and Revolution Transformed the American Performing Arts* (2008) made *The Economist*'s year's-best-books list.

Horowitz was a *New York Times* music critic (1976–80) before becoming executive director of the Brooklyn Philharmonic Orchestra. During his 1990s tenure, the BPO was reconceived as a "humanities institution," producing thematic, cross-disciplinary festivals in collaboration with schools and museums. In 2003, Horowitz cofounded PostClassical Ensemble, an experimental chamber orchestra based in Washington, D.C.; he serves as executive producer. From 2011 to 2020 he also directed Music Unwound, a National Endowment for the Humanities–funded national consortium of orchestras and universities dedicated to curating the American musical past; the topics in play were "Dvořák and America," "Charles Ives's America," "Copland and Mexico," and "Kurt Weill's America."

The documentary films Horowitz produced during the Covid pandemic—a companion series to *Dvořák's Prophecy*—were an outgrowth of American music festivals he created for PostClassical Ensemble and Music Unwound. The same is true of the Naxos CDs and DVDs he has produced celebrating Aaron Copland, Arthur Farwell, Lou Harrison, Bernard Herrmann, Silvestre Revueltas, and "Dvořák and America." They apply topics in American musical history to a larger cultural narrative, and to issues of present-day concern.

Horowitz is the recipient of fellowships from the Guggenheim Foundation, the National Endowment for the Humanities, New York University, and Columbia University, as well as a Certificate of Appreciation from the Czech Parliament. For the NEH, he also led a National Education Project and a Teacher-Training Institute, both devoted to "Dvořák and America."

His website is www.josephhorowitz.com. His blog is www.artsjournal.com/uq.